S0-AOV-775

Children of Incarcerated Parents

Yvette R. Harris, PhD, an associate professor of psychology at Miami University, received her Ph.D. in psychology from the University of Florida with a specialization in cognitive development. For the past 17 years her research has focused on exploring the environmental contributions to preschool and school age cognitive development and more recently has taken on applied focus examining the learning/ teaching patterns of African American mothers transitioning from welfare to work. She has presented her work at both national and international conferences, and her research has appeared in a variety of educational and developmental journals. Her current research focuses on the challenges of family reunification when a parent is released from prison, and she has appeared on NPR and was the keynote speaker at the National Association for Children of Incarcerated Parents Annual Meeting, and presented her recent work on reunification at the 15th National Symposium on Juvenile Services.

James A. Graham, PhD, is an associate professor of psychology at the College of New Jersey (TCNJ). He received a B.A. in psychology from Miami University. He completed graduate work at the University of Memphis where he received M.S. and Ph.D. degrees in developmental psychology. Currently, he serves as coordinator of the developmental specialization in psychology program at TCNJ, where he teaches a variety of undergraduate courses related to developmental psychology. During the summer, he travels to Johannesburg, South Africa, to teach graduate courses in child development and research methods. His scholarship focuses on the social-cognitive aspects of peer relationships among school children from both molar (peer group) and molecular (dyadic) perspectives. The overarching objective of his work and his social development laboratory is to foster prosocial thinking and behavior among children, especially those from understudied groups. He has presented his work in a variety of international, national, regional, and local conferences. He has published articles on the roles of race and gender in children's friendships, children's evaluations of social situations, children's relationships to media, and the evaluation of community programs.

Gloria J. Oliver Carpenter, PhD, is an assistant professor of psychology at Northern Kentucky University. She earned a B.S. in psychology from Florida Agricultural and Mechanical University and completed a Ph.D. in clinical psychology from Miami University, Ohio. Dr. Carpenter has also completed a National Institutes of Health postdoctoral fellowship at Cincinnati Children's Hospital Medical Center, where she focused on research and clinical interventions with children coping with comorbid conditions and the relation of these conditions to health status and outcomes. In addition, she actively worked with community programs conducting program evaluations related to schools and health disparities. Her research interests focus on parent and youth involvement in medical decision-making and school outcomes, as well as community engagement initiatives in community-based participatory research. Dr. Carpenter's teaching areas include lifespan development, the psychology of race and gender, childhood psychopathology, and health psychology.

Children of Incarcerated Parents

Theoretical, Developmental, and Clinical Issues

YVETTE R. HARRIS, PhD
JAMES A. GRAHAM, PhD
GLORIA J. OLIVER CARPENTER, PhD

SOUTH UNIVERSITY LIBRARY
COLUMBIA, SC 29203

SPRINGER PUBLISHING COMPANY

New York

Copyright © 2010 Springer Publishing Company

All rights reserved.

No part of this publication may be reproduced, stored in a retrieval system, or transmitted in any form or by any means, electronic, mechanical, photocopying, recording, or otherwise, without the prior permission of Springer Publishing Company, LLC, or authorization through payment of the appropriate fees to the Copyright Clearance Center, Inc., 222 Rosewood Drive, Danvers, MA 01923, 978-750-8400, fax 978-646-8600, info@copyright.com or on the web at www.copyright.com.

Springer Publishing Company, LLC
11 West 42nd Street
New York, NY 10036
www.springerpub.com

Acquisitions Editor: Sheri W. Sussman
Project Manager: Becca Mosher
Cover Design: TG Design
Composition: Publication Services, Inc.

E-book ISBN: 978-0-8261-0514-1

10 11 12 13/5 4 3 2 1

Library of Congress Cataloging-in-Publication Data

Children of incarcerated parents : theoretical, developmental, and clinical issues / Yvette R. Harris . . . [et al.].
    p. cm.
ISBN 978-0-8261-0513-4 (alk. paper)—ISBN 978-0-8261-0514-1 (ebook)
    1. Children of prisoners—United States. 2. Children with social disabilities—United States.   I. Harris, Yvette R.   HV8886.U5C53 2010
    362.82'95—dc22

                                                                2010003011

Printed in the United States of America by the Hamilton Printing Company

The author and the publisher of this Work have made every effort to use sources believed to be reliable to provide information that is accurate and compatible with the standards generally accepted at the time of publication. Because medical science is continually advancing, our knowledge base continues to expand. Therefore, as new information becomes available, changes in procedures become necessary. We recommend that the reader always consult current research and specific institutional policies before performing any clinical procedure. The author and publisher shall not be liable for any special, consequential, or exemplary damages resulting, in whole or in part, from the readers' use of, or reliance on, the information contained in this book.

The publisher has no responsibility for the persistence or accuracy of URLs for external or third-party Internet Web sites referred to in this publication and does not guarantee that any content on such Web sites is, or will remain, accurate or appropriate.

Contents

Contributors

Adela Beckerman is a professor of social work and director of the Bachelor in Social Work (BSW) Program at Florida Memorial University. Dr. Beckerman earned her Ph.D. in social welfare from the State University of New York at Albany and her M.S.W. at the State University of New York at Stony Brook. She has published articles in numerous journals on issues related to foster care, social work education, drug courts, and HIV/AIDS among at-risk populations, as well as on birth defects in the Haitian communities in Florida. She has also conducted program evaluations for substance abuse, education, and health planning agencies. She recently completed research for the University of Kentucky Center for Poverty Research that examined child welfare caseworkers' decision making regarding permanency planning when a parent is incarcerated.

Kimberly Belmonte is currently enrolled as a graduate student at the State University of New York, New Paltz.

Marty Beyer is a child welfare and juvenile justice consultant with a Ph.D. in clinical/community psychology from Yale University. She assisted Alabama and Oregon in implementing strengths/needs-based child welfare practice and serves on the Katie A. Advisory Panel in Los Angeles. Marty invented "visit coaching" and was invited by the Administration for Children's Services (ACS), the New York City child welfare agency, to train visit coaches working in private foster care agencies and in the Children of Incarcerated Parents Program (CHIPP, the ACS visiting with incarcerated parents program).

Sarah Zeller-Berkman has her M.A. from Hunter College and is a doctoral candidate at the CUNY Graduate Center. She is concurrently the director of the Beacons National Strategy Initiative for the Youth Development Institute in New York City. For the past six years she has provided technical assistance to youth development programs in the NYC area by conducting trainings and onsite capacity building. She has worked in partnership with young people who have a parent in prison to create research on the stressors and supports in their lives. She has also worked as an evaluator of youth initiatives and as a researcher of adult-youth partnerships for social change.

Kathy Boudin is director of the Criminal Justice Initiative: Supporting Children, Families, and Communities, located at the Columbia University School of Social

Work. Dr. Boudin earned her Ed.D. from Columbia University Teachers College. She is an adjunct lecturer at both Columbia University School of Social Work and New York University School of Social Work on issues related to incarceration and reentry. She has developed programs and has been a teacher and counselor both inside and outside of prison in areas that include mother-child relationships across the separation of prison, the HIV/AIDS epidemic, basic literacy, higher education, and "long-termers" in prison. She has carried out research on the role of higher education in a maximum security prison for women, adolescents with incarcerated mothers, and developmental processes of people in prison serving long sentences for violent crimes and their recidivism rates, examining parole and sentencing policy. She founded Teen College Dreams, a program to aid youth with incarcerated parents in their college-going process.

He Len Chung is a licensed psychologist and assistant professor of psychology at the College of New Jersey. Dr. Chung earned her M.A. and Ph.D. in psychology from Temple University and her B.A. from Washington University in St. Louis. She completed a clinical internship at Western Psychiatric Institute and Clinic and NIMH research fellowships in Psychiatric Epidemiology and Mental Health & Substance Use Services. She has published articles on issues related to neighborhood effects on antisocial behavior, community reentry following incarceration, the mental health of juvenile offenders, and the transition to adulthood for adolescents in the juvenile justice system. She has also contributed to technical reports on promoting well-being through evidence-based community programs and building pathways out of serious adolescent offending.

Holly Foster is an associate professor of sociology at Texas A&M University. Her work examines the implications of incarceration for families and children. She has published research on families and incarceration with John Hagan in the *Annals of the American Academy of Political and Social Science* and *Social Problems.*

Randi Blumenthal-Guigui coordinated Memphis Children Locked Out, a community-wide initiative designed to assess and address the needs of Memphis area children with a parent in prison. Ms. Guigui developed Project REACHH (Re-energizing Attachment, Communication, Health, and Happiness), an innovative visiting program for children in Memphis, Tennessee, whose parents were incarcerated. Ms. Guigui was also a founding member of the Alliance for Tennessee's Children of Prisoners. Ms. Guigui works at Osborne Association, a New York City-based nonprofit founded in 1931 with a 20-year history of providing innovative prison and jail-based services to families, including in-prison family centers, parenting education programs, healthy relationships courses, and a visit program that reconnects incarcerated fathers with their children.

Vanessa A. Harris is currently a graduate student at Miami University. Ms. Harris earned her B.A. in psychology at California State University Fullerton. She has conducted research examining the effects of losing a twin, as well as the unmet needs of twins with disabilities. She is currently at Miami University, conducting research in the area of family reunification after maternal incarceration.

Tabitha R. Holmes is an assistant professor of psychology at the State University of New York, New Paltz. Her scholarship and teaching have centered upon how individuals develop within an ecological context. She also studies how individuals' belief systems help shape interactions between family members.

Kerry Kazura received a B.A. in psychology from the University of Southern Maine and an M.A. and Ph.D. in Child Development and Family Studies from the Auburn University, Alabama. She is currently an associate professor of family studies at the University of New Hampshire. For six years, Dr. Kerry Kazura was the co-director of the Family Connections Project at the New Hampshire Lakes Region Prison Facility. She has experience in developing, implementing, and evaluating parenting/family programs for incarcerated parents. During that time, Dr. Kazura's research objectives were to evaluate the effectiveness of incarcerated parent programs, and examine the differential effects of maternal and paternal incarceration on children's social and emotional development.

Tanya Krupat is currently the director of the New York Initiative for Children of Incarcerated Parents at the Osborne Association, which aims to raise awareness about and reform policies and practices that impact the thousands of children in New York state whose parents are incarcerated. She helped develop and then directed the Children of Incarcerated Parents Program (CHIPP) and the Family Visiting Unit within NYC's child welfare agency, the Administration for Children's Services. Prior to this, she was the Family Services Coordinator at a women's prison in New York State.

Daniel McFadden received his B.A. in psychology from the College of New Jersey. He works with children and adolescents in special education classes in the Bridgewater-Raritan school district and plans to pursue a Ph.D. in clinical psychology.

Sophie Naudeau holds a Ph.D. in child development from Tufts University, where she conducted research on positive youth development with a focus on children of incarcerated parents. She has authored numerous articles on children and youth development and has done extensive fieldwork with children and youth in various cultures, including in Bosnia, Guinea-Conakry, Sierra Leone, Thailand, and Cambodia. She is currently a Human Development Specialist at the World Bank, where she focuses on (1) analyzing the opportunities and challenges that children and youth face in low and middle-income countries, (2) developing tools and implementing projects that respond to the specific needs of this population, and (3) designing impact evaluations of early childhood programs.

Susan D. Phillips is an assistant professor at the Jane Addams College of Social Work, the University of Illinois, Chicago. She is nationally recognized for her expertise on the effects that parental arrest and incarceration have on children and families. Dr. Phillips' understanding of this population is grounded in first-hand experience in developing and administering programs for children with parents in prison and relatives who care for them, as well as involvement on the front lines of policy reform efforts. Her research on children of incarcerated parents is widely cited. In addition,

Dr. Phillips is currently a consultant to the National Resource Center for Children of Incarcerated Parents and the Council of State Governments on matters relating to research on children whose parents are involved in the criminal justice system.

Kristina Toth is the administrator for the Family Connections Center of the New Hampshire Department of Corrections. In 1998, Kristina co-created one of the first family support centers in a state prison. This center has expanded to three prisons and works with incarcerated fathers and mothers, their children, and their children's caregivers to create healthy family relationships during the tumultuous time of a parent's incarceration. Ms. Toth earned a B.A. at the University of New Hampshire. She has co-published several articles on the family connections center and speaks at many state-wide conferences on the subject. In 2008 Kristina Toth was recognized by New Hampshire's only state-wide newspaper, the *Union Leader*, as one of New Hampshire's "40 under 40." In 2009 Kristina graduated from the prestigious Leadership New Hampshire, a year-long educational program for future leaders of New Hampshire.

Kathleen Tillman is a lecturer of psychology at the State University of New York, New Paltz. Ms. Tillman received her M.A. in community counseling and school counseling from Eastern Mennonite University and is a Ph.D. candidate in counseling psychology with a specialization in child development at the University of North Dakota. Ms. Tillman has worked as a child therapist in a variety of therapeutic settings and completed an APA-accredited predoctoral internship in clinical child psychology.

Margaret Wentworth is currently enrolled as a graduate student at the State University of New York, New Paltz.

Preface

The desire to produce this edited book developed from our many conversations with friends and colleagues on the plight of children with parents in the United States criminal justice system. We were disturbed by their numbers—there are over 1.5 million children under the age of 18 with parents in the criminal justice system; the racial disparities—African American children comprise 53% of that number, followed by Caucasian children (23%) and Latino children (23%); the lack of attention to their persistent adverse developmental and clinical outcomes—low self esteem, depression, decrease in academic performance; and the overall inconsistent focus on their life challenges and general well-being. Thus, our major goal in creating this book was to stimulate discourse among a diverse group of social scientists, to pose questions and offer suggestions on research directions for children of incarcerated parents, and at some level to influence public policy and public opinion on this frequently marginalized group of children.

To this end, we assembled an esteemed group of social scientists with expertise on theory, developmental trajectories, neighborhood issues, challenges inherent in parenting from prison, reunification, legislative concerns, and service planning and intervention.

It is our desire that *Children of Incarcerated Parents: Theoretical, Developmental, and Clinical Issues* will serve as a comprehensive source for psychologists, educators, students, researchers, and policy makers who work with (or will work with) or pursue research on children of incarcerated parents, as well as the frontline responders who provide immediate assistance to these children.

Acknowledgments

We would like to take this opportunity to acknowledge the many people who helped to make this book possible.

Thanks to our family and friends for their love and encouragement. We appreciate your belief in our having the vision to create this textbook. We thank you for keeping us grounded through the editing and writing process.

We would like to extend our sincere appreciation to the authors and publishers whose works are included in this text. We are grateful for your courage to investigate topics on children of incarcerated parents and their families. Your work served an instrumental role in the creation of this volume.

We would also like to thank our respective universities (Miami University, The College of New Jersey, and Northern Kentucky University) for providing us with the time and resources to complete such an undertaking.

Thanks to the editorial, production, and marketing staff at Springer Publishing Company. We value your time and expertise in making this text possible.

Finally, a big thanks to Sheri W. Sussman, our editor at Springer Publishing Company. This book could not be possible without your editorial feedback, guidance, and belief in our work.

Framework

The Changing Landscape in the American Prison Population: Implications for Children of Incarcerated Parents

1

JAMES A. GRAHAM
YVETTE R. HARRIS
GLORIA J. OLIVER CARPENTER

Over the past 15 years, numerous studies from a variety of academic disciplines have examined the impact of parental incarceration on children (see Johnston, 1995; Parke & Clarke-Stewart, 2002; Braman, 2004; Travis, 2005; and Farrington & Welsh, 2007 for reviews). Given the increasing growth in the nation's prison population, it is important to examine the potential impact of parental incarceration on children. Regardless of how one feels about the criminal justice system in America, it is evident that parental incarceration disrupts families emotionally, socially, and financially.

Children of incarcerated parents (CIP) are a subset of American children at risk for anti-social and delinquent behavior. The level of risk may vary in children of prisoners compared to children in the general population. Assuming a normal distribution for both populations, Figure 1.1 shows some children are less at-risk and some are more at-risk, with the majority being in-between; however, the CIP fall into a higher-risk zone.

Due to the societal challenges and informational demands, an examination of demographic characteristics of parental incarceration is relevant to developmental scientists for two major reasons. First, there is a dramatic increase in the number of children growing up without a parent due to incarceration. Many children face varying amounts of

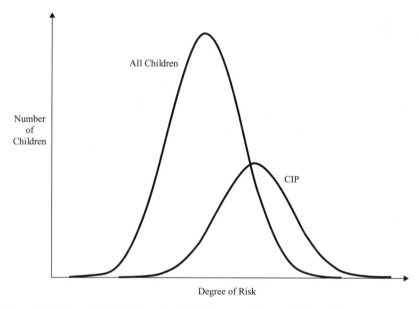

Figure 1.1 Normal distributions for all children at risk and CIP at risk.

time without their parents; thus it is important to examine the developmental trajectories that these children experience prior to their parents' incarceration, during imprisonment, and upon reunification with them. Second, parental incarceration is a multifaceted issue that encompasses varying layers of complexity, from individual to dyadic, familial, community, and societal. The impact of parental incarceration on children is studied from a variety of disciplines, theories, and methodologies. Given the complexity of this issue, it is important to continually add to, modify, and enhance research on the impact of parental incarceration on children. We explore these concerns throughout this volume. In this introductory chapter, we start with a brief review of the Bureau of Justice Statistics report on the demographic trends of incarcerated parents and their children. One should carefully examine such reports often because they often focus on the parental perspective of incarceration, rather than the child's perception of having an incarcerated parent. A common limitation of much of the work in the field is that it fails to account for the bidirectional perspectives of the incarcerated parent and the child. In this chapter, we discuss this issue as well as other conceptual and methodological biases inherent in research on children of incarcerated parents. The end of the chapter focuses on how the chapters in this volume contribute to the sparse literature base on this understudied and multidimensional group.

INCREASES IN THE NUMBER OF CHILDREN GROWING UP WITHOUT A PARENT DUE TO INCARCERATION

With 2.3 million people in prisons or jails, the United States is the leader of incarceration rates around the globe—a 500% increase over the past 30 years. Based on the 2004 Survey of Inmates in State and Federal Correctional Facilities about incarcerated parents and their minor children, Glaze and Maruschak (2008) compare estimates of the numbers by gender, age, race, and Hispanic origin in state and federal prisons in 1991, 1997, 1999, 2004, and 2007.

Population Statistics

According to the Bureau of Justice Statistics (BJS), a leading source of information pertaining to reports on incarcerated parents, an estimated 809,800 prisoners of approximately 1.5 million held in the nation's prisons at the middle of 2007 were parents of minor children (Glaze & Maruschak, 2008). Parents held in the nation's prisons—52% of state inmates and 63% of federal inmates—reported having an estimated 1,706,600 minor children, accounting for 2.3% of the U.S. resident population under age 18 (Glaze & Maruschak, 2008). The percentage of incarcerated parents of minor children increased by 79% from 1991 to the middle of 2007 (see Figure 1.2).

Age

According to estimates by the Bureau of Justice Statistics, over 700,000 children will reach the age of 18 while their parents are incarcerated. The percentage of minor children with a parent in state or federal prison is greatest among children from birth to 9 years, followed by 10- to 17-year-olds (see Table 1.1). Parents between 25 to 35 years old were more likely held in state and federal prisons, followed by prisoners ages 35 to 44, and 24 years and younger.

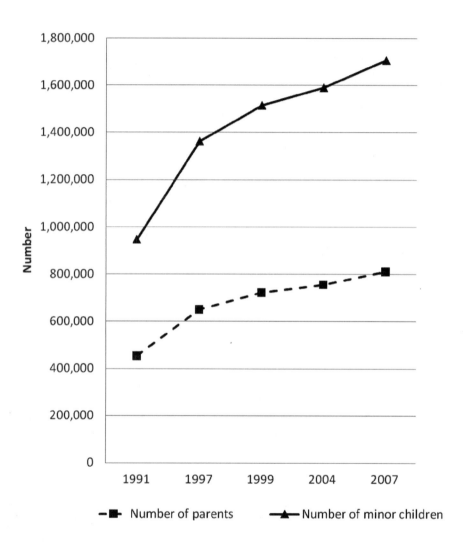

Figure 1.2 Estimated number of parents in state and federal prisons and their minor children. Bureau of Justice Statistics (Glaze & Maruschak, 2008).

Table 1.1

AGE DISTRIBUTION OF CHILDREN OF PARENTS IN STATE AND FEDERAL PRISONS AT TIME OF STUDY, BY GENDER (GLAZE AND MARUSCHAK, 2008)

Age of Minor Child	CHILDREN OF PARENTS IN STATE PRISON (AGE GROUP PERCENTAGES)			CHILDREN OF PARENTS IN FEDERAL PRISON (AGE GROUP PERCENTAGES)		
	Total	Male	Female	Total	Male	Female
Less than 1 year	2.4	2.5	1.6	0.7	0.7	1.1
1–4 years	20	20.3	16.7	15.1	15.3	12.6
5–9 years	30.2	30.3	29.1	33.8	34	30.1
10–14 years	31.6	31.4	33.8	35.1	35	35.8
15–17 years	15.8	15.5	18.8	15.3	15	20.4

Race and Ethnicity

As Figure 1.3 depicts, Black children are approximately 8 times more likely, and Hispanic children are nearly 3 times more likely, than white children to have an incarcerated parent (Glaze & Maruschak, 2008). Out of the 1.5 million children with an incarcerated father, nearly half are black. Approximately 200,000 children have an incarcerated mother. These mothers were more likely to be white (45%), followed by Black (30%) and Hispanic (19%). There is a disproportionate representation among black and Hispanic children with incarcerated parents. These data must be carefully interpreted, as higher numbers may be a reflection of larger societal issues (such as poverty, urbanization, and discrimination) rather than just a problem among certain social groups.

Gender

The impact of parental incarceration on a child may differ depending on the gender of the parent and the child. A child's experiences of separation from a mother may vary from the child's experiences of paternal separation. The nation's federal and state prisons held approximately 744,200 fathers and 65,600 mothers in the middle of 2007. According to Glaze and Maruschak (2008), since 1991 the number of children with a mother in prison has more than doubled, and the paternal incarceration statistics demonstrate a 77% increase. How does the difference in incarceration rates among mothers and fathers affect the living arrangements of their children?

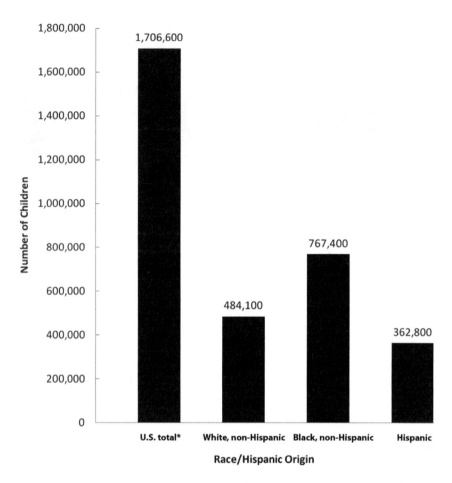

Note: Children were assumed to have the same race/ethnicity as the incarcerated parent. Percentages were calculated based on the U.S. resident population under age 18 as of July 1, 2007.

*Includes children of other races. Other races include American Indians, Alaska Natives, Asians, Native Hawaiians, other Pacific Islanders, and persons identifying two or more races.

Figure 1.3 Minor children in the U.S. resident population with a parent in state or federal prison, by race and Hispanic origin, 2007. Bureau of Justice Statistics (Glaze & Maruschak, 2008).

Family Structure

The number of children with incarcerated parents has increased dramatically over the years. In the month before their arrest or just prior to imprisonment, 64% of mothers held in state prisons and approximately 50% of incarcerated fathers reported living with their minor children. In the month before their mothers' arrest, children were much more likely to be financially supported by their mothers and living in a single-parent household than children with incarcerated fathers.

The impact of parental incarceration on children may vary depending on whether or not the parent lived with them prior to incarceration. Incarcerated parents differed in their reports of who were the primary caretakers of their children prior to their arrest. Incarcerated fathers were more likely to report mothers as being the primary caretaker of their children in the month before arrest. As shown in Table 1.2, incarcerated mothers were more likely to report that they were the primary providers for their children before arrest, and they were more likely to report that grandmothers (42%) or other relatives (23%) are the current caretakers of their children (Mumola, 2000; Glaze & Maruschak, 2008). Regardless of age, race/ethnicity, gender, or living arrangements, most incarcerated parents influence the emotional, social, and financial lives of their children in some way.

Table 1.2

PERCENTAGES OF CURRENT CAREGIVERS OF MINOR CHILDREN OF PARENTS IN STATE PRISON BY GENDER

Children's Current Caregiver[a]	Total	Male	Female
Other parent	84.2	88.4	37
Grandparent	15.1	12.5	44.9
Grandmother	14	11.6	42.1
Grandfather	4.3	3.6	12
Other relatives	6.2	4.7	22.8
Foster home or agency	2.9	2.2	10.9
Friends, others[b]	2.9	2.4	7.8
Estimated number of parents in state prison	636,300	585,200	51,100

[a]Includes all parents with minor children. Detail may sum to more than 100% because some prisoners had multiple minor children living with multiple caregivers.
[b]Includes inmate's friends, friends of the inmate's children, cases where the parent reported that the child now lived alone, and others.

CONCEPTUAL AND METHODOLOGICAL BIASES IN RESEARCH ON CHILDREN OF INCARCERATED PARENTS

Systematic investigations of research concerning children of incarcerated parents are limited. A review of the literature suggests a range of historical and ongoing concerns regarding the methods used in studies of children with an incarcerated parent.

Conceptual Biases

Children of incarcerated parents are considered an at-risk population, but not all of these children are at-risk (Johnston, 1995), and if they are at-risk it may be for different reasons among children (Phillips, Erkanli, Costello, & Angold, 2007; Phillips & Erkanli, 2008). Research on children of incarcerated parents typically recruit participants from high-risk environments characterized by poverty, crime, urbanization, and the like. Such narrow recruitment methods and limited social contexts minimize the amount of work on normative development and mutes potentially positive developmental outcomes in children (McLoyd, 1998).

Unfortunately, delinquency and negative developmental outcomes have been the main focal point of much of the research in this arena. There is an inclination to believe that children of incarcerated parents are more likely to end up in prison because they are following their parents' example. There is no clear empirical evidence to support this claim; however, a lot of research and legislative reform uses this ideology to guide public policy decisions.

As reported earlier in this chapter, parental incarceration is more common among black and Hispanic children compared to white children even though children from all socioeconomic classes and ethnicities experience parental incarceration. Researchers and social service agencies need to be aware of the connection between discrimination and other social issues inherent in the criminal justice system, housing, education, and employment sectors, which place these groups of color at differing levels of risk for incarceration.

Methodological Constraints

Historically, much of the research on understudied populations, such as children of incarcerated parents, is confounded in a number of ways. Unfortunately, methodological limitations, such as deficiencies in validity and reliability, continue to trouble research today. We briefly explore these two issues in the sections to follow.

As Harris and Graham (2007) point out, attempts to increase internal validity often enhances the "scientific rigor" of the research, but it often comes at a price—a decrease in external validity. This demand for internal validity makes it more challenging to conduct scientifically rigorous research with certain populations. Researchers who work with some understudied populations, such as African American children or children of incarcerated parents, may encounter difficulties with recruiting participants, developing valid measures, using valid theories, and training research assistants to be culturally sensitive (Sue, 1999). These factors may discourage many social scientists to initiate empirical investigations that examine complex developmental and clinical issues among children of incarcerated parents.

As mentioned earlier in this chapter, much of the research views the child of an incarcerated parent from a homogenous rather than a heterogeneous perspective. We need more research to uncover the complexities of CIP, but it is just as important to create a knowledge base that extends beyond the stereotypical urban, lower-income community of color. We need to create a more balanced representation of the child of an incarcerated parent, one that includes varying socioeconomic, educational, and residential backgrounds. According to McLoyd (1998), the external validity of many studies on understudied groups is highly variable because of the lack of specification of many demographic variables of the participants (including the white comparison group). Because there is a widening divide among children of incarcerated parents, it is important that research provide objective specification of demographics (such as race, ethnic origin, social class, gender, neighborhood, etc.), given the cultural complexity of parental incarceration, even in race-homogenous studies.

An additional methodological constraint is the type of research design that one chooses to use in the examination of the influence of parental incarceration on child development. Most social scientists fall within two camps: one group primarily employs quantitative methodologies, and the other approaches research from a qualitative perspective. The study of parental incarceration on child development is interdisciplinary. The research in the field has focused on the interaction of a variety of disciplines, such as anthropology, biology, education, juvenile justice, psychology, social work, and sociology. An interdisciplinary examination of child development can provide insight into various pathways of development often overlooked by a one-dimensional focus of study, such as the use of methods or designs that are only quantitative or only qualitative. The utilization of both quantitative and qualitative research approaches (e.g., case study, ethnography, focus groups, surveys) may be helpful in the study of child development (Sue, 1999) and may be particularly relevant to CIP because the field is ripe for both basic and applied research.

The reliability of some research in the field of children with incarcerated parents is highly variable. To minimize such variability, many leaders and organizations that focus on parental incarceration and child development are creating initiatives to address the growing need for more reliable research in the field. Because of some of these initiatives, Bouchet (2007) reports on key issues that hinder reliability of studies on children of incarcerated parents.

In general, the reliability challenges faced in CIP studies revolve around three areas: (1) research, (2) practice, and (3) public policy. Research needs to address some key challenges (Bouchet, 2007). First, it is difficult to gather information about children with incarcerated parents because the population is virtually invisible for several reasons, such as stigma, lack of communication among social service agencies, and limited definition of "family" from the U.S. criminal justice system. Second, many studies that generalize to the population of children of incarcerated parents may be largely based on reports from correctional agencies that solely focus on the parent's perspective (rather than parent and child), while the sample sizes in others studies may be too small or outdated. Third, there is no consistent method of data collection on the characteristics of children and incarcerated parents. Furthermore, there is not a central repository of reliable data sources that can be shared with persons interested in this topic area to raise public awareness or to promote advocacy.

Some may question the reliability of some studies on children of incarcerated parents because of the challenges associated with practice and public policy. In terms of service delivery and practice, many social service agencies grapple with several issues relating to children of incarcerated parents. These agencies have limited funding, which makes it difficult to create a quality program that addresses the needs of children with incarcerated parents while concurrently working to maintain the integrity of their other social service programs (Bouchet, 2007). Many social service agencies and practitioners lack the cultural knowledge to provide adequate assistance to this heterogeneous group of children and their families. The lack of revenue among some agencies may exacerbate the problem; agencies may not have adequate resources to provide cultural training for workers in their incarceration programs.

Reliable interventions and research may be difficult due to the nature of the topic. Some parents, children, and families may be reluctant to take advantage of services due to the social stigma, shame, and fear (Bouchet, 2007).

Public policy and system reform movements in this area face a number of challenges that may influence the reliability of work done in this field. In order to move forward in this area, advocates, politicians, and legislators need to base their efforts on and gather knowledge from reliable sources of information. There are a number of challenges in this arena. There is a lack of public awareness or education on the impact of parental incarceration on children. Many incarcerated parents do not clearly understand the parental termination risks associated with incarceration under the Federal Adoption and Safe Families Act of 1997. Moreover, creating partnerships with correctional institutions and their constituents (such as guards, social workers, psychologists, and unions) may pose as a barrier to policy reform. A final issue impeding progress and the reliability of reform in parental incarceration is determining which level of entry is best—the federal, state, or local level?

The purpose of this chapter is to identify fundamental issues facing research on children of incarcerated parents, rather than to provide an in-depth analysis of the topic. Research and policy decisions are mired in controversy, in the absence of valid and reliable data on children and families of incarcerated parents. In addition, the lack of a common knowledge base that contains scientifically sound research on the impact of parental incarceration and effective interventions poses a threat to research and work in this area (Christian, 2009).

ORGANIZATION OF THE VOLUME

This volume is divided into five parts. The chapters provide detailed information from a variety of developmental and clinical perspectives to shed light on this complex and increasingly significant topic. The chapters in this edited volume offer a mixture of basic and applied research using varying methodologies (e.g., quantitative, qualitative), theoretical frameworks, and experiences with this phenomenon at individual, community, state, and national levels. The contributors to this edited book offer illuminating and practical insights into the world of children with incarcerated parents. The authors identify some of the issues that plagued earlier research and continue to hinder some of the current work in the field. This edited volume recommends ways that we can minimize some of these issues, thus advancing our knowledge of the developmental trajectories of children with incarcerated parents.

Part I: Framework

This section provides the overall rationale for the book, and begins with an introduction and overview of the material to be covered in subsequent chapters.

Chapter 1: The Changing Landscape in the American Prison Population: Implications for Children of Incarcerated Parents

Graham, Harris, and Oliver Carpenter begin with a discussion of the demographic trends of parental incarceration and the percentages of children, by race and age, with parents who are currently incarcerated in jails and state and federal prisons. The chapter continues with a brief overview of the conceptual and methodological limitations of research on the developmental outcomes for children with incarcerated parents.

Chapter 2: Parents "in the System": An Ecological Systems Approach to the Development of Children with Incarcerated Parents

Chapter 2, by Holmes, Belmonte, Wentworth, and Tillman, presents a discussion of the theoretical models guiding the research and intervention programs for children with incarcerated parents. The chapter answers such questions as: How is the problem conceptualized? Who is the focus of the intervention? and What are the factors that promote risk and resiliency in these children?

Part II: Developmental Trajectories

The two chapters in the second part of the book focus on describing the developmental outcomes of children (including school-age and adolescents) with incarcerated parents. The section includes chapters that address such questions as: (1) What are the effects of parental arrest, incarceration, and re-entry on children's developmental outcomes?

(2) How do they cope (both positively and negatively) with parental arrest, incarceration, and preparation by parents to re-enter the parenting role? (3) How do parental arrest, incarceration, and re-entry impact children's education, their social-emotional development, their peer relationships, and their sibling relationships? (4) How is the parent-child attachment relationship altered because of parental arrest, incarceration, and re-entry into the parenting role?

Chapter 3: Children of Incarcerated Parents: Developmental Tragectories Among School-Age Children

Chapter 3 by Naudeau focuses on the developmental trajectory of school-age children. According to statistics released by the Department of Justice (2007), over 50% of the children with incarcerated parents are infants under the age of 10. Their developmental outcomes significantly differ from those of adolescents. Naudeau discusses the negative and the positive outcomes that children and families are likely to experience during all phases of parental incarceration. Using a positive development perspective, the chapter discusses how school-age children of incarcerated parents may grow from the experience when provided with adequate support.

Chapter 4: Children of Promise

In Chapter 4, Boudin and Zeller-Berkman provide information on the experiences of adolescents with incarcerated parents. Some evidence suggests that parental incarceration may predispose adolescents to juvenile incarceration, and they may experience such problems as school suspensions, truancy, and a high dropout rate. The chapter discusses the adolescents' experiences with parental incarceration, and details their reactions as the parent is arrested, incarcerated, and released from prison. This chapter reports the findings from three studies that explore key supportive relationships in the lives of adolescents with incarcerated mothers and the role of the adolescents themselves in coping with the challenges.

Part III: Environmental Considerations

Part III focuses on children of incarcerated parents and consists of two chapters. Chapters 4 and 5 discuss the community effects and familial living arrangements of children of incarcerated parents, as well as challenges encountered in these environmental contexts.

Chapter 5: The Effects of Incarceration on Neighborhoods and Communities

Chapter 5 by Chung and McFadden reviews two lines of research that help to explain the consequences of incarceration for communities and the children living in them: (1) the effects of mass imprisonment on community functioning, and (2) community-level effects on child development. The chapter recommends programmatic efforts during imprisonment and reintegration to promote healthy child development in high-incarceration areas.

Chapter 6: Living Arrangements of Children of Incarcerated Parents: The Roles of Stability, Embeddedness, Gender, and Race/Ethnicity

In Chapter 6, Foster first reviews literature on child living arrangements prior to and during parental incarceration, with particular attention to parental gender and race/ethnicity. The second part presents new research on how living arrangements influence parental expectations of living with their children upon release from prison from a Texas dataset. The findings include information on children of both incarcerated mothers and fathers from African American, Hispanic, and non-Hispanic white groups.

Part IV: Parenting from Prison

Part IV discusses the effective clinical interventions and programs that help children to develop resiliency and coping strategies. This section concludes with a chapter on programs that focus on rebuilding the parent-child relationship.

Chapter 7: Building Partnerships to Strengthen Families: Intervention Programs and Recommendations

In Chapter 7, Toth and Kazura highlight programs that help parents reconnect with their children and improve parenting skills, and that help provide services to other family members to help incarcerated parents transition back into the community and reunite with their children successfully. This chapter serves as a catalyst for an examination of matters related to children's visitation programs and the long-term impact on developmental adjustment.

Chapter 8: Strengthening Parent-Child Relationships: Visit Coaching with Children and Their Incarcerated Parents

In Chapter 8, Beyer, Blumenthal-Guigui, and Krupat describe how visit coaching and family centers in prisons and jails offer an attachment-based, culturally competent developmental framework to help incarcerated parents and children's caregivers better understand and meet the needs of their children and manage the uncertainties about the future due to incarceration. In addition, they discuss ways to support children in navigating their relationship with their incarcerated parent.

Part V: Current and Future Directions

This section begins with a discussion of the controversial Adoption and Safe Families Act of 1997, which mandates termination of parental rights after a length of time of parental absence. The section continues with a discussion of the various national-, state-, and community-level programs designed for children with incarcerated parents. The section concludes with suggestions for next steps in research, intervention, legislation, and social policy for children of incarcerated parents.

Chapter 9: Child Welfare Legislation and Policies: Foster Children with a Parent in Prison

Chapter 9 by Beckerman discusses variability in how child welfare agencies and correctional facilities deal with incarcerated parents and their families, and how legislation affects the well-being and developmental outcomes of children. In addition, the chapter describes the findings of a recent study of foster care caseworkers who manage cases of children with incarcerated parents.

Chapter 10: Service Planning and Intervention Development for Children of Incarcerated Parents

Chapter 10 by Phillips discusses national-, state-, and community-level programs that are available for children with incarcerated parents. The chapter describes the strengths and limitations in service planning and intervention development efforts for children of incarcerated parents from two frameworks: (1) a procedural justice perspective and (2) a developmental epidemiology perspective.

Chapter 11: The Challenges of Family Reunification

Harris, et al., discuss the challenges inherent in family reunification. They specifically address the challenges that the re-entering mother faces, as well as those of the children and their current caregivers. The chapter proposes components necessary for family reunification and closes with suggestions for framing research directions and questions on family reunification in the twenty-first century.

Chapter 12: Research and Intervention Issues for Moving Forward with Development in Children of Incarcerated Parents

The volume closes with Chapter 12, with a reflection by Oliver Carpenter, Graham, and Harris on the status of science, practice, and policy on children with incarcerated parents. The chapter includes a summary of the information presented in previous chapters, continues with a discussion of the issues that remain unaddressed, and concludes with recommendations for new directions with reference to legislation, social policy, and programs that impact the quality of life for children of incarcerated parents.

REFERENCES

Bouchet, S. M. (2008). *Children and families with incarcerated parents.* Baltimore, MD: The Annie E. Casey Foundation.
Braman, D. (2004). *Doing time on the outside: Incarceration and family life in urban America.* Ann Arbor, MI: University of Michigan Press.
Christian, S. (2009). *Children of incarcerated parents.* National Conference of State Legislators. http://www.ncsl.org/documents/cyf/childrenofincarceratedparents.pdf
Farrington, D. P., & Welsh, B. C. (2007). *Saving children from a life of crime: Early risk factors and effective interventions.* New York, NY: Oxford University Press.
Glaze, L. E., & Maruschak, L. M. (2008). *Parents in prison and their minor children* (NCJ 222984). Washington DC: Bureau of Justice Statistics.
Harris, Y. R., & Graham, J. A. (2007). *The African American child: Development and challenges.* New York, NY: Springer Publishers.
Johnston, D. (1995). *Effects of parental incarceration.* In K. Gabel and D. Johnston (Eds.), Children of Incarcerated Parents (pp. 59–88). New York, NY: Lexington Books.
McLoyd, V. C. (1998). Changing demographics in the American population: Implications for research on minority children and adolescents. In V. C. McLoyd & L. Steinberg (Eds.), *Studying minority adolescents: Conceptual, methodological, and theoretical issues* (pp. 3–28). Mahwah, NJ: Erlbaum.

Mumola, C. J. (2000). *Incarcerated parents and their children.* (NCJ 182335). Washington DC: Bureau of Justice Statistics.

Parke, R., & K. Clarke-Stewart, A. (2002). *Effects of parental incarceration on young children,* Paper produced for the *From Prison to Home* Conference funded by the U.S. Department of Health and Human Services on January 30–31, 2002. (Available at www.urban.org/RossParke).

Phillips, S. D., Erkanli, A., Costello, E. J., & Angold, A. (2007). Differences among children whose mothers have a history of arrest. *Women & Criminal Justice, 17(2/3),* 45–63.

Phillips, S. D., & Erkanli, A. (2008).Differences in patterns of maternal arrest and the parent, family, and child problems encountered in working with families. *Children & Youth Services Review, 30,* 157–172.

Sue, S. (1999). Science, ethnicity, and bias: Where have we gone wrong? *American Psychologist, 54,* 1070–1077.

Travis, J. (2005). *But they all come back: Facing the challenges of prisoner reentry.* The Urban Institute Press: Washington DC.

Parents "in the System": An Ecological Systems Approach to the Development of Children with Incarcerated Parents

TABITHA R. HOLMES
KIMBERLEY BELMONTE
MARGARET WENTWORTH
KATHLEEN TILLMAN

Over the past 30 years, researchers, educators, and clinicians have recognized the importance of understanding how children are affected by parental absence. Although child-parent separation occurs for a variety of reasons (e.g., parental death, emigration), most research in this area has focused upon children with separated or divorced parents, a research trend influenced by the social changes affecting American families in the 1980s and 1990s. Thus, as divorce rates burgeoned, so too did research inquiries regarding how children are influenced by the psychological, social, and economic upheaval that typically accompanies the dissolution of a two-parent home (e.g., Hetherington, Bridges & Insabella, 1998). At the same time, however, a second group of children faced with parent-child separation—children of imprisoned parents—was steadily increasing in size due to an additional set of changing social conditions. These conditions included a conservative shift in policy that dictated unprecedented prison sentences for drug offenders, many of whom were women (Blumstein & Beck, 1999; Western, Kling & Weinman, 2001). As a reflection of these changes, the prison population increased from approximately 1.8 million in the mid-1970s to 5.6 million in 2001, with a parallel surge in the number of children with imprisoned parents. Despite this trend, these children have largely been absent from most research agendas. This gap in the literature is particularly worrisome given current data that estimate that in 2007 over 1.7 million minor children in the United States had parents in state or federal prison, an 82% increase since 1991 (Glaze & Maruschak, 2008). Such a statistic speaks to the urgency with which the research community needs to contribute, both theoretically and empirically, to the understanding of this emergent population.

Although there is a paucity of research on how a child develops after a parent is sent to prison, researchers across disciplines have begun to address some of the issues related to separation and reunification in families with incarcerated parents. In psychology, inquiries typically involve proximal factors that affect parent-child relationships and processes. Though this research is useful, the narrow scope of this work suggests that development exists in a localized vacuum where children are passively and exclusively influenced by the direct processes that occur in their daily lives; research on children of incarcerated parents (CIP) has rarely addressed the indirect and distal factors that affect developmental processes and outcomes. This approach is problematic given that CIP are often catapulted into a series of complex systems—legal, political, cultural, and institutional—that extend far beyond that of the familial context. Accordingly, a framework for conceptualizing how families are affected by incarceration should examine how children are embedded in a network of overlapping and interactive systems.

Bronfenbrenner (1979) provided such a framework with the Ecological Systems Model when he expanded on traditional definitions of "environment" by describing a set of nested contexts that influence individual development directly and indirectly. After acknowledging the significance of the immediate settings in which an individual lives and develops, he went on to underscore the importance of the relationship between settings and the larger contexts in which settings are embedded. In addition to providing a detailed, differentiated description of the structure of the ecological environment, Bronfenbrenner also described how individuals develop and change over time through ecological transitions. These transitions occur "whenever a person's position in the ecological environment is altered as the result of a change in role, setting, or both" (p. 26). Given that such changes are ubiquitous in the lives of families affected by the incarceration of parents (e.g., grandparents become primary caregivers, children move to new neighborhoods), the Ecological Systems Model is a particularly useful theory for understanding CIP.

The most direct and immediate context in the Ecological Systems Model is the microsystem, a setting in which a developing person interacts "face-to-face" with the physical, social, and symbolic features of the environment. It encompasses a child's family, school, and peer group, along with the physical elements (e.g., noise, pollution, cultural artifacts) that are contained within the environment. The second level, the mesosystem, is a system comprised of two or more microsystems. Accordingly, the mesosystem serves as a link between the information, knowledge, and attitudes that exist between an individual's social worlds and relationships. The exosystem, on the other hand, is a remote system that involves settings that do not contain the developing child; the events that occur in these settings indirectly influence the immediate environment in which the child lives. Examples include a parent's workplace and social and community institutions. Finally, the macrosystem, the most complex and distal system, encompasses the overarching social structures, customs, values, and beliefs that define a particular culture or subculture at a point in historical time. This system is often referred to as a cultural blueprint, encompassing "patterns of ideology and lifestyles that are reflected in goals and practices of socialization" (Bronfenbrenner, 2005b, p. 47).

Given the importance of understanding the ecological complexities of families' lives, along with the "products and producers" (Bronfenbrenner, 1979, p. 26) of developmental change, the next section of this chapter will describe relevant research as it applies to each of Bronfenbrenner's four systems.

THE ECOLOGICAL SYSTEMS MODEL: BEYOND THE IMMEDIATE SETTING

Microsystem

Parent-Child Relationships During Incarceration

As might be expected, most research on CIP in psychology focuses on the microsystem, the face–to–face dyadic interactions created, maintained, and disrupted when a parent is imprisoned. Importantly, a child's entire microsystem is often rearranged after a parent is first arrested, as seen when children are separated from siblings to ease the burden on replacement caregivers. Although separation from their parents is potentially traumatic, children do not generally receive sympathy and support from others, as would be the case if their parents were hospitalized for an illness. Philbrick (2002), for instance, found that even children assigned to social workers did not receive emotional support and were not provided an outlet for the discussion of their parents' imprisonment. The inadequate support for the children's emotional needs reveals just one of the challenges faced by children of incarcerated parents.

The bulk of research on the microsystems of CIP has centered upon the parent-child relationship. Johnson (2006), for example, points out that the separation that occurs when a parent enters prison plays the single most detrimental role in generating negative developmental outcomes in children, although the effects are worse for children if the primary caregiver is imprisoned (Murray, 1999). It is important to note, however, that it is a common misconception that incarceration typically disrupts traditional, intact, nuclear families. Less than half of imprisoned parents live with their children prior to incarceration, and three quarters of imprisoned parents are divorced or unmarried (Hairston, 2007; Mumola, 2000). Exposure to poverty and familial involvement in drugs, criminal behavior, and violence often encompass more significant risk factors than parental imprisonment alone. Thus, compounding risk factors frequently precede incarceration and separate families before parents enter the criminal justice system (Miller, 2006).

Once a parent is imprisoned, there appears to be wide variability in the degree to which family members are given opportunities to foster healthy relationships. During the period of incarceration, less than one quarter of parents see their children on a monthly or more frequent basis (Hairston, 2007; Mumola, 2000), and approximately half have no contact with their children (Snell, 1994). Reasons for lack of regular contact include practical (e.g., location of prison, inconvenient visitation schedules, financial difficulties), institutional (e.g., unsafe visitation rooms, aggressive treatment of visitors), attitudinal (e.g., the belief that children will be harmed by visitation), and relational (e.g., tension in the parent-child relationship) barriers (Hairston, 2007; Parke & Clarke-Stewart, 2003; Seymour, 1998). Although letters and phone calls provide alternative means of maintaining contact, these modes of communication, like visitation, may be fraught with multiple complications.

The degree to which regular visits with incarcerated parents provide children risk or protective factors remains unclear. In some instances, visitation can reassure a child that his or her parent is managing life in prison, thereby ameliorating the stress and distress associated with the separation (Johnson, 1995). At the same time, many children experience negative emotions such as fear and frustration upon seeing a parent in the prison system (Nesmith & Ruland, 2008). Moreover, many children appear to struggle with prison conditions such as lack of physical contact and privacy (Arditti, Lambert-Shute & Joest, 2003), and negative behavioral reactions (e.g., defiant behavior) to a visit are common (Johnson, 1995). Importantly, most research in this area has relied on caregiver reports to describe children's functioning. Replacement caregivers, for example, will often refuse to allow children to visit their incarcerated parent, citing the negative impact that such visits can have on the child (Myers, Smarsh, Amlund-Hagen & Kennon, 1999; Roy & Dyson, 2005; Clopton & East, 2008). Research, however, does not necessarily support this view. Few studies have utilized standardized youth report measures, and even fewer studies have collected data using child interviews, behavioral observations of children, teacher report forms, or information from multiple sources (Myers, Smarsh, Amlund-Hagen & Kennon, 1999). Thus, the effects of prison visitation remain unclear.

In contrast to the issues raised above, some children may not be aware that their parent is incarcerated. Within the family unit, a parent's incarceration may be a source of shame and anger (Myers et al., 1999); children may be kept from knowing the truth about where their parents are and what crimes they were charged with committing. Even for those who do know about their parents' situations, some children are told to keep this information to themselves, a request that may have consequences for the parent-child relationship and the mental health of the child. Pennebaker and Francis (1992) addressed the importance of being able to speak about a trauma, reporting that non-disclosure of trauma is associated with elevated psychological distress and decreased health. Importantly, many children are not given the opportunity to disclose the trauma of their parents' arrest because they do not have anyone in whom they can confide.

Parent-Child Relationships After Incarceration

Most incarcerated parents plan to reunite with their children following release (Poehlmann, 2005; Tuerk & Loper, 2006); however, the prison experience often fails to prepare ex–convicts for the resumption of their roles and duties as parents (Hairston, 2007; Young & Smith, 2000). Recognizing that the design and purpose of the criminal justice system runs contrary to offender–friendly policies, most correctional facilities' treatment programs do not help to resolve problems that contribute to incarceration and the dissolution of families in the first place (Young & Smith, 2000). Furthermore, detriments to self–esteem and personal responsibility incurred during imprisonment undermine ex–convicts' confidence and security in the parental role. In prison, parents are faced with many psychological hurdles such as the loss of self-efficacy and diminished opportunity for identity development, factors that may contribute to feelings of suspiciousness, aggression, or emotional disconnection. Such psychological states are maladaptive when an ex-inmate is reunited with his or her family and may impede normative relations. Similar to the literature on military culture (Hall, 2008), imprisoned parents may learn to survive in prison by adopting skill sets and coping mechanisms that do not translate positively into family life.

Replacement Caregivers

When a parent is incarcerated, the replacement caregiver takes on a critical role for CIP, functioning as an interim primary caregiver and attachment figure. For obvious reasons, the experiences for caregivers differ dramatically depending on the contexts in which they take on additional childcare responsibilities. Although many replacement caregivers do an exemplary job of caring for CIP, financial pressures and stress can jeopardize the caregiver's capacity to provide adequate attention, supervision, and emotional support while parents are imprisoned (Hairston, 2007; Seymour, 1998).

When fathers are incarcerated, children are usually cared for by their biological mothers, a transition that often causes mothers to become more independent, financially and emotionally (Edin, 2000; Travis, 2005). Mothers also tend to act as gatekeepers by restricting or encouraging access and relationships between children and their fathers (Roy & Dyson, 2005). This dynamic is described as "an active process of negotiating overlapping role expectations as partners and parents" (p. 305). Conversely, when mothers are incarcerated, the care of children will often be placed on grandparents (Hairston, 2007; Mumola, 2000), a potentially vulnerable population.

In general, the needs of grandparents caring for CIP are understudied and misunderstood, particularly for grandfathers. Ruiz (2000) identified some of the logistical challenges faced by grandmothers caring for their grandchildren, including declining health, financial strain, and the emotional strain or stress of caring for grandchildren.

In addition, grandmothers are often in need of emotional validation and support, given the difficulty of dealing with CIP who may exhibit emotional problems and behavioral issues in the home and at school (Dressel & Barnhill, 1994).

In terms of nonfamilial childcare arrangements, statistical reports most likely underestimate the percentage of children who enter foster care due to parents' reluctance to report this information and the prevalent use of relatives as "kinship" foster parents (Genty, 1998; Hairston, 2007). Research in this area is scarce and should be a target of future inquiries.

Peer Relationships

Peer relationships also influence the outcomes of children with incarcerated parents by virtue of the powerful socializing roles that peers play in the experiences of young people. In structured intervention settings, for example, peers enduring similar reactions to parental absence due to incarceration may be able to promote empathy and support (Hairston, 2007; Lopez & Bhat, 2007; Miller, 2006). Thus, the significance of peers in reciprocally transmitting and maintaining values contributes to the outcomes of this population in context–dependent ways. Little research, however, has explored this aspect of the microsystem.

The Mesosystem

Neighborhood Effects

Undoubtedly, CIP grow up in diverse neighborhoods that vary in terms of resources, norms, and expectations. In communities in which parental incarceration is rare, children and families may become ostracized and the target of stigma and negative attention (Clopton & East, 2008; Travis & Waul, 2004). Conversely, in some neighborhoods, parental incarceration may be normative rather than stigmatized, a characteristic that can contribute to disorganized communities that have no clear behavioral expectations or tools for socializing children to become productive, law-abiding citizens. In these neighborhoods, high rates of incarceration and reentry (i.e., coercive mobility) often result in high residential mobility rates that disrupt social networks and create an atmosphere of mistrust, isolation, and low social cohesion (Crutchfield,

1989). This in turn may contribute to even greater social disorganization (Western, Lopoo & McLanahan, 2004) and diminished opportunities for children to establish and maintain positive social relationship
(Rose & Clear, 2003). Male role models may be particularly scarce in
neighborhoods where a gender imbalance emerges due to incarceration patterns (Travis, 2005).

In general, CIP are often forced to move, either permanently or temporarily, from their neighborhoods. Harassment or financial hardships,
for example, can force families to relocate, thereby exposing children to
additional life disruptions (Western, Lopoo & McLanahan, 2004). Such
disruptions are also likely to occur when CIP are forced to move from
their homes to live with replacement caregivers (e.g., grandparents or
foster parents) or because their primary caregiver can no longer support the family on one income. Regardless of the motivation behind a
family's move, CIP appear to move frequently. Children with incarcerated mothers, for example, are four to five times more likely to move in
a five year period than children without mothers in prison (Clopton &
East, 2008).

One important element of neighborhood effects on CIP centers
upon social capital. Social capital, as defined by Coleman (1988), refers
to the positive relationships cultivated and maintained by parents and
other adults in the community that contribute to children's development in positive ways. For a variety of reasons, CIP are likely to experience reduced social capital that can negatively influence developmental
outcomes.

As researchers have pointed out, when children are uprooted from
their neighborhoods, social capital may decrease (e.g., McLanahan &
Sandefur, 1994). Residential mobility, for example, is related to how frequently parents talk with other parents; parents who move frequently
are less likely than other parents to talk with the parents of their children's friends (Pettit & McLanahan, 2003). Thus, when families with an
incarcerated parent are forced to move, children are exposed to a reduction in their mesosystem or linked microsystems.

Although research has not extensively examined neighborhood
effects on CIP, some of the work discussed above suggests that this
is an important area to explore in the future. Although it may appear
beneficial to remove criminals and ex-convicts from certain neighborhoods, thereby decreasing local crime rates and increasing social stability, research in community psychology suggests that high levels of
incarcerated community members creates a unique set of problems

for families affected by incarceration that must be addressed (Rose & Clear, 2003).

Parent-Caregiver Relationship

The relationship between an imprisoned parent and the designated caregiver for his or her children is an important mesosystem that can influence the parent-child microsystem. First, the relationship between inmates and their family members prior to incarceration can inform the degree to which relatives are willing to adopt the role of custodial caregiver (Enos, 2001). An inmate who has a history of positive exchanges with her family, for example, may be more likely to receive assistance from family members in a time of crisis than an inmate who has been estranged from her family due to previous prison sentences or a history of addiction or violence. Equally important is the degree to which imprisoned parents believe that family members will provide safe and reasonable care for their children. Thus, the bidirectional relationship between parents and family members can play a role in whether or not children are raised in a familial or nonfamilial setting.

The ongoing relationship between the imprisoned parent and the custodial caregiver also plays a critical role in whether or not children are permitted to visit or stay in contact with their parents while they are in prison (Hairston, 2003); custodial caregivers serve as gatekeepers between children and their imprisoned parents. Nurse (2001), for example, found that the quality of the relationship between an incarcerated father and his children was dependent on the nature of the mother-father relationship. Similarly, incarcerated parents often report that ongoing conflict and disagreements between family members serve as barriers to the ongoing relationships with their children.

The degree to which parents and replacement caregivers view parenting in similar ways is also an important aspect of the mesosystem that may offer insight into the adjustment of CIP (McHale, 2009). Research on co-parenting originally focused on the significance of understanding the extent to which parents work in complementary, consistent ways during separation due to divorce. In this work, researchers found that children who have parents who support one another's parenting values, goals, and strategies adjust to divorce better than children with parents who undermine each other's parenting efforts (Coiro & Emery, 1998). Applying these findings to CIP, it seems likely that children would benefit enormously from co-parenting alliances between an imprisoned parent and the replacement caregiver, be it a marriage partner, family member, or foster parent. This notion requires researchers to move beyond the traditional co-parenting framework to include nontraditional co-parents (Jones, Zalot, Foster, Sterrett & Chester, 2007) such as grandparents and foster parents.

The Exosystem

Effect of Incarceration on an Imprisoned Parent

Schnittker and John (2007) found that incarceration has long-term effects on the physical and mental health of ex-convicts, regardless of the length of incarceration. Moreover, given that mental illness and drug abuse occur at significantly higher rates in offenders than in the general population, Dallaire (2007) notes that incarceration may exacerbate preexisting medical and/or emotional conditions in a way that further erodes ex–convicts' parenting abilities and increases the likelihood of recidivism (Mumola, 2000). Drug offenders, for instance, frequently undergo recurring cycles of release and reentry, placing severe strain on the parent-child relationship (Tuerk & Loper, 2006).

An aspect of the exosystem that is particularly important for understanding CIP involves parents' work contexts (or lack thereof) after incarceration and reunification. Due to the stigma associated with incarceration and the loss of the work experience and education that individuals experience while in prison, ex-inmates may have difficulty finding employment or may find that their earning potential has been greatly reduced post-incarceration. Using the Fragile Families database, for example, Lewis, Garfinkle, and Gao (2007) determined that there is a negative labor market outcome associated with incarceration. Looking specifically at un-wed fathers, they found that fathers who had been incarcerated earned 28% less per year than fathers who had not been incarcerated. Although previous research found that incarceration was associated with reduced wage rates, Lewis et al. (2007) did not find a drop in wage rates, suggesting that the earning potential of previously incarcerated fathers was negatively affected by their inability to find and keep steady employment. Supporting this idea, ex-convict fathers were found to work fewer weeks and fewer hours per week. They were also more likely to engage in unofficial, illegitimate, or "off-the-books" work.

At greatest risk are families in which a previously incarcerated parent cannot find employment. The most obvious negative consequence of parents' unemployment is that their children will have fewer financial resources at their disposal. Job loss and unemployment, however, are also associated with negative psychological, physiological, and social changes for the unemployed worker, with obvious indirect costs for their children. According to a meta-analysis of 104 studies on job-loss, unemployed people had lower levels of psychological and physical well-being than people who were employed (McKee-Ryan, Song, Wanberg & Kinicki, 2005); many report symptoms associated with depression and anxiety (Catalano, 1991; Vinokur, Price & Caplan, 1996; Price, Friedland & Vinokur, 1998). At the same time that unemployment leads to an increase in anxiety and depression, reemployment leads to a decrease in negative affect, as evidenced by several longitudinal studies tracking changes in employment (Liem & Rayman, 1982; Ryan et al, 2005). In addition to manifest psychological symptoms, Liem and Rayman (1982) assert that job loss itself is associated with feelings of guilt, responsibility, and inadequacy. In families with more traditional gender roles, for example, the inability for men to contribute to their family's financial security can cause particular discomfort and stress (Al Gharaibeh, 2009).

Importantly, the negative emotions resulting from unemployment often impact the entire family system. Wives of unemployed men, for example, experience more anxiety and depression when compared to wives of employed men (Liem & Rayman, 1982). As Price, Friedland, and Vinokur (1998) suggest, the loss (or lack) of a job is a network event that can change family ties, social networks, and friendships. Unemployment also can represent a stigmatized social status. Thus, job loss can lead to financial loss and a loss in social capital (Coleman, 1988) for individuals and families. Accordingly, an important area for future research involves the degree to which CIP may be particularly vulnerable to the effects of unemployed parents, given their likely exposure to stigma and fractured social networks independent of a parent's job loss.

In addition to work-related issues, parents who spend time in prison may also have a hard time developing or maintaining positive intimate relations after incarnation. The stigma associated with incarceration, coupled with the loss of finances, subsequent difficulties gaining employment, and legal constraints that prohibit ex-convicts from utilizing public assistance make finding a marriage partner particularly difficult for many men (Edin, 2002; Western, Lopoo & McLanahan, 2004). Research on the relationships that women develop and maintain post-incarceration have not been extensively studied.

Parenting within the Parameters of Policies

A variety of policies related to prison terms and prisoner rights directly and indirectly affect children and families. At the same time, policies often vary from state to state. For example, how individual child welfare agencies go about preserving and strengthening parent-child bonds during incarceration varies dramatically between states (Genty, 1998). One policy that affects all CIP regardless of state residency is the Adoption and State Families Act of 1997. This federal law requires states to terminate parental rights after a child has resided in foster care for 15 of the last consecutive 22 months. Children's date of entry into the foster system is legally designated as 60 days after removal from their homes. This law forces incarcerated parents to relinquish legal rights to their children if they cannot find adequate caretakers for their children. In effect, the law makes it difficult for incarcerated parents to return to their lives and families after serving jail time (Travis, 2005). Although the law is intended to protect children, it does not facilitate their return to their natural family units after their parents' sentences are complete.

Mandatory minimum sentencing is another policy that indirectly precipitates a number of challenges for inmates and CIP (Arditti, Lambert–Shute, & Joest, 2003). Mandatory minimums lead to the fixed, lengthy incarceration of nonviolent drug offenders and dangerous prison overcrowding, conditions that threaten the health and safety of incarcerated parents and disregard individual family circumstances in the course of sentencing procedures. Compounding the repercussions of mandatory minimum sentencing is the considerable and increasing power that prosecutors possess and exercise in the courts, especially with regard to plea bargaining (Arditti, Lambert–Shute & Joest, 2003).

Macrosystem

View of Prison and Prisoners

In general, people around the world have negative opinions of the prison system, viewing prison both as too comfortable a punishment and unlikely to result in rehabilitation (e.g., Roberts & Hough, 2005). By extension, many believe that people who commit crimes are no longer able to contribute positively to society. This viewpoint is illustrated through mechanisms of social stigma according to which normative exclusion is legalized (Murray, 2009). In some states, for example, laws prohibit ex-convicts from voting and accessing welfare benefits or other forms of public assistance (Travis, 2005). Clearly, these permanent sanctions can affect the day-to-day living conditions of CIP, as stigma is transmitted inter-generationally (Gofman, as cited in Murray, 2007). By denying rights to their parents, CIP are denied resources and are consequently excluded from participating in normative society. In addition, the societal messages of disapproval filter down to CIP, who are forced to reconcile mixed messages about parental figures.

Not everyone in society, however, views incarceration as negative. In certain neighborhoods, incarceration is linked to status or street credibility rather than social exclusion (Anderson, 2000). In urban communities where "prison culture" dictates that a young man comes of age by embarking on his first jail sentence rather than by entering college, peer pressure may perpetuate the cycle of intergenerational incarceration (Dallaire, 2007). In these instances, disregard for authority is encouraged, as it represents a kind of rebellion against the White majority. In some African-American neighborhoods, for example, incarceration is not tied to stigma because it is believed that arrests are the result of racism (Schnittker & John, 2007; Anderson, 2000).

APPLYING THE ECOLOGICAL MODEL

Future Research: Systems and Beyond

In addition to revolutionizing the way in which researchers define environmental influences, Bronfenbrenner (1992) championed a series of important ideas about how individuals develop over time. A full review of his contributions is beyond the scope and intent of this chapter; however, several of his ideas are particularly relevant for the study of CIP and may inform the direction of future inquires.

Bronfenbrenner posited that contextual influences are bidirectional and reciprocal—neighborhoods influence families and families influence the communities in which they live; parents play a role in a child's development at the same time that a child contributes to his or her parents' development. Although this interchange makes intuitive sense, reciprocal exchanges have rarely been explored in the literature on CIP. Thus, future research needs to examine such things as how the development of replacement caregivers is affected by the added responsibility of caring for children after parents are sent to prison and how the caregivers' varied coping mechanisms and well-being, in turn, affect the children in their care. A recent qualitative study of the subjective experiences of CIP, for example, found that children are very cognizant of the needs and emotions of their caregivers (Nesmith & Ruhland, 2008). We have little understanding, however, of how these perceptions develop, change, or affect the caregiver-child relationship.

Such perceptions are critical for our understanding of how CIP develop over time, particularly given Bronfenbrenner's (2005a) assertion that human development is influenced by both objective and subjective properties of the environment. In particular, inquires should continue to explore the role of perceptions about prison, people who are incarcerated, and the stigma associated with both. Thus, as argued earlier, public perception of prison and prisoners may affect how families with an incarcerated parent are treated during and after a parent's incarceration, and caregivers' perceptions of the prison environment influence whether or not children are given opportunities to visit their parents while they are incarcerated (Myers, Smarsh, Amlund-Hagen & Kennon 1999; Roy & Dyson, 2005; Clopton & East, 2008).

Second, developmental processes and outcomes are jointly affected by the properties of the person and the environment; individuals are active agents who contribute to their own development (Bronfenbrenner, 1992). Although this idea has been explored in the risk and resilience literature, it has generally not been extended to the study of CIP. Thus, we know very little about the characteristics of CIP that contribute to their development in constructive and destructive ways. For example, an important research question involves whether or not incarcerated parents experience more stress than non-parents, given the fact that they have children. This could be examined as a function of the children's characteristics (e.g., degree of distress due to incarceration). A corollary question could examine how parents' differential responses to their children's varying distress further influence the children, particularly those with certain characteristics. Such a series of inquiries reflect what Bronfenbrenner (1988) referred to as a process-person-context model. This model, an extension of the original ecological systems model (1979), advocates for the understanding of the particular characteristics of the person and context, as affected by mediating and moderating processes.

Finally, in the spirit of the ecological model, future research is needed on the dimension of time, as it influences CIP. This can be accomplished by the use of what Bronfenbrenner labeled a chronosystem paradigm, a research design that "permits one to identify the impact of prior life

experiences, either singularly or sequentially, on subsequent development" (Bronfenbrenner, 2005a, p. 83). This can take two forms, a long- or
short-term approach (Bronfenbrenner, 1993), both of which are important for a complete understanding of CIP. In a short-term approach,
research examines developmental outcomes before and after a life transition (e.g., the removal of a parent from the home due to incarceration). What, for example, is the developmental impact of a child seeing
a parent arrested? Do significant adults in a child's life change their
behavior after a child's parent is arrested? A long-term approach, on the
other hand, requires examination of cohort affects or the cumulative life
course; the effects of a sequence of transitions. This could include, for
instance, examination of the developmental differences of groups of CIP
who are differentially affected by policy decisions that place them with
familial or nonfamilial replacement caregivers.

Rethinking Intervention with CIP

There are several types of interventions that have been designed to meet
the needs of incarcerated parents and their children. These programs aim
to promote positive socio-emotional functioning of children, strengthen
parent-child relationships, and assist incarcerated parents with developing and implementing positive parenting practices. Although the programs intervene at different structural levels, each intervention is built
upon the belief that parents and children who are separated as a result
of parental incarceration face unique challenges and need assistance to
cope successfully with issues related to parental incarceration. Thus, the
focus of intervention has been aimed at proximal processes manifest in
family members' microsystems. In this section, we will briefly outline
three types of interventions for incarcerated parents and their children:
parent education programs, parent-child interventions, and child-focused interventions. We will then offer suggestions for how the ecological model can inform future intervention efforts.

Parent Education Programs

Incarcerated parents often question their effectiveness as parents and can
have difficulty managing their own emotions and responding effectively
to negative child behaviors. Parent education programs aim to address
these and other issues through curriculum-based interventions that
include instruction on child development, positive parenting skills, and

issues unique to parenting from a correctional facility. These programs are offered to select parents and tend to be implemented in women's correctional facilities (Hairston, 2007). One such example is Partners in Parenting (PIP), a skills-based parent education program that involves a developmental curriculum that addresses risk and resilience in children. The program also assists parents with reintegration by preparing parents to develop positive social support networks and connect with their children's schools (Gonzalez, Romero & Cerbana, 2007). Importantly, parents who attend these programs while incarcerated increase their knowledge of effective parenting practices, improve their parenting skills, and increase their confidence as parents (Gonzalez, Romero & Cerbana, 2007; Thompson & Harm, 2000).

Parent-Child Interventions

A number of different interventions seek to strengthen parent–child relationships when a child is separated from a parent due to parental incarceration. These interventions involve both the parent and child and focus on strengthening or repairing parent-child relationships and promoting positive outcomes in affected children (Hairston, 2007). Girl Scouts Beyond Bars, for example, facilitates frequent visits between daughters and imprisoned mothers and attempts to reduce the distress that mothers and children often experience by providing an accepting and non-stigmatizing environment that fosters positive relationships between incarcerated mothers and their daughters. Girl Scouts Beyond Bars follows the format of conventional Girl Scout troops by providing regularly scheduled mother-daughter troop meetings that include structured team-building activities, physical activity, instruction in life skills, and time to engage in leisure activities. The Girl Scouts Beyond Bars curriculum also includes discussions about violence prevention, family functioning, and drug prevention. Troops are typically co-facilitated by therapists and incarcerated mothers, thereby encouraging mothers to function as positive role models for their daughters while implementing positive parenting skills and effectively resolving conflict during meetings (Hairston, 2007; Miller, 2006).

Caregivers of girls who have participated in Girl Scouts Beyond Bars report that girls participating in the program have improved their communication skills and decreased delinquent behavior (Miller, 2006). A similar program, Living Interactive Family Education, is an example of a parent-child intervention that provides boys and their incarcerated fathers with opportunities to strengthen their relationships through joint activities.

Filial Therapy, a form of empathetic, therapeutic response and inter-action, is another example of a parent-child therapeutic intervention that aims to strengthen the parent-child bond while decreasing problematic child behaviors (Harris & Landreth, 1997). In Filial Therapy, trained therapists teach parents to accurately identify and respond to the needs of their children so that parents can function as the primary facilitators of change in their children's lives. In the initial stage of treatment, par-ents receive instruction on basic child-centered play therapy skills (e.g., active listening, identifying and responding to their children's feelings, setting limits in therapeutic ways, increasing their children's self-esteem, and structuring weekly play sessions with their children). In order to facilitate this learning process, parents engage in role-plays and group discussions and then meet with their children several times weekly for special play time. These sessions are videotaped and are reviewed dur-ing supervision. Parents learn to listen empathically, fully engage in their child's play, and to enjoy spending time with their children while provid-ing structure and effectively setting limits (Landreth, 2002).

Child-Focused Interventions

Therapeutic counseling, support groups, and mentoring programs are child-focused interventions that aim to promote the positive socio-emotional functioning of children with incarcerated parents. Some interventions derive their theoretical foundations from grief and loss mod-els (e.g., Deferred Prosecution Unit–Social Workers in Family Services) where facilitators of the programs help children work through the four stages of grief and make connections between their parents' behavior and their own choices. Other mentorship interventions, such as the Amachi Program, are grounded in developmental attachment theory, cultivating supportive bonds between adult role models and children with parents in prison (Hairston, 2007). Informally, many Big Brothers/Big Sisters Pro-grams aim to address the needs of CIP.

Although child-focused interventions programs tend to be scarce, there are a handful of programs that offer individual counseling, group counseling, and structured social activities to children with parents in prison (Hairston, 2007). School-based interventions for children with incarcerated parents are also relatively rare. One recently–developed school-based intervention for third to fifth graders aimed to create a safe and supportive environment, impart information, and encourage group empathy, but has yet to undergo any rigorous evaluation (Lopez & Bhat, 2007).

Ecologically Based Interventions

The ruptured parent-child relationship has historically served as the focal point of interventions designed to assist CIP. As a common theme across an otherwise diverse range of scenarios, disruption in the parent-child attachment constitutes a universal focal point for approaching, understanding, and addressing CIP. With this in mind, successful interventions should promote reciprocal, adaptive exchanges between children of incarcerated parents and important attachment figures such as mothers, fathers, siblings, caregivers, teachers, and peers (Dallaire, 2007; Young & Smith, 2000). However, as demonstrated throughout this chapter, a focus on the microsystem is incomplete and inadequate. Intervention efforts necessitate collaboration and networking between schools, correctional facilities, and social service agencies. In addition, consideration must be given to more distal features of the environment, even those that involve settings with which children do not directly interact. For example, intervention efforts should address replacement caregiver needs, along with the relationships between caregivers and incarcerated parents.

Finally, interventions must accommodate and prioritize among the needs of subgroups; important considerations in this arena include the child's developmental stage, the respective genders of the child and the imprisoned parent, and the interplaying roles of race and culture (Arditti, Lambert-Shute, & Joest, 2003; Engstrom, 2008; Miller, 2006).

CHAPTER SUMMARY

In summary, Bronfenbrenner's ecological model provides a useful framework for understanding the complex, dynamic systems that influence and are influenced by CIP. Accordingly, it allows researchers and clinicians to move beyond the view of the individual child or parent as the primary problem to be studied or "fixed" through intervention. Instead, the model acknowledges that when a parent is incarcerated, a multitude of direct and indirect ecological factors—both in the child's immediate environment and in more distal, macro-level settings—influence how the child will develop. This requires that those interested in understanding CIP excavate below the surface of what is traditionally thought to influence children and families; it requires examination of contexts that are potentially hidden from obvious scrutiny. As Bronfenbrenner (2005c) pointed out

> The responsibilities of the researcher extend beyond pure investigation, especially in times of national crisis. Scientists in our field must be willing to draw on their knowledge and imagination in order to contribute to design of social interventions: policies and strategies that can help sustain and enhance our most precious human resource—the nation's children (p. 272).

By many accounts, we have a national crisis involving incarcerated parents and the children they leave behind (e.g., Glaze & Maruschak, 2008). By providing a framework for how to conceptualize the complexities that characterize the lives of CIP, we hope to contribute to a new dialogue about how to best understand and help families dealing with this issue.

REFERENCES

Al Gharaibeh, F. (2008). The effects upon children in Jordan of the imprisonment of their fathers: A social work perspective. *International Social Work, 51(2)*, 233–246.

Arditti, J. A., Lambert–Shute, J. & Joest, K. (2003). Saturday morning at the jail: Implications of incarceration for families and children. *Family Relations, 52(3)*, 195–204.

Blumstein, A., & Beck, A. J. (1999). Population growth in U.S. prisons, 1980–1996. In M. Tonry & J. Petersilia (Eds.), *Prisons* (pp. 17–61). Chicago, IL: University of Chicago Press.

Bronfenbrenner, U. (1979). *The ecology of human development: Experiments by nature and design.* Cambridge, MA: Harvard University Press.

Bronfenbrenner, U. (1988). Interacting systems in human development. Research paradigms: Present and future. In N. Bolger, A. Caspi, G. Downey, & M. Moorehouse (Eds.), *Persons in context: Developmental processes* (pp. 25–49). Cambridge: Cambridge University Press.

Bronfenbrenner, U. (1992). Ecological systems theory. In R. Vasta (Ed.), *Six theories of child development: Revised formulations and current issues* (pp. 187–248). Philadelphia: Jessica Kingsley.

Bronfenbrenner, U. (1993). The ecology of cognitive development: Research models and fugitive findings. In R. H. Wozniak & K. W. Fischer (Eds.), *Development in context: Acting and thinking in specific environments* (pp. 3–44). Hillsdale, NJ: Erlbaum.

Bronfenbrenner, U. (2005a). Interacting systems in human development: Research paradigms: present and future. In U. Bronfenbrenner (Ed.), *Making human beings human: Bioecological perspectives on human development* (pp. 67–93). Thousand Oaks, CA: Sage.

Bronfenbrenner, U. (2005b). Lewinian space and ecological substance. In U. Bronfenbrenner (Ed.), *Making human beings human: Bioecological perspectives on human development* (pp. 41–49). Thousand Oaks, CA: Sage.

Bronfenbrenner, U. (2005c). Strengthening family systems. In U. Bronfenbrenner (Ed.), *Making human beings human: Bioecological perspectives on human development* (pp. 260–273). Thousand Oaks, CA: Sage.

Catalano, R. (1991). The health effects of economic insecurity. *American Journal of Public Health, 81,* 1148–1152.

Clopton, K. L., & East, K. K. (2008). Are there other kids like me? Children with a parent in prison. *Early Childhood Education Journal, 36,* 195–19.

Coiro, M. J., & Emery, R. E. (1998). Do marriage problems affect fathering more than mothering? A quantitative and qualitative review. *Clinical Child and Family Psychology Review, 1,* 23–40.

Coleman, J. C. (1988). Social capital in the creation of human capital. *American Journal of Sociology, 94,* 95–120.

Crutchfield, R. D. (1989). Labor Stratification and violent crime. *Social Forces, 68*(2), 489–512.

Dallaire, D. H. (2007). Incarcerated mothers and fathers: A comparison of risks for children and families. *Family Relations, 56*(5), 440–453.

Dressel, P., & Barnhill, S. (1994). Reframing gerontological thought and practice: The case of grandmothers with daughters in prison. *The Gerontologist, 34,* 685–690

Edin, K. (2000). Few good men: Why poor mothers don't marry or remarry. *The American Prospect, 11,* 26–31

Engstrom, M. (2008). Involving caregiving grandmothers in family interventions when mothers with substance use problems are incarcerated. *Family Process, 47*(3), 357–371.

Enos, S. (2001). *Mothering from the inside: Parenting in a women's prison.* Albany, NY: State University of New York Press.

Genty, P. M. (1998). Permanency planning in context of parental incarceration. *Child Welfare, 77*(5), 543–559.

Glaze, L. E., & Maruschak, L. M. (2008). Parents in prison and their minor children. *Bureau of Justice Statistics Special Report.* Washington, DC: Bureau of Justice Statistics.

Gonzalez, P., Romero, T., Cerbana, C. B. (2007, December). Parent Education Program for Incarcerated Mothers in Colorado. *Journal of Correctional Education, 58.*

Hall, L. K. (2008). *Counseling military families: What mental health professionals need to know.* New York: Routledge.

Hairston, C. F. (2007). *Focus on children with incarcerated parents: An overview of the research literature.* Baltimore, MD: The Annie E. Casey Foundation.

Harris, Z. L. & Landreth, G. L. (1997). Filial therapy with incarcerated mothers: A five week model. *International Journal of Play Therapy, 6*(2), 53–73.

Hetherington, E. M., Bridges, M., & Insabella, G. M. (1998). What matters? What does not? Five perspectives on the association between marital transitions and children's adjustment. *American Psychologist, 53,* 167–184.

Johnston, D. (1995). Effects of parental incarceration. In K. Gabel & D. Johnston (Eds.), *Children of incarcerated parents* (pp. 59–88). New York: Lexington Books.

Johnston, D. (2006). The wrong road: Efforts to understand the effects of parental crime and incarceration. *Criminology and Public Policy, 5(4),* 703–720.

Jones, D. J., Zalot, A., Foster, S., Sterrett, E. & Chester, C. (2007). Childrearing in African American single mother families: A coparenting framework. *Journal of Child and Family Studies, 16, 671–683.*

Landreth, G. L. (2002). *Play therapy: The art of the relationship* (2nd ed.). New York: Brunner Routledge.

Lewis, C., Garfinkel, I. & Gao, Q. (2007). Incarceration and unwed fathers in fragile families. *Journal of Sociology & Social Welfare, 34*(3), 77–94.

Liem, R., & Rayman, P. (1982). Health and social costs of unemployment. *American Psychologist* 37(10), 1116–1123.

Lopez, C. & Bhat, C. S. (2007). Supporting students with incarcerated parents in schools: A group intervention. *The Journal for Specialists in Group Work, 32*(2), 139–153.

Nurse, A. (2001). Coming home to strangers: Newly paroled juvenile fathers and their children. Paper presented at the Conference on the Effects of Incarceration on Children and Families, Chicago, IL, Northwestern University.

McHale, J. (2009, April). The caregiver's perspective—how coparenting adaptations made in response to parental incarceration affect children's adjustment [panel presentation]. In J. A. Poehlmann (Chair), *The Effects of Parental Incarceration on Children and Families: Diverse Theoretical, Empirical, and Intervention Perspectives.* Symposium conducted at the Biennial Meeting of the Society for Research on Child Development, Denver, CO.

McKee-Ryan, P.M., Song, Z., Wanberg, C.R., & Kinicki, A. J. (2005). Psychological and physical well-being during unemployment: A meta-analytic study. *Journal of Applied Psychology, 90,* 53–76.

McLanahan, S, S., & Sandefur, G. (1994). *Growing up with a single parent: What hurts, what helps?* Cambridge, MA: Harvard University Press.

Miller, K. M. (2006). The impact of parental incarceration on children: An emerging need for effective interventions. *Child and Adolescent Social Work Journal, 23*(4), 472–486.

Mumola, C. J. (2000). *Incarcerated parents and their children* (Bureau of Justice Statistics Special Report No. NCJ 182335). Washington DC: Office of Justice Programs, U.S. Department of Justice.

Murry, J. (2007). The cycle of punishment: Social exclusion of prisoners and their children. Criminology *and Criminal Justice, 7*(1), 55–81.

Myers, B., Smarsh, T., Amlund-Hagen, K., & Kennon, S. (1999). Children of Incarcerated Mothers. *Journal of Child and Family Studies* 8(1), 11–25

Nesmith, A., & Ruhland, E. (2008). Children of incarcerated parents: Challenges and resiliency, in their own words. *Children and Youth Services Review, 30*(10), 1119–1130.

Parke, R. D., & Clarke-Stewart, K. A. (2003). The effects of parental incarceration on children: Perspectives, promises, and policies. In J. Travis & M. Waul (Eds.), *Prisoners once removed* (pp. 189–232). Washington, DC: The Urban Institute Press.

Pennebaker, J. W., Francis, M. E. (1992). Putting stress into words: The impact of writing on physiological, ansentee, and self-reported emotional well-being measures. *American Journal of Heath Promotion, 6*(4), 280–287.

Pettit, B., & McLanahan, S. (2003). Residential Mobility and Children's Social Capital: Evidence from an Experiment. *Social Science Quarterly,* 84(3): 632–649.

Philbrick, K. (2002). Imprisonment: The impact on children. *Issues in Forensic Psychology, 3,* 72–81.

Poehlmann, J. (2005). Incarcerated mothers' contact with children, perceived family relationships, and depressive symptoms. *Journal of Family Psychology, 19*(3), 350–357.

Price, R. H., Friedland, D. S., & Vinokur, A. D. (1998). Job loss: Hard times and eroded identity. In J.H. Harvey (Ed.), *Perspective on loss: A Source Book* (pp. 303–316). Philadelphia, PA: Taylor and Francis.

Roberts, J. V., & Hough, M. (2005). Sentencing young offenders: Public opinion in England and Wales. *Criminal Justice, 5*(3), 211–232.

Rose, D. R., & Clear, T. R. (2003). Incarceration, reentry, and social capital: Social networks in the balance. In J. Travis & M. Waul (Eds.), *Prisoners once removed* (pp. 313–341). Washington DC: The Urban Institute Press.

Roy, K. M., & Dyson, O. L. (2005). Gatekeeping in context: Babymama drama and the involvement of incarcerated fathers. *Fathering, 3*(3), 289–310.

Ruiz, K. M. (1999). Intergenerational households maintained by African American grandmothers: New roles and challenges for the 21st century. *African American Research Perspectives, 6*(2), 1–122.

Schnittker, J., & John, A. (2007). Enduring stigma: The long-term effects of incarceration on health. *Journal of Health and Social Behavior, 48*(2), 115–130.

Seymour, C. (1998). Children with parents in prison: Child welfare policy, program, and practice issues. *Child Welfare, 77*(5), 469–493.

Simmons, C. W. (2000). Children of incarcerated parents. *California Research Bureau, 7*(2), 1–11.

Snell, T. L., & Morton, D. C. (1994). Women in prison: Survey of state prison inmates, 1991 (NCJ 145321). Washington, DC: U. S. Department of Justice.

Travis, J. (2005). Families and children. *Federal Probation, 69*(1), 31–42.

Travis, J., & Waul, M. (Eds.). (2004). *Prisoners once removed: The impact of incarceration and reentry on children, families, and communities.* Washington, D.C: Urban Institute Press.

Tuerk, E. H. & Loper, A. B. (2006). Contact between incarcerated mothers and their children: Assessing parenting stress. *Journal of Offender Rehabilitation, 43*(1), 23–43.

Vinokur, A. D., Price, R. H., & Caplan, R. D. (1996). Hard times and hurtful partners: How financial strain affects depression and relationship satisfaction of unemployed persons and their spouses. *Journal of Personality and Psychology, 71*(1), 166–179.

Weissman, M. & LaRue, C. M. (1998). Earning trust from youths with none to spare. *Child Welfare, 77*(5), 579–594.

Western, B., Kling, J., & Weinman, D. (2001). The labor market consequences of incarceration. *Crime and Delinquency, 47,* 410–27.

Western, B., Lopoo, L., & McLanahan, S. (2004). Incarceration and the bonds between parents in fragile families. In M. Patillo, D. Weiman, and B. Western (Eds.), *Imprisoning American: The social effects of mass incarceration* (pp. 21–45). New York: Russell Sage Press.

Young, D. S. & Smith, C. J. (2000). When moms are incarcerated: The needs of children, mothers, and caregivers. *Families in Society, 81*(2), 130–141.

ADDITIONAL RESOURCES

Bronfenbrenner, U. (2004). On making human beings human. Newbury Park, CA: Sage.

The Center for Children of Incarcerated Parents (CCIP): http://www.e-ccip.org.

Luster, T., & Okagaki, L. (Eds.). (2005). Parenting: An ecological perspective, 2nd ed. Mahwah, NJ: Lawrence Erlbaum.

Developmental Trajectories

PART II

3

Children of Incarcerated Parents: Developmental Trajectories Among School-Age Children

SOPHIE NAUDEAU

There are two main reasons for focusing on the impact that parental incarceration may have on school-age children. First, parental incarceration has become increasingly prevalent in today's American society (Mumola, 2000). Current estimates indicate that between 1.5 million and 2 million American children have an incarcerated parent, and that tens of thousands of others have experienced or will experience the incarceration of a parent at some point in their lives (Mumola, 2000; Seymour & Hairston, 2000; Travis & Waul, 2004).

Second, children of incarcerated parents may experience a range of immediate and long-term problems, such as strains of economic deprivation, feelings of abandonment, loneliness, shame, guilt, sadness, anger, resentment, eating and sleeping disorders, diminished academic performances, and disruptive behaviors at home or at school (Travis & Waul, 2004). In fact, children of incarcerated parents are five times more likely than other children to be incarcerated themselves in the future (Seymour & Hairston, 2000). However, literature on parental incarceration is scarce, and little is known about the impact that parental incarceration may have on children, families, and society at large (Parke & Clarke-Stewart, 2004; Travis & Waul, 2004). If anything, incarcerated individuals tend to be viewed by the media, the general public, and many politicians as being unfit for society, and undeserving of sustained positive attention (Abramsky,

2002). When these incarcerated individuals are parents, they are implicitly viewed as irresponsible caregivers, just like abusive or neglectful parents. Their children, in turn, are denied the attention and support that children usually receive when separated from their parent for other reasons, such as death or divorce.

Despite this lag in adequate knowledge, parental incarceration continues to impact children and families. Therefore, it is of both scientific and social importance to understand how individuals and families are impacted, so that their needs can be properly addressed and their resources enhanced through adequate and evidence-based support. In particular, it is important to understand how parental incarceration may impact school-age children, so that school systems (including teachers and school counselors) and other institutions serving this age group (e.g., organizations providing recreational services, faith-based organizations, etc.) may adapt their programs and practices accordingly.

This chapter draws from several streams of literature and summarizes the state of our current knowledge about how parental incarceration may impact the developmental trajectories of school-age children. We discuss the many negative outcomes that children and families are likely to experience when a parent goes to jail or prison, but we also emphasize that the experience is grounded in a process that often starts before the separation itself and is likely to continue afterwards. That is, we explain that multiple variables beyond parental incarceration per se need to be taken in consideration while appraising its effect on children's development. In addition, using a positive development perspective and learning from the history of the study of other parent-child separations such as divorce, we discuss how school-age children of incarcerated parents may in fact develop quite well and even grow from the experience when provided with adequate support.

PARENTAL INCARCERATION AND EXPECTED NEGATIVE OUTCOMES AMONG SCHOOL-AGE CHILDREN

The rate of incarceration in prisons and jails in the United States has recently escalated at an extremely fast pace. According to the Bureau of Justice Statistics Bulletin (2001), the proportion of incarcerated U.S. residents has increased from 1 in every 218 to 1 in every 142 between 1990 and 2000. This trend seems to have affected both men and women. Yet the increasing incarceration rate for women is of particular concern because these women are often the only caregivers of their children. Although no specific agency or social services system is charged with collecting data about incarcerated mothers and their children, conservative estimates indicate that 65 % of female inmates have children (Mumola, 2000), and that at least 6% of women entering prison or jail are pregnant (Beck & Karberg, 2001). As a result, conservative estimates are that approximately 200,000 children in this country have an incarcerated mother (Mumola, 2000; Travis & Waul, 2004).

In parental incarceration, as in parental death, children and families are likely to experience a sense of loss that may impact their emotional adjustment (Parke & Clarke-Stewart, 2004). John Bowlby's (1960, 1973, 1988) work on attachment, separation, and loss is quite informative in this respect. In his view, having a responsible attachment figure, usually the mother, provides children with a sense of security that leads to positive development. In turn, Bowlby also suggests that separation from this attachment figure may lead to a range of negative outcomes in children, especially young children, as they develop and mature. More recently, Corr & Corr (2004) have highlighted the many challenges faced by children when coping with the death of a parent, as well as the types of interventions that can support children through the grieving process.

Despite the scarcity of precise information on the topic of parental incarceration, and on the extent to which children of various age groups are likely to be impacted, most studies usually conclude that children of incarcerated parents (CIP) are likely to experience a range of negative and sometimes contradictory feelings (Parke & Clarke-Stewart, 2004; Sack, Seidler, & Thomas, 1976; Travis & Waul, 2004). Among the most commonly cited effects are loss of parental socialization through role modeling, support, and supervision; feelings of abandonment, loneliness, shame, guilt (including survivor guilt), sadness, anger, and resentment; eating and sleeping disorders; diminished academic performances; and disruptive behaviors at home or at school. In addition, feelings of being stigmatized by peers, teachers, and society in general might emerge among school-age children unless the incarceration is seen as a direct result of social prejudice. In such cases, children might feel discriminated against rather than stigmatized (Gabel 1992; Gaudin & Sutphen, 1993).

The whole family often undergoes negative changes as well. Indeed, parental incarceration often sets in motion a number of family circumstances, such as loss of income, family relocation to a different community, and greater reliance on the remaining parent or caregiver for all child care responsibilities (Travis & Waul, 2004). In addition, when conflict exists between the parents both before and during the separation, children and families may experience the loss of important relationships with family friends or extended family members (Hairston, 2004).

Yet despite all these expected negative consequences, parental incarceration can sometimes be positive for children. In particular, the incarceration of specific family members can be beneficial for some families when the removed parents used to be violent with his or her spouse, children, or other household members (Travis & Waul, 2004). Acknowledging that problems can and often do arise before a parent is actually incarcerated reminds us that incarceration itself often constitutes only one part of a broader, longer process.

PARENTAL INCARCERATION AS A PROCESS

Issues are likely to arise for school-age children not only during the incarceration period per se, but also before and after it, if and when the absent parent comes home. Here, several streams of literature can inform our understanding of the dynamics that may take place at the child and family levels at all stages of the incarceration process.

Recently, new conceptual and methodological tools for investigating subjective experiences of change have emerged (Flowerdew & Neale, 2003). The life course perspectives on family change and the newer ecological approaches (see Bronfenbrenner, 2001; Elder, 1994, 1998; Lerner, 2002), for instance, enable us to understand different types of parent-child separations as processes, not as discrete events. These approaches also suggest the need to take into account children and families' life experiences, and their cumulative "weight" or "layering" (Flowerdew & Neale, 2003). Such understanding of change as a process, not a single event, can inform our understanding of the distinct stages within the process, namely before, during, and after parental incarceration.

Before Parental Incarceration

In many cases of parent-child separations, research indicates that children may already be at risk of experiencing both internalizing and externalizing negative outcomes before the separation itself. In divorce, for instance, it is imperative to take pre-divorce hostility and conflict into account (Price & Kunz, 2003). Indeed, divorce is a "non-random event" (Burns & Dunlop, 2003), and many of the problems traditionally thought to result from divorce are in fact present within the family life before the actual separation (Hetherington, 2003). Perhaps more obviously than in other types of separation, a parent's incarceration does not necessarily signal the onset of a family's problems (Travis & Waul, 2004). Rather, it often adds to the stress of a family already struggling with such life circumstances as poverty, discrimination, instability, violence, and limited access to sources of support.

During Parental Incarceration

The incarceration period is probably the most documented period in terms of its effects on children and families. However, not all children experience parental incarceration in the same ways. In particular, and among many other variables, parent-child separations resulting from parental incarceration vary in length, in the amount of contacts that parents and children are able to maintain, and in the likelihood that the absent parent will eventually come home. In addition, because separations due to parental incarceration happen over a period of time (i.e., the length of the incarceration period) and not simply as a one point in time event, it is important to understand that children and families' reactions may vary within this period of time.

Children's Adjustment to Parental Incarceration

Bowlby's (1980) work on the grief process that most children go through after parental death can inform our understanding of how children may adjust to other losses, even temporary ones. In particular, Bowlby's (1980) work can inform our understanding of how children may react to the loss of a parent following this parent's incarceration.

Bowlby (1980) pointed out various phases or stages in the grief process. These phases often overlap, and different children may go through them at different rates depending on their developmental level and a range of other variables (Sigelman & Shaffer, 1991). Yet these phases can help us understand the range of reactions that school-age children of incarcerated parents are likely to display and the specific needs that they may experience at different times.

In the first phase, often referred to as the "numbness phase," children seem to not fully realize that a separation has occurred. This psychological numbness may serve as a way to protect children, albeit temporarily, against the painful and sometimes overwhelming feelings that can be associated with the loss of a loved one.

In the second or "yearning" phase, children often become more aware of the feelings of sadness, loneliness, and "separation pain" or "separation anxiety" that they may experience (Bowlby, 1980, Raphel, 1983). They also become increasingly preoccupied with what has been lost (i.e., the parent himself/herself and all that this loss may represent in terms of time spent together, financial well-being, etc.). During this period, children may also develop an ideal image of their absent parent (Whiting, 1990). Disruptive behaviors are likely to emerge (Sigelman & Shaffer, 1991), and children may "recycle" their sadness and pain into misdirected anger toward the adults and children in their environment (e.g., teachers, peers, siblings, the parent who remained home, etc.).

In the third phase, that of "disorientation and depression," children modify their thinking and feelings about the separation, and they often realize that being reunited with the absent parent is not possible in the present. This new realism may lead to apathy and to moderate levels of depression. Here, it is important to note that such reactions are not necessarily problematic, provided that they remain within a normative range. Indeed, although in other circumstances these reactions could be perceived as pathological, Boss (1999) correctly noted that "complicated grieving can be a normal reaction to a complicated situation and is not [due to] internal personality defects" (p.10). Children who experienced a loss, albeit temporary, and who are in this phase of the grieving process, often need time to adjust. Giddens' (1992) concept of "psychological traveling time" is useful in this respect. Indeed, it takes time to accept and come to terms with major life events, and different individuals may "travel" at different paces across contexts (Flowerdew & Neale, 2003). This "traveling" time is needed for children to find a new balance, or equilibrium, in which they can function normally again, and many children who experience a loss do in fact find this new balance.

In the fourth and last phase, the "reorganization phase," children who have reached a new equilibrium pull themselves together. They are often ready to take on new challenges in their lives, and as we will explain later, they may turn this challenging life-event into an opportunity for positive development.

Here it is important to reemphasize that different children go through these phases at different rates, with some children delaying their negative reaction to the separation and others reaching a new equilibrium more quickly (Corr & Corr, 2004). We will explore these differences later, when we discuss the several variables, in addition to the child's age, that need to be taken into consideration when assessing the impact of parental incarceration.

Families' Adjustment to Parental Incarceration

We also need to consider the adjustment process that the whole family may undertake when experiencing the temporary or permanent loss of a family member as a result of his or her incarceration. In this regard, the classic studies on family stress that followed the Great Depression of 1929 (e.g., Angel, 1936; Cavan & Ranck, 1938; Elder, 1974) are highly informative, especially because their findings were later corroborated by more recent studies (e.g., Elder, 1998; McCubbin, Boss, Wilson, & Lester, 1980). What this literature indicates is that, similar to individuals, families go through several phases when adjusting to change. Provided that they have the internal resources to do so (i.e., integration, or a sense of unity and adaptation, or flexibility), families that experience a life stressor or a major change are likely to first go into a stage of crisis and disorganization, followed by a state of reorganization and recovery. Finally, and if all goes well, families reach a new level of organization, or new equilibrium.

Both individuals and family systems, then, go through several phases before they can finally attain balance again. The problem, however, is that reentry of the formerly incarcerated parent may occur before this new equilibrium is found, and at a time when neither the formerly incarcerated parent nor the family and children are ready for the reentry process to begin.

After Parental Incarceration: Reentry

In cases when reentry does take place, many scholars and practitioners have observed that the family's reunion may be more stressful than the separation itself, especially when the incarceration period was long and when the absent parent and remaining family members experienced significant change during the separation period (Parke & Clarke-Stewart, 2004). Inmates' families change in their absence, and returning prisoners often find it difficult to resume their former roles, both as partner and parent (Travis & Waul, 2004). Returning parents may find it difficult, for instance, to reestablish bonds with and authority over their children, which may lead to high amounts of stress and tension.

In addition to the problems they may encounter at home, within their families, returning prisoners also face a host of other challenges that often translate into important issues for the well-being of their children and families (Travis & Waul, 2004). These challenges may include the following: continuing substance abuse problems and a need for treatment; homelessness; difficulty on finding steady employment, especially with a criminal record; and limited access to public assistance and governmental benefits (Parke & Clarke-Stewart, 2004). Reentry, then, is not easy.

Therefore, parental incarceration calls for adjustments at the child and family levels not only during the incarceration period per se but also before and after it. Of course, not all school-age children and families go through the experience in the same way. Significant differences can be expected in regard to the child's specific age, gender, and a host of other variables at the individual, family, and broader contextual levels. As Boss (1986) puts it, a stressor does not act directly on the family; "rather, it is the perception of the event as mediated by internal and external contexts that determines whether the family will cope or fall into crisis" (p. 720).

KEY MODERATING AND MEDIATING VARIABLES

Several important variables may impact how parental incarceration influences the development of school-age children. Among these variables, some are more likely to play a role at the child, family, or sociocultural level, respectively.

Variables at the Child Level

Just as in other types of parent-child separations such as parental death or divorce, several characteristics of the child may impact how he or she will react to the incarceration process (e.g., child's age, gender, and sibling order, as well as his or her temperament, intelligence, physical appearance, and social skills). The interaction among the child's gender, the child's age, and the incarcerated parent's gender may be particularly important in children of incarcerated parents. Indeed, the lack of a masculine positive role-model at home may become particularly problematic in sons of incarcerated fathers, as they may try to understand their own current behavior and life course trajectories through the behavior and life course trajectories of their absent father. They may, then, engage in aggressive behavior or even in criminal or illicit activities as a result of a real or perceived lack of alternative options (Eddy & Reid, 2004).

When children are separated from their mother as opposed to their father, different reactions can be expected in boys and girls, and at different ages. During World War II, Freud and Burlingham (1943) evaluated the impact of parent-child separations following the German bombing of Great Britain, and found that separation from the mother was often more traumatic than separation from the father. In the following years, and within the framework of attachment theory (see Bowlby, 1960), maternal separation was also found to create more distress for children than father absence. Yet the children involved in these studies were usually quite young, and scholars of divorce (e.g., Hetherington, 2003) found in more recent studies that children are not necessarily more affected by maternal separation as compared to paternal separation. This shift in how children react to maternal and paternal separations may reflect a historical shift in the involvement of fathers in their children's lives. In fact, in today's American society there is little evidence of any significant differences in the care-giving skills and competences of mothers as compared to fathers, and boys and girls alike can develop well in either type of care (Hetherington, 2003).

The issue, then, is not so much the gender of the absent parent, but rather the capacity of the remaining parent or caregiver to be involved with the child and to engage in authoritative parenting. Yet children of incarcerated parents are more likely to be placed with an alternative caregiver than with their biological father when their mother is incarcerated. Indeed, although 90% of children of incarcerated fathers are cared for by their mothers, 79% of children of incarcerated mothers reside with grandparents or other relatives but not with their fathers (Mumola, 2000; Travis & Waul, 2004). In many cases, it might be particularly difficult for these fathers to become involved with their children, especially—as is often the case—when they were not present in their children's lives prior to the mother's incarceration (Seymour & Hairston, 2000).

Variables at the Family Level

The configuration of the family prior to the incarceration period and the capacity of the remaining parent or caregiver to function effectively are likely to act as key variables in how children and families may adjust to a parent's incarceration. In many cases, however, remaining parents are either not involved in the child's care giving (especially, as just discussed, when they were not involved prior to the incarceration) or they are so affected by the incarceration themselves that they cannot engage in positive parenting. Living with a depressed, disturbed, or character-disordered parent after parental incarceration is likely to place children at risk of impaired emotional, social, and academic achievement. In turn, living with a parent who is psychologically competent often acts as a protective factor in children of incarcerated parents (Hairston, 2004). In essence, then, children's symptoms following parental incarceration are often mediated by their remaining parent or caregiver's capacity to function well and to engage in positive parenting.

Moreover, communication within the family, both between the children and the remaining parent and with the incarcerated parent can dramatically improve how children cope and adjust to the separation process and to the family structural changes that ensue. However, in many cases, children are not fully informed about their parent's incarceration, or when they are, they might not be able to maintain frequent contacts with that parent.

Children of incarcerated parents often receive a distorted explanation of where their parent is and why he or she is there. Some parents and scholars argue that lying to children is a way to protect them and to minimize the negative consequences associated with such a separation (Hairston, 2004). Following this type of reasoning, nearly one third of American families of incarcerated parents do in fact engage in some form of total or partial deception and may refer to prison as an army camp, a hospital, or even a school (Parke & Clarke-Stewart, 2004). In some cases, there may be legitimate reasons for the remaining parent or caregiver to partially or totally hide the truth from the children. Indeed, family jobs, housing, welfare payments, and child custody may be jeopardized when a parent's incarceration becomes public knowledge (Johnston, 1995). In addition, and depending on the circumstances, most children do not need to know all the details of their parent's crime or illicit behaviors and arrest.

However, the uncertainty and lack of information that results from what Johnston (1995) calls "forced silence" often undermines children's ability to cope (Parke & Clarke-Stewart, 2004). In turn, providing children with the information they deserve to have, in ways that are developmentally appropriate, allows them to begin the process of grieving the loss of their parent and to adjust to their new situation. Moreover, when children do know where their parent is, regular contacts and visits are more likely to take place. Children then get an opportunity to better understand their parent's situation, to see them realistically, and to express their emotional reactions to the separation (Naudeau, 2003). Regular visitation also allows parents and children to maintain their existing relationship, thus allowing the family to reunite more success-fully following separation (Johnston, 1995).

Yet despite these beneficial aspects of visitation, approximately one half of incarcerated parents in the United States do not receive any vis-its from their children, and many others receive only infrequent visits (Hairston, 2004; Seymour & Hairston, 2000). Many factors may inter-fere with regular contacts. The costs associated with collect calls from and to prisons, and with transportation to correctional facilities that are located far away from where the family lives are prohibitive for many families (Mumola, 2000). In addition, visits to prison are often charged with intense emotions (Hairston, 2004), and the unfriendliness of the prison environment often makes the experience so distressing that many incarcerated parents do not want their children to visit in such condi-tions (Covington-Katz, 1998). Finally, the remaining parent or caregiver may not wish the children to maintain regular contact with their incar-cerated parent. This view is particularly likely to occur when there is a high amount of conflict between the two parents, or when the remaining parent or caregiver believes that the incarcerated parent would set a bad example for his or her children (Hairston, 2004).

In sum, then, the reaction of the remaining parent or caregiver fol-lowing the incarceration, the level of communication that takes place between the two parents and with the children, and the amount of con-tacts that children can maintain with their incarcerated parent can act as key mediators of how parental incarceration may impact children. In addition, several important variables at the community level may also influence how children and families adjust to separations due to parental incarceration, especially in the case of school-age children who become increasingly socialized with friends, teachers, and other community members as they grow older and more independent.

Variables at the Sociocultural Level

The historical, societal, and political context of parent-child separations due to parental incarceration may impact the meaning of the loss for the child, his or her family, and society at large. Further, the level of communi-cation that takes place around parental incarceration and the support that children and families may receive often vary depending on this meaning.

Children who experience the death of a parent are likely to receive support from multiple sources (Corr & Corr, 2004). In turn, children of incarcerated parents are most likely to experience stigma and shame. In today's American society, somewhat similarly to how divorced parents were perceived and treated in the 1950s and 1960s, incarcerated parents are seldom viewed as worthy of positive attention (Parke & Clarke-Stewart, 2004). On the contrary, popular beliefs such as "the apple does not fall far from the tree" or "like father, like son" tend to influence how society behaves toward the children of incarcerated parents. At best, the specificity of their situation and the pain that they may experience is simply ignored, and as Clark (1995) noted, they become the "unseen victims" of their parent's incarceration. At worst, they are seen as "bad seeds" that are predisposed to engage in illicit activities themselves (Eddy & Reid, 2004; Hairston, 2004).

In any case, the lack of interest and/or the social stigma that most children of incarcerated parents experience often prevents them from getting the support they need. Indeed, many children and families do not tell even their closest friends about a parent's incarceration for fear of being exposed to ostracism and discrimination (Hairston, 2004; Fishman, 1990; Koenig, 1985). In fact, many children of incarcerated parents who are victims of such ostracism or who voluntarily distance themselves from their peers and teachers because of fear of sharing their family's experience end up falling behind academically and eventually dropping out of school (Eddy & Reid, 2004).

Depending on the crime their parent committed and on the prevalence of imprisonment in their neighborhood, children and family members may not experience as much stigma or shame (Hairston, 2004; Schneller, 1976). In fact, children and families may experience a combination of resentment and pride—not shame—when a parent's incarceration is viewed as a direct result of injustice (e.g., in the case of political prisoners) or social prejudice against minorities (Gabel, 1992). Indeed, in today's American society, certain minorities are more affected by incarceration than others. For instance, 12% of Black males in their twenties and thirties were in prison or jail in 2000, as compared to 4% of Latino males and 1.7% of White (non-Latino) males (Bureau of Justice Bulletin, 2001). As we will further discuss later in this chapter, such ambivalent feelings may trigger positive outcomes in these children's development, especially in regard to character, but they can also lead to further alienation.

The level of support available to children and families depends upon the local and societal normality of the experience and the meaning associated with it. Yet the amount of support that children and families receive during the separation process plays a critical role in how they may adjust to their parent's incarceration (Travis & Waul, 2004). Support may come from a variety of sources: the extended family, the children's school and recreational services, faith-based institutions, the community, and the government. It may also come in many forms, such as emotional, financial, or practical (e.g., care giving) support.

Some scholars have argued that economic support is most likely to be forthcoming in European American families, and African American families are more likely to provide help in services. A grandmother, for instance, may provide practical support in housework and childcare and emotional support for her son or daughter and grandchildren (Parke & Clarke-Stewart, 2004). Yet the involvement of a grandmother may also lead to increased stress within the family and to negative outcomes in the children if the relationship between the grandmother and the remaining parent is tense. In fact, many mothers with incarcerated husbands and overly involved parents report feeling infantilized (Parke & Clarke-Stewart, 2004). This is not to say that the presence and help of grandparents cannot be positive. On the contrary, it can be. But when positive effects are gained, they are usually indirect and obtained through the type of support that leads the remaining parent to engage in improved parenting.

Finally, positive peer relationships and a structured school environment are likely to act as powerful buffers of the children's experience, especially for school-age children. Indeed, although children who become increasingly involved in a delinquent peer group are likely to develop antisocial behaviors and academic problems, a positive and supportive relationship with a single friend or with a caring adult outside the family (e.g., with a teacher, coach, or other mentor) may help buffer the negative impact of the separation (Rhodes, 2002). Similarly, children who experience the incarceration of one or both parents and who are placed in chaotic schools characterized by erratic discipline, low expectations by teachers, and a mutual lack of respect between teachers and students are more likely to engage in conduct disorders than children who find themselves in a supportive and structured school environment where teachers and counselors are available and sensitive to their needs (Parke & Clarke-Stewart, 2004).

In general, given the fact that parental incarceration remains a non-normative experience that is often perceived negatively by society, CIP appear more likely than other children to experience stigma and shame, to receive little or inadequate support, and to experience a range of internalizing and externalizing problems. However, we know from recent literature on divorce that positive outcomes can result from at least certain types of parent-child separation depending on the broader context and on the level of support that children receive throughout the separation process and the family structural changes that ensue.

THE POTENTIAL FOR POSITIVE DEVELOPMENTAL OUTCOMES

The view that parental incarceration presents a risk in children's lives and developmental trajectories is consistent with the fact that most studies still place an overriding emphasis on the harmful factors associated with parental separation, especially resulting from incarceration, rather than on the positive outcomes that children may derive from the experience. However, several scholars have begun to report that many children do adjust quite well to the experience of having an absent parent, and that some children even develop new strengths in the process.

Over the past few years, for instance, scholars have increasingly documented instances of positive development among children of divorced parents. Although not minimizing the stress and risks to children that divorce may create, both Kelly (2003) and Smart (2003) explain that the vast majority of these children (i.e., 75% to 80%) do not have any problems in adjustment, intimate relationships, or career attainment later in life. In fact, they say, many of these children develop positive attributes in the process of adjusting to their parents' divorce. In the Virginia Longitudinal Study of Divorce and Remarriage, Hetherington (2003) further explains that divorce can lead to a range of outcomes in children. Indeed, although 20% of the sample seemed to experience difficulties in regard to internalizing, externalizing, social and cognitive competence, and self esteem, half of the sample scored within the norm on these various outcome variables, and 30% demonstrated high (i.e., above the norm) levels of competence in several areas. Adolescents in all three competent clusters were low in problem behaviors and high in social skills, popularity, and academic performance.

The literature on positive development among children of incarcerated parents is much scarcer. In a sense, this absence of information is not very surprising. Indeed, the political implications of saying that children can turn out fine when one or both of their parents are incarcerated are many, and any policymaker or practitioner must use caution when making such statements. Unlike children of divorced parents, and for reasons noted above, most children of incarcerated parents do not receive much support to cope with the separation process. Therefore, and perhaps rightly so, the few scholars who write about the impact that parental incarceration may have on children tend to focus on these children's needs rather than on their inner strengths and resources.

What these scholars tend to ignore is that the millions of American children who currently experience the incarceration of a parent will become adult citizens one day. Therefore, it is of paramount importance to understand not only how they can grow up into harmless and problem-free young adults but also how they can go much further and develop into responsible, society-minded, and contributing adult citizens—people that others would embrace as friends, neighbors, and community leaders.

To address the question of how school-age children experiencing parental incarceration may become fully contributing adult members of society, we need to better understand how parental incarceration may impact children's character and character development. Yet character is one of those essential attributes of human life that is difficult to capture in words. As Ryan and Bohlin (1999) put it: "like all abstractions, you can't see character, you can't touch it, [and] you can't taste it" (p. 5), and Berkowitz (2002) further explains that no real consensus exists among psychologists and researchers about how the term character is or should be defined (see Naudeau, 2005, for a full review on this topic). For the purpose of this chapter, we use Lerner's definition of character as "a central tendency of a person (. . .) that constitutes his or her probability in acting good (or bad), socially right (or wrong), and admirably (or not admirably) in the context of opportunities or presses to behave alternatively" (personal communication, December 31, 2004).

Just as character is not so simple to define, little consensus exists on how character develops (see Naudeau, 2005, for a full review on this topic). However, a certain amount of consensus exists. Indeed, although scholars, educators, and laypersons alike often agree that character development first takes place within the family, many also believe that friends, schools, and other institutions within the community (e.g., youth development programs, faith and/or spiritual communities, the mass media, government, etc.) have an influence on children's character and should therefore participate in the promotion of their character development (Damon, 1997; Hoff Sommers, 2002).

This focus on character and character development, rather than on any of the other attributes of positive development, is particularly relevant because CIP are often considered particularly at risk of growing into deprived and arguably depraved individuals with no moral compass. Indeed, parental incarceration often raises the fear in people's minds that the children will end up becoming criminals themselves, and sooner rather than later.

Following the idea of "inborn criminality" first developed by the nineteenth century Italian philosopher Lombroso (1874), many concerned citizens and policymakers have difficulties conceiving of children of incarcerated parents as moral individuals. Instead, they focus on the fact that children of incarcerated parents are five times more likely than other children to end up in jail or prison at some point in their lives (Eddy & Reid, 2004). Yet beyond these statistics and the much contested genetic explanation offered by Lombroso (see Farrington, 1993; Trasler, 1962), much remains to be understood about why children of incarcerated parents are more likely than other children to become criminals—and maybe more interestingly, how (i.e., with what types of support) these same children can develop in positive ways.

NEGATIVE LIFE EXPERIENCES AND CHARACTER DEVELOPMENT

Could negative life experiences, or contradictions in life, have the potential to trigger positive development among school-age children? This question is particularly important in light of our focus on parental incarceration. Indeed, the experience of being separated from one or both parents as a result of parental incarceration is painful for most children and potentially harmful as well. However, as Damon (1997) explained when speaking of family breakup and loss, "the effects can be managed. Children are resilient. They can come through such experiences as strong or stronger than they were prior to the difficulties. [. . . .]. In fact, adversity in the home, much like any other hardship, can facilitate the child's character development, particularly when the child is offered proper guidance and support." (p.85)

Several scholars, particularly in the cognitive development tradition (Piaget, 1932, 1973; Kohlberg, 1968, 1970, 1984) have explained that progression from one stage of character development to the next involves a disequilibrium followed by a new and more advanced type of equilibration. Using Kohlberg's (1968) stages of moral development,

Turiel (1998) investigated the effects of contradictions on moral thinking. He hypothesized that the best way to induce moral development in children and adolescents was to present them with conceptual contradictions at one stage above their current level of moral reasoning. Once children perceive a conflict between two arguments, they usually feel challenged and motivated to solve it (Turiel, 1998), especially if enough support is present in the environment (Damon, 1997).

School-age children of incarcerated parents may experience and/or perceive a lot of contradictions between their absent parent's behavior and/or beliefs and the other moral messages they are likely to receive from various sources (e.g., the other parent or alternative caregiver, other family members, friends, school, the media, and society at large). They are likely to experience conflicting value systems, both within their own family (e.g., when the incarcerated parent's behavior is condemned by other family members as immoral) and outside of it. As previously discussed, many CIP experience a range of negative feelings, including stigma, and others may also experience a combination of resentment and pride, especially when their parent's incarceration is viewed as a direct result of prejudice (Gabel, 1992; Gaudin & Sutphen, 1993).

In addition, children who do not receive any support to cope with the separation process or whose right to communicate with their incarcerated parent is being challenged may also develop a lack of respect for authority and a feeling of anger toward society (Gabel, 1992; Johnston, 1995). We may expect, then, that exposure to conflicting value systems may lead to character growth in at least some CIP, especially if the types of conflicting values they are presented with are just slightly above their own level of cognitive development, and if they receive enough emotional support to cope with their parent's incarceration.

RECENT FINDINGS AND IMPLICATIONS FOR FUTURE RESEARCH

A recent study of positive development among children of incarcerated parents (see Naudeau, 2005) investigated how incarceration of one or both parents may impact the development of sixth-grade children, particularly their character and character development. A sub-sample of participants (N = 54) was derived from the 4-H Study of Positive Youth Development (PYD), a national longitudinal investigation assessing the development of key characteristics of positive youth development (i.e., the "Five Cs" of competence, confidence, connection, character, and caring), and a sixth C, contribution. Both quantitative and qualitative data were collected through student questionnaires (completed by students at their local school or 4-H site under the supervision of trained study staff) and through parent questionnaires (completed at home). Two major conclusions were drawn from the results of this exploratory study.

First, when several key theoretical and/or empirical variables (i.e., child's sex, race/ethnicity, and site of testing; household's income; caregiver's education, relationship to the child, and health) were controlled for, parental incarceration was not related to increased problem behaviors (i.e., intra-punitive behaviors (e.g., depression and risk behaviors such as smoking cigarettes, drinking alcohol, and using drugs) and extra punitive behaviors (e.g., bullying and delinquent behaviors)) or to lower scores in regard to character, or the other markers of positive development (i.e., competence, confidence, connections, caring, and contribution). Second, there was significantly more variance within the group of children of incarcerated parents than within the comparison group in regard to character.

The fact that CIP in this sample did not engage in more intra-punitive or extra-punitive behaviors than children in the control group (i.e. children who had not experienced parental incarceration) and did not exhibit lower scores on character and other positive attributes could be interpreted in several ways.

On the one hand, it is possible that CIP in this sample did not experience high levels of stress in their family lives as a result of parental incarceration. Alternatively, they had enough individual resources and external support to cope with such stress and were able to develop in positive ways, including in regard to character. The exploratory qualitative results in this study seem to corroborate this second interpretation. Indeed, children in the comparison group were significantly more likely to speak of conventional aspects of character (e.g., "being a good/nice person" and "behaving well") when asked to describe a person who is doing really well in all areas of his/her life. In turn, CIP were significantly more likely to mention other dimensions of character (e.g., "being brave/courageous," "doing what is right," "trying one's best," "respecting self and others," and "being responsible") that were coded as somewhat more mature.

It is also possible that a delay in reaction may occur when it comes to how parental incarceration can impact children's character and overall development. Children in this sample are still young (11 years old on average) and their character is far from being fully developed. Indeed character, much like identity (see Erikson, 1959), has the potential to develop not only during childhood and adolescence but also throughout life, at least in individuals who remain open to novelty and change throughout their lives (Colby & Damon, 1992). In the process, individuals' character may move backward and forward, depending on the particular situation they face and the environment they evolve in at a given time (Berger, 1999). Accordingly, 11-year-old children who score higher than other same-age children on character today might score lower a few months or a few years later. Similarly, individuals who score lower than others in this study may develop positively later on in adolescence, when they are further along in their individual developmental trajectory. Therefore, only longitudinal research can properly assess change over time in the development of children of incarcerated parents—and sustained efforts should be deployed to ensure that children of incarcerated parents receive adequate support through schools and other relevant institutions, even when they appear to develop well.

It is also interesting to note that CIP in this sample differed significantly from one another in regard to character. Indeed, results from the exploratory study described above indicated significantly more variance within the CIP group than within the comparison group on the quantitative measure of character.

These findings are hardly surprising, as several cognitive, contextual, and social factors may lead to differences in character and character development among individuals who experience similar events or contradictions in life. Therefore, children who experience parental incarceration are likely to react in different ways when it comes to character.

In addition, several scholars (e.g., Colby & Damon, 1992; Hart, Yates, Fegley, & Wilson, 1995; Walker at al., 1995) explain that individuals' own interpretation of the negative events or contradictions they experience in life and the meaning they derive from these experiences play a key role in how their character may further develop. Indeed, differences in how people make meaning of their life seem to account for much of the difference in how they react to certain events (Colby & Damon, 1992, Kegan, 1982).

Over time and across experiences, character becomes more complex and coherent insofar as people develop the capacity to develop adaptive schemas and to unify their experience and their actions accordingly (Erikson, 1956; Horowitz, 1998). Kegan (1982) refers to this process as the "evolution of meaning" (p. vii). Learning to make meaning of certain events—especially negative ones—in a way that is both realistic and adaptive is a lifelong process.

As previously noted, character development is far from being complete in childhood and early adolescence. For one thing, the overall stage of logical thought within which school-age children and young adolescents function often limits their capacity to make meaning of certain experiences (Piaget, 1932; Turiel, 1998). On the other hand, late childhood is also a time of strong idealism (Elkind, 1967), and the capacity of children to derive a positive meaning from negative experiences might come from aspects of their overall development that go well beyond their cognitive growth.

Implications for Future Research

Clearly, the findings discussed above are very preliminary and are limited insofar as they rely on a small sample size of children whose scores on various measures were collected at only one point in time. Recruiting large numbers of children of incarcerated parents for research purposes can prove quite difficult. Indeed, parental incarceration remains such a taboo topic in much of today's American society (Abramsky, 2002; Johnston, 1995) that both children and parents are likely to underreport such painful experiences. In addition, parents or caregivers who are raising children alone as a result of parental incarceration are likely to experience increased levels of stress (Kelly, 2003). As a result, they may be less likely to participate in a research study with their children, unless the direct benefits they see in doing so outweigh the constraints (e.g., time commitment, etc.).

However, larger sample sizes are necessary for further research to be conducted on the topic of how parental incarceration may impact the developmental trajectories of their school-age children. Indeed, larger sample sizes would allow researchers to conduct hierarchical regression analyses in order to assess which variables (e.g., child's age, sex, race/ethnicity; household's income; caregiver's education; relationship to the child; level of family stress; types and levels of support received by the child and his/her family, etc.) exert a mediating or moderating influence on various developmental outcomes of interest.

Unfortunately, conducting quantitative research on this topic with a large sample size is a challenging endeavor at this point in time given the constraints previously listed. As an alternative and/or complementary strategy, conducting in-depth qualitative studies with a limited numbers of parents and children who experienced parental incarceration may be more feasible at this point and may help researchers generate more hypotheses, provided that enough participants could be recruited for in-depth interviews. In particular, researchers could use qualitative methods to assess how participants make meaning of their parent's incarceration, and how different meaning-making strategies may lead to different outcomes in their developmental trajectories.

CONCLUSION

In sum, much remains to be learned about how parental incarceration may impact the developmental trajectories of school-age children. Given that parental incarceration has become so prevalent in today's American society, it is both of scientific and social importance to move this research agenda forward.

It is also critical to break the taboo of parental incarceration and to provide timely and sensitive support to school-age children of incarcerated parents and their families. As discussed in this chapter, childhood is a time of great plasticity when it comes to character and character development. A supportive school environment (i.e., one in which peers, teachers, coaches, and counselors are willing to listen to and respond to the specific needs of CIP) is likely to act as a powerful buffer to these children's negative experience and to help them develop to their full potential as young members of society—for the benefit of all. Therefore, promoting such positive and structured school environments in communities where parental incarceration is particularly prevalent should be a priority for both policymakers and civil society.

CHAPTER SUMMARY

This chapter draws from several streams of literature and summarizes the state of our current knowledge about how parental incarceration may impact the developmental trajectories of school-age children. We discuss the many negative outcomes that children and families are likely to experience when a parent goes to jail or prison, but we also emphasize that the experience is grounded in a process that often starts before the separation itself and is likely to continue afterwards. That is, we explain that multiple variables beyond parental incarceration per se need to be taken in consideration while appraising its effect on children's development. In addition, using a positive development perspective and learning from the history of the study of other parent-child separations such as divorce, we discuss how school-age children of incarcerated parents may in fact develop quite well and even grow from the experience when provided with adequate support.

REFERENCES

Abramsky, S. (2002). *Hard time blues: How politics built a prison nation.* New York: St Martin's Press.

Angel, R.C. (1936). *The family encounters the Depression.* New York: Charles Scribner.

Beck, A., & Karberg, J. (2001). *Prison and jail inmates at Midyear 2000.* Bureau of Justice Statistics Bulletin. U.S. Department of Justice: Washington DC. NCJ 185989.

Berger, E. (1999). *Raising children with character: Parent, trust, and the development of personal integrity.* Northvale, NJ: Jason Aronson Inc.

Berkowitz, M.W. (2002). The science of character education. In Damon, W. (Ed.), *Bringing a new era in character education* (pp.43–63). Stanford, California: Hoover Institution Press.

Boss, P. (1986). Family stress: Perception and context. In Sussman, M., & Steinmetz, S. (Eds.), *Handbook on marriage and the family* (pp. 695–723). New York: Plenum Press.

Boss, P. (1999). *Ambiguous loss: Learning to live with unresolved grief.* Cambridge, MA: Harvard University Press.

Bowlby, J. (1960). Grief and mourning in infancy and early childhood. *Psychoanalytic Study of the Child, 15,* 9–52.

Bowlby, J. (1973). *Attachment and loss, II: Separation.* New York: Basic Books.

Bowlby, J. (1980). *Attachment and loss, III: Loss, sadness, and depression.* New York: Basic Books.

Bowlby, J. (1988). *A secure base: Parent-child attachment and healthy human development.* New York: Basic Books.

Bronfenbrenner, U. (2001). Human development, bioecological theory of. In N. J. Smelser & P. B. Baltes (Eds.), *International encyclopedia of the social and behavioral sciences* (pp. 6963–6970). Oxford: Elsevier.

Bureau of Justice Statistics Bulletin (2001, March). *Prison and jail inmates at midyear 2000.* Washington DC: U.S. Department of Justice.

Burns, A. & Dunlop, R. (2003). Parent and child similarities in divorcing and non-divorcing families: A ten year study. *Journal of Divorce & Remarriage, 39*(1–2), 45–63.

Cavan, R.S., & Ranck, K.H. (1938). *The family and the Depression.* Chicago: University of Chicago Press.

Clark, J. (1995). The impact of the prison environment on mothers. *The Prison Journal, 75 (4),* 306–329.

Colby, A. & Damon, W. (1992). *Some do care: Contemporary lives of moral commitment.* New York: The Free Press.

Corr, C., & Corr, D.M. (2004). *Handbook of childhood death and bereavement.* New York: Springer Publishing Company

Covington-Katz, P. (1998). Supporting families and children of mothers in jail: An integrated child welfare and criminal justice strategy. *Child Welfare, 77 (5)*, pp. 495–511.

Damon, W. (1997). *The youth charter: How communities can work together to raise standards for all our children.* New York: The Free Press.

Eddy, J.M., & Reid, J.B. (2004). The adolescent children of incarcerated parents: A developmental perspective. In Travis, J., & Waul, M. (Eds.). *Prisoners once removed: The impact of incarceration and reentry on children, families, and communities.* Washington, DC: The Urban Institute Press.

Elder, G. H., Jr. (1974). *Children of the Great Depression.* Chicago, IL: University of Chicago Press.

Elder, G.H., Jr. (1994). Time, human agency, and social change: Perspectives on the life course. *Social Psychology Quarterly, 57*, 4–15.

Elder, G.H., Jr. (1998). The life course as developmental theory. *Child Development, 69*, 1–12.

Elkind, D. (1967). Egocentrism in adolescence. *Child Development, 38 (4)*, pp. 1025–1034. Erikson, (1959). Identity and the life-cycle. *Psychological Issues, 1*, 18–164.

Farrington, D.P. (1993). The psychosocial milieu of the offender. In Gunn, J., & Taylor, P.J. (Eds.), *Forensic psychiatry: Clinical, legal, and ethical issues* (pp. 252–285). Oxford, UK: Butterworth-Heineman,

Fishman, L.T. (1990). *Women at the wall: A study of prisoners' wives doing time on the outside. Albany.* State University of New York Press.

Flowerdew, J., & Neale B. (2003). Trying to stay apace: Children with multiple challenges in their post-divorce family lives. *Childhood, 10*(2), 147–161.

Freud, A., & Burlingham, D.T. (1943). War and children. New York: Ernest Willard.

Gabel, S. (1992). Behavioral problems in sons of incarcerated or otherwise absent fathers: The issue of separation. *Family Process 31*, 303–314.

Gaudin, J.M. & Stutphen, R. (1993). Foster care vs. extended family care for children of incarcerated mothers. *Journal of Offender Rehabilitation, 19 (3/4)*, 129–147.

Hairston, C.F. (2004). Prisoners and their families: Parenting issues during incarceration. In Travis, J., & Waul, M. (Eds.). *Prisoners once removed: The impact of incarceration and reentry on children, families, and communities.* Washington, DC: The Urban Institute Press.

Hart, D., Yates, M., Fegley, S., & Wilson, G. (1995). Moral commitment in inner-city adolescents. In Killen, M., & Hart, D. (Eds.), *Morality in everyday life: Developmental perspective.* Cambridge, MA: Cambridge University Press.

Hetherington, E. M. (2003). Social support and the adjustment of children in divorced and remarried families. *Childhood, 10*(2), 217–236.

Hoff Summers, C. (2002). How moral education is finding its way back into America's schools. In Damon, W. (Ed.), *Bringing a new era in character education* (pp. 23–41). Stanford, California: Hoover Institution Press.

Johnson, D. (1995). Parent-child visitation in the jail or prison. In Gabel, K., & Johnston, D. (Eds.), *Children of incarcerated parents.* New York: Lexington Books.

Kegan, R. (1982). *The evolving self: Problem and process in human development.* Cambridge, MA: Harvard University Press.

Kelly, J. B. (2003). Changing perspectives on children's adjustment following divorce: A view from the United States. *Childhood, 10*(2), 237–254.

Koenig, C. (1985). *Life on the outside: A report on the experiences of the families of offenders from the perspective of wives of offenders.* Canada, Pacific Region: Chilliwack Community Services and Correctional Service of Canada

Kohlberg, L. (1968). The child as a moral philosopher. *Psychology Today, 2,* 25–30

Kohlberg, L. (1970). Education for justice: A modern statement of the Platonic view. In Sizer, N.F., & Sizer, T.R. (Eds.), *Moral education: Five lectures* (pp. 56–83). Cambridge, Harvard University Press.

Kohlberg, L. (1984). *Essays on moral development: The psychology of moral development.* San Francisco: Harper & Row.

Lerner, R. M. (2002). *Concepts and theories of human development* (3rd ed.). Mahwah, NJ: Erlbaum.

Lombroso, C. (1874). *L'uomo delinquente.* Torino, Italy: Bocca.

McCubbin, H.I., Boss, P.G., Wilson, L.R., Lester, G.R. (1980). Developing family invulnerability to stress: Coping patterns and strategies wives employ. In Trost, J. (Ed.), *The family and change* (pp. 1–27). Vasteras, Sweden: International Library.

Mumola, C.J. (2000). Incarcerated parents and their children. Bureau of Justice Statistics Special Report. Washington, D.C.: U.S. Department of Justice.

Naudeau, S. (2003). Children of incarcerated parents. In J. R. Miller, R. M. Lerner, L. B. Schiamberg & P. M. Anderson (Eds.), *Human Ecology: An encyclopedia of children, families, communities, and environments* (pp. 123–125). Santa Barbara, CA: ABC-Clio.

Naudeau, S. (2005). Positive development among children of incarcerated parents: A focus on character. Unpublished doctoral dissertation, Tufts University, Boston.

Parke, R.D., & Clarke-Stewart, K.A. (2004). The effects of parental incarceration on children: Perspectives, promises, and policies. In Travis, J., & Waul, M. (Eds.). *Prisoners once removed: The impact of incarceration and reentry on children, families, and communities.* Washington, DC: The Urban Institute Press.

Piaget, J. (1932, 1965). *The moral judgment of the child.* New York: Free Press.

Piaget, J. (1973). The child and reality. New York: Viking.

Price, C. & Kunz, J. (2003). Rethinking the paradigm of juvenile delinquency as related to divorce. *Journal of Divorce & Remarriage, 39*(1–2), 109–133.

Raphel, B. (1983). *The anatomy of bereavement.* New York: Basic Books.

Ryan, K., & Bohlin, K.E. (1999). *Building character in schools: Practical ways to bring moral instruction to life.* San Francisco: Jossey-Bass Publishers.

Sack, W.H., Seidler, J., and Thomas, S. (1976). The children of imprisoned parents: A psychosocial exploration. American Journal of Orthopsychiatry, 46(4), 618–628.

Schneller, D.P. (1976). *The prisoner's family: A study of the effects of imprisonment on the families of prisoners.* San Francisco: R and E Research Associates.

Seymour, C., & Hairston, C. F. (Eds.). (2000). *Children with parents in prison: Child welfare policy, program & practice issues.* New Brunswich: Transaction Publishers.

Sigelman, C.K., & Shaffer, D.R. (1991). *Life-span human development.* Pacific Grove, CA: Brooks/Cole.

Smart, C. (2003). Introduction: New perspectives on childhood and divorce. *Childhood, 10*(2), 123–129.

Trasler, G.B. (1962). *The explanation of criminality.* London: Routledge & Kegan Paul.

Travis, J., & Waul, M. (2004). Prisoners once removed: The children and families of prisoners. In Travis, J., & Waul, M. (Eds.). *Prisoners once removed: The impact of incarceration and reentry on children, families, and communities.* Washington, D.C.: The Urban Institute Press.

Turiel, E. (1998). The development of morality. In Damon, W. (Series Ed.) & Eisenberg, N. (Vol. Ed.), *Handbook of child psychology: Vol. 3. Social, Emotional, and Personal Development* (5th ed., pp. 863–932). New York: Wiley.

Walker, L., Pitts, R.C., Hennig, K.H., & Matsuba, M.K. (1995). Reasoning about morality and real-life moral problems. In Killen, M., & Hart, D. (Eds.), *Morality in everyday life: Developmental perspective.* Cambridge, MA: Cambridge University Press.

Whiting, P. (1990). *The experience of personal loss: A comprehensive vision.* Unpublished manuscript, Vanderbilt University, Nashville, TN.

ADDITIONAL RESOURCES

Children's books/resource guides for practitioners

Bender, J.M. (2003). My Daddy is in jail: Story, discussion guide, and small group activities for grades K-5. Youthlight, Inc.

Brisson, P. (2004). Mama loves me from away. Boyds Mills Press.

Stanglin, J.A. (2006). What is jail, Mommy? Lifevest Publishing, Inc.

Woodson, J. (2002). Visiting Day. Scholastic Press.

Wright, L. & Seymour, C.B. (2000) Working with children and families separated by incarceration: A handbook for child welfare agencies. CWLA Press.

Yaffe, R.M (2000). When a parent goes to jail: A comprehensive guide for counseling children of incarcerated parents. Rayve Productions.

Organizations providing support/information to children of incarcerated parents and their families

Aid to Children of Imprisoned Mothers: http://www.takingaim.net/history.asp

Big Brothers Big Sisters – Mentoring Children of Promise/Amachi program: http://www.bbbs.org/site/c.diJKKYPLJvH/b.1632625/k.A4D2/Other_Programs.htm?gclid=CNrBtM2w85gCFQUWGgodU18T1A

The Center for Children of Incarcerated Parents: http://www.e-ccip.org/

Child Welfare League of America (CWLA): http://www.cwla.org/programs/incarcerated/

4

Children of Promise

KATHY BOUDIN
SARAH ZELLER-BERKMAN

It's not good for kids to go through what we went through. I listen to the kids talk about all the people in their lives that are locked up and we need to do something to change this! . . .

—Trisha Ferrer, age 17
Participatory Action Research Team Member
Writer, activist, child of a formerly incarcerated mother

INTRODUCTION

The dramatic expansion of the prison population over the past 20 years has left at least 2.4 million children in the United States with a mother or father in jail or prison (Bernstein, 2005). One in 10 children (more than 7 million) has a parent under criminal justice supervision right now, including parole, probation, and incarceration, (Bernstein, 2005) and approximately 10 million children in the United States have had one or both parents incarcerated in their lifetime (Reed & Reed, 2004). Although there are more fathers in prison than mothers, the number of mothers in prison has more than doubled (122%) from 1991–2007 (Schirmer, Nellis, & Mauer, February 2009). Findings indicate that there is generally a much greater disruption in the lives of youth when their mother goes to prison (Dallaire, 2007). Race and ethnicity are a defining aspect: more than 70% of the children of parents in prison are children of color (Schirmer et al., February 2009).

The negative impact of maternal incarceration reverberates across the lifespan of these children from newborns to adolescents, yet children with incarcerated mothers have largely been an invisible population. More recently there has been a growing interest in younger children with mothers in prison, however, few studies have focused on the needs and interventions for adolescents with incarcerated mothers even though an estimated 40% of the children of incarcerated parents are between the ages of 10 and 17 (Mumola, 2000).

This chapter discusses findings from three studies that explore key supportive relationships in the lives of adolescents with incarcerated mothers and the role of the adolescents themselves in coping with the challenges that they face. The goals of this chapter are first to communicate the findings that affirm the value of relationships of adolescents with their incarcerated mothers and of peer support among the adolescents themselves; second, to demonstrate that the adolescents can play a positive role in creating their own well-being through the relationships that they build and through their active engagement in issues raised by maternal incarceration that impact their lives; and third, to communicate the urgent need for adults as policymakers, clinicians, program administrators, and educators to create positive conditions to support adolescents faced with the challenges of maternal incarceration and to draw on the strengths, knowledge, and skills of the adolescents themselves in making these changes.

BACKGROUND

What happens to children once their mother is incarcerated? Children are often moved from house to house, lied to about their mother's incarceration, and feel the loss of their primary source of comfort (Hagen & Myers, 2003). The caretakers, even those with the best intentions of providing a stable, loving home, are overwhelmed and do not have enough supports in place (Bloom & Steinhart, 1993; Dressel & S., 1994). Two central factors that predict how a child will adjust to the separation and incarceration of the parent are the nature and quality of the alternative caregiving arrangement and the quality of the incarcerated parent-child relationship, including the ability to maintain contact with the absent parent (Parke & Clarke-Stewart, 2003). Other factors include whether the child was living with the parent, the economic significance of the incarceration, and the broader family and social network.

There is generally a much greater disruption in the lives of youth when their mother goes to prison. Incarcerated fathers report that before their arrest, their child's mother was the primary caregiver and 90% report that after their imprisonment, these mothers continue the caregiving responsibility. However, when mothers are in prison, only about 30% of fathers assume parental responsibility. Most commonly, the grandparent becomes the caregiver (53%). In addition, other relatives in the kin network pick up the parent role for another 30% of the cases and friends step in about 10% of the time. Fewer than 10% of mothers in state prisons report that their children were placed in foster care (Mumola, 2000).

All children, regardless of age, may experience emotions of fear, anxiety, sadness, loneliness, anger, and confusion when a parent goes to prison (Osborne Association, 1993b). And most children have already experienced challenges before a mother goes to prison related to parental or community problems, including but not limited to poverty, racial discrimination, substance abuse, mental illness, or violence (Covington, 2003). Incarceration is only one of many interconnected issues (Johnson & Waldfogel, 2004).

Adolescents face many of the same challenges as younger children when a mother goes to prison. However, adolescence is a unique period of growing independence and a critical period for establishing future life paths. Without supports, the combined effects of parental incarceration with the other challenges faced by adolescents, especially adolescents of color, can result in higher levels of aggression, perennial delinquent activity, and intergenerational incarceration (Bernstein, 2005; Eddy & Reid, 2003). Adolescents with incarcerated parents need support and understanding from adults that takes into account the specific realities of teenagers. Unfortunately, most often these teens are defined by their deficits and problems, and by the potential dangers they present for society: "their conduct disorders;" "potential next generation criminals" (Eddy & Reid, 2003). Most studies focus on the problems rather than the strengths of these youth (Eddy & Reid, 2003; Phillips, Burns, Wagner, Kramaer, & Robbins, 2002). Although they face real challenges, defining this group of adolescents at best as "disadvantaged" and at worst as solely a "potential threat" misses the opportunity to know their complexity and engage them through their strengths.

Youth development theory emphasizes the strengths of young people, promotes the conditions that lead to positive development, and posits that the problem-solving around this issue will be enhanced with youth input (Benson, 1997; Damon, 2002; Pittman & Cahill, 1992; Pittman, Martin, & Williams, 2007, July). What would it mean to view adolescents who are dealing with parental incarceration in this way? Like other academics who utilize a positive youth development framework, we emphasize youth as resources, not problems to be solved (Roth, Brooks-Gunn, Murray, & Foster, 1998). Youth development theory also stresses the need for researchers to explore the optimum conditions and settings for positive development to occur (National Research Council & Institute of Medicine, 2002; Perkins, Borden, Keith, Hoppe-Rooney, & Villarruel, 2003). In this chapter we talk about key relationships and the infrastructure that supports them as settings for positive development. Our research methods and designs are based upon the idea that research benefits when young people have a say in the process. All three studies used participatory methodology and two of the three used a participatory action research design.[1]

Although the authors of this chapter use positive youth development as a framework, the convergence of maternal incarceration and adolescent development is too complex to be seen through only one theoretical lens. Drawing on an ecological model of development (Bronfenbrenner, 1977, 1988), we explore immediate relationships such as family and peers as important for positive development, along with environmental conditions such as correctional facility programs and criminal justice policies. We utilize a developmental perspective to focus on the particular experience of adolescents with incarcerated mothers. Social constructionist theory contributes to seeing these relationships and developmental trajectories as malleable in contexts such as between prison and the outside world. (Burton, Allison, & Obeidallah, 1995; Glenn, 1994). Although fully aware of the impact of the social context on development, we continually evoke the ways in which human agency reshapes development and social contexts.

THE THREE STUDIES

The first study, "Children of Promise" (Boudin, 2007), relied on qualitative interviews and focus groups with youth who participated in a prison program, Teen Time[2], for teens with incarcerated mothers. The participants were four young men and four young women ages 18 to 22. Five of them were African American, including all four young women and one young man; two young men were Latinos and one young man was White. As high school teens, all of the youth in this study had been separated from their mothers in prison for at least five years and up to 14 years; all of their mothers were still incarcerated with one exception. Only two had fathers in their lives, and all were raised by other family members. Each of the teens struggled to defy social expectations of predicted failure while simultaneously negotiating overcrowded schools with high drop-out rates, neighborhoods with drug dealers and crime, violence, and poverty.

Their mothers were incarcerated at a maximum security prison for women, Bedford Hills Correctional Facility, located near New York City. The New York State Department of Correctional Services (NYSDOCS) and the administrative leadership of Bedford Hills C.F. supported the teens' relationships with their mothers. Programs provided regular visits and positive visiting conditions for both individual time with mothers and group activities. Their mothers participated in a variety of parenting programs, including one called "Mothers of Adolescents." Their mothers also could utilize a children's advocacy program that allowed them to connect to the caregivers of their children, work on custody issues, and connect to institutions such as schools, after-school programs, and medical personnel in order to help their teens. Teen Time had a peer support component for the teens themselves. The teens spent time with one another outside of the prison in adult-chaperoned activities and in a rap group once a month during their one monthly weekend visit with their mothers. A social network of support developed among the teens. The program also involved all of the teens and all of the mothers spending time together in the special visiting room area and sharing activities such as arts, crafts, and games. The mothers carried out traditions for their teens such as birthdays, holiday events, and end-of-the-school-year "Celebration of Achievement." The teens participated in the program until they turned 18.

The interviews took place with the teens when they were 18–21 years of age looking back at their high school years. They discussed the challenges and positive conditions that supported them as adolescents. They focused on the positive value of three sets of relationships: with their mothers; with the other teens whose mothers were incarcerated, and with all the mothers and all of the teens[3].

The second and third studies, participatory action research projects, reveal how research designs can emanate from a strength-based perspective. The main tenet of participatory action research is that a researcher would include as co-researchers members of the community that they want to understand; these community members will participate in the development and execution of the research process. In these studies, having young people who have experienced parental incarceration as co-researchers was considered integral to producing relevant, powerful, and useful research on this topic. The strength, knowledge, and skill of people impacted by parental incarceration form the basis for an exploration into the complex relationship between forced parental separation and healthy development.

In the study entitled "The Stressors and Supports for Children with Incarcerated Parents," a participatory action research design was chosen in which young people impacted by parental incarceration were co-researchers in partnership with the author, an academic scholar who was also the child to a father in prison. For a year and a half, the Participatory Action Team consisting of 4–6 young people ages 15–18 and one of the authors met at the City University of New York Graduate Center over 40 times for at least three hours each time over the course of 2005–2006 to conduct the research. Young people in the research group developed the research questions, created the research protocols, conducted focus groups with 36 youth in three NYC-based nonprofits who were impacted by incarceration, engaged in thematic analysis, created products from their research, and ultimately joined a policy initiative for children with incarcerated parents. In addition to working at the Graduate Center on a regular basis, the team went on two weekend retreats, a demonstration in Washington DC, and two members attended a conference in California.

The third study called "Invisible Experts" was also a participatory action research project conducted by members of the research team in the second study and two other youth researchers. The research collective conducted a total of eight focus groups with over 50 youth, ages 8–21, from the New York City area (Bronx, Brooklyn, Manhattan, and Queens) in part to fill the vacuum of information about these young people's experiences and needs. The study aimed to create a series of policy recommendations by youth, for youth impacted by parental incarceration, and a Bill of Rights for Children of Incarcerated parents in New York City under the auspices of an Osborne Association policy initiative.

The three studies are not representative. The experience of the teens in "Children of Promise" differs in key aspects from the vast majority of situations faced by teens with mothers in prison; these differences include regularity of visiting with mothers, sharing activities with peers with incarcerated mothers both in and out of the prison, and sharing activities with all of the peers and their mothers in a space designed for shared activities in the prison. Most teens with incarcerated parents do not have the experience of participating in a PAR project about their experience. The potential for learning from the atypical case is different and sometimes a superior criterion to representativeness (Merriam, 1988; Reinharz, 1992; Stake, 2000). These studies, although not representative, offer an opportunity to develop knowledge that could contribute to thinking about the broader issues of teens with incarcerated mothers.

RELATIONSHIPS OF MOTHERS IN PRISON AND THEIR ADOLESCENT CHILDREN

> I need somebody to talk to; she's there to talk to. I want somebody to listen to me, she's listening. I need her advice, she gives me the best advice she could give me. If I need something, she tries her best to get it. She does what a mother could do, you know. That's why . . . it's real hard. And I don't think anybody could understand it or know what it is unless they're in . . . in their mother's shoes, or their child's shoes, to understand why I feel like my mother's a good mother even though she committed a crime. Because if my mother didn't help me, . . . I wouldn't be the person I am today. (Allah)

The greatest challenge named by the adolescents in all three studies was the loss of their mother and the need/desire to stay connected. This challenge was named by youth in all of the studies regardless of what age they were when their mothers were arrested, the character of that relationship, or the variety in the current custodial situations. Research has documented the importance for most children of having contact with their mothers after arrest, during the separation of incarceration, and in anticipation of coming home (Baunach, 1985; Blinn, 1997; Bloom & Steinhart, 1993; Gamer & Gamer, 1983; McGowan & Blumenthal, 1978; Osborne Association, 1993a; Reed & Reed, 2004).

A central role that ongoing contact with a mother in prison plays is to reassure the teen that her or his mother has not abandoned or forgotten him. The mother has left the child as a consequence of the action that led to her arrest. The teen can realize that she or he remains loved and central to that parent's life through contact with the mother, including visits, phone calls, and mail (Osborne Association, 1993b).

A second key role of contact with mothers is to allow the adolescent to know that the mother is safe. For adolescents as well as for younger children the safety of the mother is central to a sense of safety for themselves. The media of prison can be very frightening, and firsthand connections matter in terms of the teens' sense of their own safety. Although this is particularly critical immediately following the arrest in which there can be trauma of either watching the arrest or the sudden disappearance of a mother, contact is often a lasting and ongoing reassurance as to the safety of the mother (Bernstein, 2005; Bloom & Steinhart, 1993).

A third reason for contact with mothers that participants expressed was to provide the opportunity for mothers and adolescents to work toward healing ruptures and trauma, and to cope with the common emotions accompanying arrest and incarceration, including fear and anxiety, sadness and isolation, anger, and guilt (Baunach, 1985; Bloom & Steinhart, 1993; Osborne Association, 1993a). Teens in the focus groups in the "Invisible Experts" study spoke about their feelings as a result of their parents' arrest and incarceration:

> " . . . I feel like angry and confused 'cause when my mother got arrested I didn't know what was going on." "It was depressing" "I had mixed feelings." "It was annoying."
>
> "When my mother went to jail, I was rebellious to people I was with. I was angry at her for not coming back to get me and I was disappointed with her. There was a little bit of hate also and I felt resentful because I had to seek responsibility for my little brothers and sisters."

Contact with the mothers along with positive visiting and parenting programs gave the teens in the Teen Time program the possibility of asking questions and talking through issues related to their mothers' arrests, issues that would go unprocessed if there were not time, space, and support to have these conversations. In general, the teens in the studies worked at understanding the crime, their mothers, and their mothers' lives. The supportive conditions such as teen rap groups and mothers' parenting programs also allowed the teens to express anger and criticism, feeling safe enough to do so because there was a regularity to contact and the opportunity to recover from the divide that anger can cause.

Parenting classes for the mothers are critical for helping the mothers cope with the feelings of their adolescent children. For example, if the mother can work to understand and tolerate the anger, contact with mothers allows the teens to express their anger and the mother to respond in a manner that is constructive and that can move the relationship forward.

Common roles of parents such as nurturing, protection, and guidance take place from prison and are often accompanied by role reversal.

The teens emphasized the positive ways that their mothers actively parented them across the separation. All eight participants in "The Children of Promise" study spoke about the nurturing that they received from their mothers through visits, phone calls, letters, and cards. At least four of the participants spoke about the feeling of being protected by their mothers. The youth gave examples of protective actions by their mothers such as helping a teen find an alternative to their school to replace one that was not working for the teen; helping the teen find a younger relative to live with when the older relative could no longer cope with the responsibility; protecting the teen emotionally from hurt; and making certain she or he had money. All the participants spoke to this issue using different phrases such as "she's there for me" even though she's not there; the caring, the special love, the nurturing. The participants wanted and felt an unconditional love from their mothers. Most of these youth had no father in their lives. For these young people, their mothers were the biological parent who could communicate a special commitment and love. The youth spoke about how their mothers gave them advice, communicated an unconditional love, and helped them solve problems as mothers celebrated their rites of passage and supported them through hurts, disappointments, and efforts to succeed.

At the same time, the teens spoke about the many ways in which their role involved helping their mothers: coping with their powerlessness and their general difficulties of prison by coming for visits, bringing packages, and being sensitive to their needs to feel loved and involved; protecting them from discussions about the crime that might upset them; giving guidance to those mothers who had bad tempers or other emotional or behavioral problems; and supporting them as they grew and changed. Some referred to the roles as "50/50" and taking care of each other. Others said that "she is a best friend and also a mother."

The roles of the mothers and their teens were complicated. Mothering is an act that takes place in many different situations with many different types of challenges, and it is useful to understand that it is in itself a role that is flexible, creative, and responds to different social situations. Developmentally predicted roles of parents and adolescents are not inevitable, they are socially determined (Burton et al., 1995; Fineman, 1995; Garcia Coll et al., 1996; Glenn, 1994; Lan, 1997; Roberts, 1995). Incarceration is not the only reason for parenting across a separation. Other common situations include divorce or separation, immigration, foster care, and the demands of employment. Each situation is different, yet they share commonalities. In the context of this study, several factors shaped the roles of the mothers and the adolescents, and they include but are not limited to the vulnerability, powerlessness, and problems that the mothers faced in prison and that the teens were aware of; the fact that for some of the mothers, their lives were less out of control in prison compared with their lives before the arrest because they were now separated from drugs, poverty, and domestic abuse; the strong need of the teens to have a mother who loved them and guided them, and the equally strong need of the mothers to be able to love and guide their children; and the desire to be connected as mothers and children.

The amount and quality of involvement of an incarcerated mother with her teen depends on many factors, such as the quality of the relationship before incarceration and the conditions related to visiting and support for the relationship during incarceration, the distance from the prison of the child, the frequency of contact, the resources and relationship between the mother and people raising the child, and strength of programs in the prison that connect mothers and teens.

Separation and Autonomy: A Paradox of Intimacy

Adolescent development literature emphasizes the need for young people to separate from their parents as they slowly mature into young adults with their own identities, and who are capable of making their own decisions. Teens spend increasing amounts of time with their peers, and they have worlds, secrets, and experiences that they no longer share with their parents, yet they continue to rely on their parents and need their parents (Burton et al., 1995; Erikson, 1968; Leadbeater & Way, 1996a; Seltzer, 1989; Shaffer, 2000; Wolf, 1991). Exactly how the relationships develop in the balance between peers and parents is something that is affected by particular relationships and specific contexts, and has been documented as such (Burton et al., 1995; Ward, 1996).

A consistent theme among the participants was that they shared their lives in detail with their mothers, that they wanted to tell their mothers everything, and that in many cases they defined their mothers as their best friend. The emphasis on telling their mothers the details of their lives, talking for hours with them, craving a physical closeness that they could have in the children's center—whether taking a nap on the floor close to a mother or having hair braided—is different from the prevailing view that emphasizes the need for adolescents to demonstrate their independence.

Some of the participants explained the paradox. First, they missed their mothers and wanted to make up for unusual separation through sharing the details of their lives. Second, because the mothers in prison were not there in the house watching, worrying, and regulating the teens on a day-to-day level, the relationship with the mothers was outside the zone of tight regulation or judgment, and this helped the teen to be open and intimate. The grandmothers or other caregivers played the role of disciplinarian. As numerous writers have said, adolescent development must be studied in specific contexts (Burton et al., 1995; Collins, 1991; Garcia Coll et al., 1996; Gutman, 1976; Stack, 1974). It was precisely the distance and separation that allowed for the intimacy.

Cognitive and Moral Development: Complicating the Good Mother

Adolescence is a period of cognitive and moral exploration and growth. The teens all searched for understanding about what had happened that led them to have a mother in prison. Although faced with society's assessment of their mothers not just as bad mothers but as bad people, reduced to the act that had brought them to prison, these young people had a complex experience of their mothers, and their desire for meaning led them to a deeper understanding. For some, such as Chantelle, it meant understanding their mothers' own childhoods: "But now . . . knowing the whole story . . . and knowing how my mother was and why she did what she did, and why she used to do all the stuff she used to do, I know . . . she had a reason." For others, it was about understanding problems their mothers faced as adults. Others continued to cope with the emotional issues of their mothers while feeling their support and love. Almost all reflected proudly on their mothers' personal growth and/ or contributions to others within prison. They could experience their mothers as full people.

The young adults faced society's condemnation of their mothers as bad mothers. They experienced the loss, trauma associated with the arrest, and many ongoing problems, but they also loved their mothers, needed them, visited them, and constructed and sustained relationships with them. They experienced personally contradictions inherent in being a good mother and a woman who had committed a crime. Allah emphasized the feeling that his mother is part of him, and able to change:

> She did something bad. But, no matter what, that's your mother, and a part of her is going to be inside of you. So, she probably did something back then. But prison is all about changing. . . . When, you go to prison . . . it's not more about like punishment, punishment, punishment. It's about they understand people change, be somebody different. . . . She does what any other mother could do. And she does it to the best of her ability.

The youth grappled with issues of crime and punishment on a deeply personal level. On the one hand there was a sense that punishment for a crime was acceptable and necessary. Yet they missed their mothers and they felt that the lengths of sentences were not fair. Several of the participants said sadly and with hesitation, probably it had been better for the trajectory of their own lives that their mothers had been incarcerated. Josh said

> It's sad to say, but I know on the path that my mother was going, that either she would have died, or I would have died, or we both would have died. So, it's very, very . . . hard for me to say, but it's good. I wish she didn't receive the amount of time she received, but it's good that me and her were separated and she was separated from the lifestyle she was living.

Josh's mother was addicted to drugs. For Josh and many of the other teens, their mothers' separation from abuse, drug dependency, and economic pressures of survival, combined with support from positive visiting conditions and parenting programs added up to a more focused and positive role for the mothers. Yet the teens wondered wasn't there a different way? There could have been an alternative to the problems that Josh's mother had and that were passed on to Josh. Perhaps if drug treatment had been the policy instead of punishment under the Rockefeller Drug law, Josh would have benefited from his mother's change of lifestyle without visiting prison for 12 years.

Identity Formation: My mother/myself trying to find a self and identity with relation to/with opposition to my mother

Identity development is usually defined as a central part of adolescent development, and parents are a major contributor to that process (Burton et al., 1995; Erikson, 1968; Fineman, 1995; Garcia Coll et al., 1996; Glenn, 1994; Leadbeater & Way, 1996a; Phelan, Davidson, & Yu, 1998; Roberts, 1995; Shaffer, 2000). A parent separated from a teen, including by incarceration, continues to exert an important role in shaping the adolescent's identity even when separated by incarceration (Gamer & Gamer, 1983; Nelson, 1999).

As the teens were grappling to understand their mothers' lives, they were struggling with who they were themselves, their own identities. On the one hand, the "failure of their mothers" led each to want to define themselves as different from their mothers:

> I think it [her mother's incarcerations] made me . . . want to achieve more, because everybody . . . it's in their head I'm going to . . . fail. Or I'm going . . . to go to jail. . . . I'm going to do school; I'm going to go to college . . . I guess just the fact that society or everybody thinks that you're going to be like a bad person. I think that you will just strive to be good. (Natalia)

On the other hand, they loved their mothers and wanted to feel connected and similar to them. For example, Hector respected his mother's strengths and could see how they were also tied to some of her problems, but he saw the roots of positive parts of himself as connected to his mother when he said ". . . the only thing is that I am more upgraded than my mother, more correct, more positive—but I get that from my mother, that determination, that power, . . . outgoing personality, . . . her strong minded. . . ." For Hector and the other teens, their mothers served as vital reference points for their sense of themselves, for both positive and negative qualities; their ongoing relationship with their mothers allowed them to feel connected to where they came from, who they wanted or did not want to be.

Mothering in the Context of the Broader Network of Caregivers: A Family System

The relationship between mother and teen took place inside of a larger family network. The relationship between family dyads such as the mother and the caregiver and the teen and the caregiver often impacted on the relationship between the mother and teen. In the "Children of Promise" study, when their mothers were arrested, the youth needed someone to raise them. All of the eight participants were living with their mothers at the time of the arrests; however, some of the mothers had not been able to provide a stable home due to poverty domestic violence, illegal drug involvement, and/or other illegal activities. Grandmothers had helped several of them. None were in foster care. By the time the participants were in high school, they relied on a complex extended family that the teen helped create, bringing together various combinations of relatives: the older generation including grandmothers, a grandfather, a great aunt, a few fathers, older siblings and younger siblings, and other relatives such as aunts, cousins, and people in the community. The foundation at home was a critical component for their stability, and when it fell apart as it did for several of the teens when they became adolescents, their own lives also became far less stable. The role of their mothers in prison in this extended family was central, according to the teens, through good times and hard times. The task in supporting the teen was to work with the entire family system—the caregivers and family at home, the mother in prison, and the adolescent in order to work with the family as a whole.

WITHOUT THE SUPPORT OF MOTHERS

Across studies, young people who did not have adequate support from family or did not have a visiting program available to them talked about the difficulties in retaining relationships with their mothers. Like the millions of young people who endure parental separation due to incarceration and who are not part of supportive programming (Satyanathan, 2001), young people in our PAR studies reported not visiting at all to missing years between visits:

> From the time I was seven years old to nine years old I didn't see my mother . . . (Focus group participant)

Current policy is not supportive of parent/child relationships across the divide of incarceration (Bernstein, 2005; Schirmer et al., February 2009). Close to 60% of mothers and fathers in state prisons report never having a visit with their children (Glaze & Maruschak, 2008 revised 1/8/09). For many it is due to long distances between the home communities and the prisons in which the parents serve time. Over 60% of parents in state prisons are incarcerated more that 100 miles form their last place of residence, and 43.3% of parents in federal prisons are over 500 miles from their last place of residence (Glaze & Maruschak, 2008 revised 1/8/09). Research indicates that women are on average imprisoned 160 miles from their children (Travis, et. Al, 2003), and 40% of mothers receive no weekly contact (Travis & Waul, 2003). The number of calls and or letters per prisoner is typically limited by correction officials and there is a high cost of collect phone calls, which causes economic strain on families (Bernstein, 2005; Travis & Waul, 2003).

In the "Invisible Expert" study, even young people who were able to visit their parent in prison reported dehumanizing and frustrating experiences:

> I went with my brother's mother to go visit my father. Yo, he (the prison guard) denied our visit and we had to sit outside in the hot ass sun for three hours for the visit to be over. That's not funny. She was pregnant and they said she had to sit on the curb. I was so upset.

Others mentioned "unwanted touches" when passing through security, guards who were abusing power, and random rules that when enforced wasted peoples time and patience. It is clear that instead of having the opportunity to connect to their mothers to work out emotional hardship, experiment with identity development, and experience nurturing, not supporting young people's relationship to their imprisoned parent leads to further feelings of isolation, frustration, and lack of control over such basic rights such as contact with a parent.

PEERS SUPPORTING PEERS

Teens benefited from being part of a peer support program for teens with incarcerated mothers and in carrying out the PAR research project with their peers. It helped them to cope with stigma, to share positive activities and expand their knowledge and life options, to have a context from which to help others, and to have fun. Normative adolescent development theory emphasizes the role of peers to adolescents. The increasing significance of peers in the lives of adolescents has been studied and acknowledged in both social and academic development (Erikson, 1968; Shaffer, 2000; Tierney & Colyar, 2005). In adolescence, young people spend more and more time with people their own age; by early adolescence, they spend more than twice as much time with peers as with parents, siblings, or any other agent of socialization (Shaffer, 2000).

Together, in the Prison and out of the Prison

Although the classic beliefs about teenage peer relationships were rooted in negative terms of "peer pressure" and teens were seen as pressuring others to do negative things (Tierney & Colyar, 2005), there are many examples of peer organizations and programs that have helped to construct positive meaning for youths (Burton et al., 1995; Campbell & MacPhail, 2003; Fine, Tuck, & Zeller-Berkman, 2005; Glenn, 1994; Haignere, Freudenberg, Silver, Maslanka, & Kelley, 1997; Oldfather, 1995). The three studies that provided data for this article looked specifically at supportive programs that brought adolescents together and created conditions for a number of positive roles that the peers played with one another. The literature of youth development and youth community development focuses on the positive role of teen peers with one another and the role of adults in constructing optimum conditions and settings for positive development to occur. (Cauce, Stewart, Rodriguez, Cochran, & Ginzler, 2003; Delgado, 2002; Hamilton & Hamilton, 2004; Luthar, 1999; Sokatch, 2005; Tierney & Colyar, 2005; Villarruel, Perkins, Border, & Keither, 2003).

The Challenge of Stigma, Shame, and Pity

All our mothers were in prison, you know. We all could relate just to each other. . . . we didn't have to be phony. We didn't have to lie. We just kept it round. And that . . . was so great, because, you know, nobody judged nobody. It was just like one big family. (Shirelle)

Stigma about having an incarcerated mother was one of the major challenges that the teens spoke of:

Stereotype. The biggest stereotype. You're going to be just like your mother . . . when you grow up. . . . the most likely thing that's going to come out of somebody's mouth is, "Oh, your father's in jail;" "Your mother's a crackhead." Or "Your mother's in jail," or "Your father's a crackhead." (Allah)

In high school, Allah didn't want his mother to appeal her case because of his fear that negative publicity about his mother would affect him: "something like that just might mess up my reputation. . . . I'm at every basketball game, every this. I'm just prom king, prom this. . . . It probably would have ruined my life . . ."

Josh articulated the underlying shame even though he said it was not about him, and just about his mother, he did not want to be associated with it, "I was basically ashamed . . . I don't think it was anything about me, just being ashamed of my mother . . . Because they thought your mother's this, you know, she's such and such and such. You know . . . a convict. Criminal."

Having an attribute or characteristic that represents a stigma, something that could be the reason for exclusion, derision, or denigration, can be particularly painful and difficult for teens. They want to be seen as normal, not different. To be stigmatized by ones peers, to be excluded or made fun of is particularly distressing because adolescents want acceptance by their peers (Erikson, 1968). The teens are affected by what Goffman calls secondary stigma that can be transmitted and equally "contaminate" all members of the family. They themselves do not have the attributes of what society stigmatizes i.e. incarceration or criminal behavior, but they are "contaminated" by the attribute (Goffman, 1963).

At the same time, having a group of peers who understand and share the situation of one another can be particularly valuable in terms of creating a context of peer acceptance and peer understanding. It can lead to an experience of being open and not defensive, not hiding, being able to feel natural and normal, and in that sense being able to develop inner strength (Barry, 2000). A focus group participant mentioned that "we should have more groups like this so kids wouldn't have to go in it alone like I did." The quote of this participant expresses the relief a young person feels as the isolation associated with prison stigma is alleviated, even if temporarily as part of a research project.

The teens who participated in ongoing groups where they were surrounded by children who faced similar challenges echoed this relief; spending time with other teens with incarcerated mothers helped them to overcome the feelings of isolation, stigma, and shame that they experienced in school and in their neighborhood because of having a mother in prison. This corroborates the importance of being part of a social network or group who shared the same stigmatized issues discussed by Goffman (1963). Adolescents need and want to be part of a teen group both because it provides a space for growth into adults in addition to that of their families and because one of the characteristics of being a teen is that of "belonging to" or "being excluded from" (Shaffer, 2000). Although the teens all had friends in their schools and neighborhoods and shared many other challenges, they could not generally share the whereabouts or personal experience of having an incarcerated mother.

In general they did not tell their peers in school about having a mother in prison. They kept it a secret. They lied about where their mothers were or avoided talking about it. They felt alone with such an important secret, uncomfortable about lying, and still affected by stigma. Both the stigma and the keeping a secret about their mothers were a major challenge during adolescence for the participants. Allah said,

> If you meet . . . a new friend in school, and it's like, "Oh, so, what does your father do? What does your mom do?" . . . that's when it comes up about your mother. That's when I used to get nervous. I was afraid to be at school, chilling, your mother's not there. Everybody else's mother, they have them there, and something comes up where your mom has to be . . . in school. And it's like, "Oh, well, my mom can't come because . . ."

The youth said that it felt more normal to not have a father around than to not have a mother around, and even more unusual to have a mother in prison.

As the teens moved through high school, they told special friends, but it was always a considered choice, carefully negotiated so that they could feel safe and not vulnerable. The teens indicated that the older that they became, the more likely they were to confide in certain people whom they trusted, either a close friend or a romantic partner.

They also did not want pity. Teachers especially might pity them. This was another reason why they did not want to tell anybody. Although weary of pity, children in the focus groups often wished that school was a more supportive place to contend with the feelings related to parental incarceration. Many participants reported not being asked what was contributing to dropping grades or acting out after a parent's arrest, just being punished.

The Challenge of Social Realities/Positive Times with Other Teens

Stigma was only one among many challenges that they had in common: living in an unstable home situation and having to move; rough neighborhoods where defending oneself or friends was a regular issue; stereotypes relating to being Black or Latin and or poor; and feelings of loss or abandonment were also common. They also shared many positive issues as teens, including friendships and intimacy, dreams of future careers and goals, love of music and dancing, clothes, styles, and hair. They had fun and laughed. The Teen Time Program offered different kinds of opportunities for the teens to spend time together, not just talking about their feelings in a group, but also spending two visiting days per month over a weekend together in the Children's Center with all the teens and all of the mothers. This involved talking, braiding hair, hanging out, doing group games, having lunch, playing cards, or making arts and crafts. The teens had their own time alone in the rap group before the mothers came down on Sunday mornings in which they talked about issues that they had in common such as how you pick a career, having an incarcerated mother and stigma, how you deal with violence in school, and wanting to run away from home because you don't like your guardian. The teens spent time in activities outside of the prison together such as camping or going on trips to places such as Washington DC, Great Adventures, on a boat trip up the Hudson, or doing community service like planting bulbs in Prospect Park.

All teens across the three studies were clear about meaning of peer support and about sharing in positive activities. Adolescence is a period of growth from childhood dependence to greater ability to solve problems, take responsibility, help others, make moral choices, and develop self-efficacy (Shaffer, 2000). Adolescents in these studies relied on their peers as a relationship through which they were moving in this direction. As the teens helped one another, self-efficacy and self-esteem grew. Youth development encourages supporting self-efficacy and mattering, making a real difference in the youth's community and being taken seriously; practice that includes taking on new roles, responsibilities, and meaningful challenges. The teens in the Teen Time program spoke proudly about being able to help each other cope with problems. One teen said, "We helped ourselves, we helped others, we mattered." As a group they spoke at a high school about the issues faced by themselves, teens with incarcerated parents, turning the stigmatized position into the role of an expert on a social issue.

A similar set of developmental gains occurred in the PAR projects about the stressors and supports for young people impacted by parental incarceration, as this group turned stigma into expertise. The development and growth of individuals as a result of engaging in the research process was shaped by the relationships formed within the research team. When reflecting on what they gained from being part of the Participatory Action Team, new knowledge about research and the topic area was always coupled with a reference to the relationships formed within the our collective. For example, Julio Ray stated that

> Since being a part of this project, I have learned so much and grew bonds with individuals that I worked with. Throughout our time I learned how to run focus groups, [and] consult and converse with other teens about what stresses them out in their everyday lives.

The development of our research team as individuals and our research project was a result of the trusting, caring relationships between people in our group. The collective felt like a safe place to admit ignorance, take risks, and be reflective (Zeller-Berkman, 2007). Young people reported feeling "like there's trust in the group. I feel like when we get together, it feels like a family somewhat" (Julio Ray, video footage). This sense of trust was fostered by addressing issues related to race head on, protecting varying sexual preferences, and addressing power dynamics. The research collective space was designated as open, but safe; a place where everyone would be listened to and was responsible for each other. All of these conditions led to the development of the individuals in the group and the creation of thoughtful research.

The PAR process regularly brought together this group of teens who had all experienced parental incarceration, daily hardships related to racism, classism, and ageism, as well as fun weekend retreats, flirtations, and lots of laughter. The growth and developmental possibilities that emanated from this research collective were not solely located at the individual level, nor stayed only within our research collective. The group produced recommendations for institutions, policy, and programs that if instituted, could alter the developmental trajectories for many young people (please see Appendix A for the full set of recommendations). Young people across the studies offered their wisdom about the supports that they would need from various institutions (such as prison, child welfare, schools, etc.) to improve their own chances at successful "outcomes" while enduring parental incarceration.

ALL THE TEENS AND THEIR MOTHERS TOGETHER DURING VISITS

One of the themes of adolescent development is the turn toward independence and separation from parents. Adolescents want a relationship with their parents but they also want to be separate from them and instead to be with their friends. It is an ongoing process of touching home and moving away, touching home and moving away (Kaplan, 1984; Wolf, 1991). When a teen lives with a parent, the teen can come in, go out, hang out with friends in the house ignoring the parent, but come and get money, a hug, or support. The visits to the prison with all the mothers and all the teens together allowed for this kind of back and forth, separating and coming together that characterizes the emotional dynamic between adolescents and parents.

Teens and mothers shared the formal weekend visits all together in the space of the Children's Center. They spent four days in a row visiting at the end of the summer and shared traditions such as birthdays and holidays, as well as inventing rituals such as "Celebration of Achievement" at the end of the school year. A normalization of the teen-mother relationship was made possible. Teens could spend time with their own mother or with other teens' mothers; they could play card games with a group of teens against all their mothers or make arts and crafts with their mom, sitting at the table all together and talking.

The teens said that it was more fun to visit with other teens and their moms compared to visiting alone. It helped make it feel more normal. And they got to see their mothers interacting with other people, seeing them in different roles. One mother might be a good artist and could help other mothers with arts and crafts; another mother could braid hair well and would braid hair of different teens.

> Just sitting with your mom, it was okay, we'll play like a game . . . But when it was the other teens there, we would all play . . . I think that was nice. And then my mother would talk to some of the other mothers there, instead of just talking to me. I don't think she minded just talking to me . . . but like maybe you're not even there, like maybe you're just out somewhere just talking with your friends. I think that was better. (Natalia)

Bronfenbrenner's (1988) ecological model of development is useful for explaining the significance of social context, in this case, the particular prison's philosophy that supported mother-child relationships, within prison limits. There was a separate visiting area with more flexible rules for mother and teen interactions, and there were programs for mothers and teens that brought them all together. This specific context made possible the normalization of relationships and the creation of dynamics and activities that had particular strengths. Optimal conditions for the adolescents and their incarcerated mothers, given the prison context, involved supporting the bonding of the adolescent and mother through regular visiting and a separate visiting space. Other optimal conditions included programs that supported the mother's own self-growth, parenting knowledge, and skills, increased her ability to reach beyond the prison and help her adolescent, and conditions for adolescent peers to support and enjoy one another (Boudin, 1997).

The youth defined the other teens and mothers as "family," most generally meaning a bond of caring and commitment that was deeper than just friends. There also appears to be a meaning that is drawn more specifically from African-American culture and that has also permeated more popular culture. The African-American family has had to create a form of caretaking that could meet the challenges of race, class, and gender oppression (Collins 1991 and Stack 1974). This often meant strong networks of both bloodmothers—biological mothers—and othermothers—grandmothers, sisters, aunts, or cousins acting as othermothers—by taking on responsibilities for one another's children, relating to the creation of families for survival. Many said that they liked having many mothers who could encourage them to do the right thing, cared about what they did, would scold them if they did something wrong, and who basically just mothered them. One young man spoke to this when he said that the many mothers whom he came to know in the Teen Time program were "Good influences. Which people wouldn't think again, coming out of prison—a lot of good influences. Well, people were always steering you in the right direction. They're as much . . . [proud as] . . . as my school board, you know. . . . I went right through school . . . It was like having 20 mothers going up there."

The agency of the youth constructed a new family that helped them to survive and transform the conditions that they faced with the loss of a mother to incarceration, making use of the conditions that they had. The teens created a space to develop counter-narratives about themselves, about their mothers, and about their relationships with them. They shaped an environment with their peers that freed themselves from stereotypes surrounding them or from outright stigmatizing. With adult support, they invented space for themselves that expanded the boundaries of who they were and who they might be (Barry, 2000; Weis & Fine, 2000).

RELATIONSHIPS AND YOUTH PARTICIPATION: WHY?

As a group, the young people in our studies have profoundly beat the odds. Among the adolescents who were participants in the "Children of Promise" study, all graduated from high school; two graduated from four-year bachelor degree programs, (and one of those is in a master's degree program); three additional finished associate degrees with plans to complete their bachelor's degree, and three others have been in and out of college and are self-supporting. No one of them is in prison, involved with drugs, or on welfare, and all continue to carry major family obligations. Their stories contradict the emphasis on failure or problems that is seen in some literature (Eddy & Reid, 2003)

In the research teams, teens learned about how to use various research methods, analyze data, think critically, present findings at academic conferences, in college classrooms, and to other young people. They conducted workshops for youth and adults at various places in NYC. Although the point of our group was to do important research together, there are still stories to share of resilience and overcoming the odds. Two of the young people on the team were hired by an evaluation organization that works out of the graduate center, where they continued to do research-related work for a while. As a collective, these young people are currently working, struggling to save money for college, serving in the army, and studying in high school. Due to the continuation of some of the conditions that make these young people's lives so difficult, like parental drug additions and poverty, we had one co-researcher who decided to try to sell drugs to support younger siblings when his mother relapsed into drug addiction. He is currently finishing out his sentence in a halfway house and looking forward to rebuilding his life when he gets out.

It is of course impossible to create a causal relationship between their life trajectories and the involvement of the youth in the programs described in this chapter who have strengthened their relationships with their incarcerated mothers, their peers, and engage their strengths as researchers and shapers of their own destinies. We recognize the complexity of factors that influence the life choices and directions of youth. In fact, their motion forward is powerful and fragile simultaneously. Class and race factors combine with ongoing incarceration of their mothers, family responsibilities such as caring for a terminally ill grandparent, or raising a high school younger sibling to create enormous pressures. These issues center around financial difficulties affecting the ability to continue their education and/or to find job. These pressures also affect the choices they make to reach their own personal goals while caring for family members. Nevertheless, we believe that the experiences helped to strengthen them as they confronted as adolescents and continue as young adults to confront the many challenges of their lives precisely because it supported the positive development of central relationships with mothers and peers, and engaged them in their strengths.

CHAPTER SUMMARY

The data in this chapter clearly demonstrates the power of programs that support relationship building between adolescents with their incarcerated parents and with peers with incarcerated parents. When properly supported, two relationships that are often stigmatized can promote positive developmental gains. The chapter is also about the untapped potential of adolescent youth to help figure out solutions to the issues, such as parental incarceration, that impact their lives. The adolescents across these studies, many of whom are doomed in the literature to walk the path of their parents and are characterized by "stereotypes of despair" (Leadbeater & Way, 1996b, p. 5), make abundantly clear that they are capable of helping themselves, other young people, their mothers, and adults gain valuable insight into this issue when given the opportunity. One such area for further exploration with adolescents as partners is the complicated process of reentry and its impact on families.[4] Clinicians, academics program providers, and activists should consider viewing adolescents as assets to any work related to parental incarceration, by training them to co-facilitate support groups, conduct research, and inform and promote policy. To address an issue of this magnitude will require an all-hands-on-deck approach by those most impacted and their supporters.

ENDNOTES

1. Participatory Action Research (PAR) is a design in which those impacted by an issue are the ones who study it, critique it, and problem solve possible solutions. PAR urges critical inquiry as a tool for constructing countervailing power, which low-power groups can use to move toward social change (Rahman & Fals-Borda, 1991).
2. For the purposes of the dissertation, pseudonyms were employed about the name of the program and its location, but given the power of the model it seems important to situate in a real place with real history; hence the real name of the program, the correctional facility, and its location are used in this chapter.
3. The author of the research, Kathy Boudin, served 22 years in prison, is a mother of a son who grew up during those years, and while incarcerated one of her key areas of

work was the development and teaching of parenting programs for mothers in prison and working with the children and teens of those mothers.

4. Although addressed in the research on Rights for Incarcerated Children (see appendix), a fuller examination of reentry was not in the scope of this article.

REFERENCES

Barry, R. (2000). Sheltered "children": The self-creation of a safe space by gay, lesbian, and bisexual students. In L. Weis & M. Fine (Eds.), *Construction sites*. New York: Teachers College Press.

Baunach, P. J. (1985). *Mothers in prison*. New Brunswick, New Jersey: Transaction.

Benson, P. (1997). *All Kids are our kids: What communities must do to raise caring and responsible children and adolescents*. San Francisco, California: Jossey-Bass.

Bernstein, N. (2005). *All alone in the world: Children of the incarcerated*. New York: New Press.

Blinn, C. (Ed.). (1997). *Maternal ties: A selection of programs for female offenders*. Lanham, Maryland: American Correctional Association.

Bloom, B., & Steinhart, D. (1993). *Why punish the children? A reappraisal of the children of incarcerated mothers in America*. San Francisco: National Council on Crime and Delinquency.

Boudin, K. (2007). *"Children of promise:" Being a teen with a mother in prison and sharing the experience with peers*. Unpublished doctoral thesis. New York: Teachers College Columbia University.

Boudin, K. (1997). The children's center programs of Bedford Hills Correctional Facility. In C. Blinn (Ed.), *Maternal Ties: A selection of programs for female offenders* (pp. 55–86). Lanham, Maryland: American Correctional Association.

Bronfenbrenner, U. (1977). Toward an experimental ecology of human development. *American Psychologist*, 32, 513–531.

Bronfenbrenner, U. (1988). Ecology of the family as a context for human development: Research perspectives. *Developmental Psychology*, 22, 723–742.

Burton, L. M., Allison, K. W., & Obeidallah, D. (1995). Social context and adolescence: Perspectives on development among inner-city African-American teens. In L. J. Crockett & A. C. Crouter (Eds.), *Pathways through adolescence: Individual development in relation to social contexts* (pp. 119–138). Mahwah, New Jersey: Lawrence Erlbaum Associates.

Campbell, C., & MacPhail, C. (2003). Facilitating community-led peer education among Summertown Youth. In C. Campbell (Ed.), *'Letting them die': Why HIV/AIDS prevention programmes fail* (pp. 132–148). Bloomington, Indiana: Indiana University Press.

Cauce, A. M., Stewart, A., Rodriguez, M. D., Cochran, B., & Ginzler, J. (2003). Overcoming the odds: Adolescent development in the context of urban poverty. In S. S. Luthar (Ed.), *Resilience and vulnerability: Adaptation in the context of childhood adversities*. Cambridge UK: Cambridge University Press 343–363.

Collins, P. H. (1991). *Black feminist thought: Knowledge, consciousness, and the politics of empowerment*. New York: Routledge.

Covington, S. C. (2003). A woman's journey home: Challenges for female offenders. In J. Travis & M. Waul (Eds.), *Prisoners once removed: The impact of incarceration and reentry on children, families, and communities* (pp. 67–103). Washington DC : The Urban Institute Press.

Dallaire, D. H. (2007). Incarcerated mothers and fathers: A comparison of risks for children and families. *Family Relations, 56*(5), 440–453.

Damon, W. (2002). *Bringing in a new era in character education*. CA: Hoover Press.

Delgado, M. (2002). *New frontiers for youth development in the twenty-first century*. New York: Columbia University Press.

Dressel, P., & S., B. (1994). Reframing gerontological thought and practice: The case of grandmothers with daughters in prison. *The Gerontologist, 34*, 685–691.

Eddy, J. M., & Reid, J. B. (2003). The adolescent children of incarcerated parents. In J. Travis & M. Waul (Eds.), *Prisoners once removed* (pp. 233–258). Washington DC: The Urban Institute Press.

Erikson, E. H. (1968). *Identity: Youth and crisis*. New York: W.W. Norton.

Fine, M., Tuck, E., & Zeller-Berkman, S. (2005). Do you believe in Geneva? Youth participatory action research and indigenous knowledge: CUNY Grad Center.

Fineman, M. A. (1995). Preface. In M. A. Fineman (Ed.), *Mothers in law: Feminist theory and the legal regulation of motherhood*. New York: Columbia University Press.

Gamer, E., & Gamer, C. P. (1983). There is no solitary confinement—A look at the impact of incarceration upon the family, *Association for the Professional Treatment of Offenders*. Pine Manor College Chestnut Hill, Massachusetts.

Garcia Coll, C., Lamberty, R. J., McAdoo, H. P., Crnic, K., Wasik, B. H. & Garcia, H. V. (1996). An integrative model for the study of developmental competencies in minority children. *Child Development, 67*(5), 1891–1914.

Glaze, L. E., & Maruschak, L. M. (2008 revised 1/8/09). Parents in prison and their minor children. In *U. S. D. o. Justice* (Ed.) (Vol. NCJ 222984): United States Department of Justice, Bureau of Justice Statistics.

Glenn, E. N. (1994). Social constructions of mothering: A thematic overview. In E. N. Glenn, G. Chang & L. R. Forcey (Eds.), *Mothering: Ideology, experience, and agency* (pp. 1–29). New York: Routledge.

Goffman, E. (1963). *Stigma: Notes on the management of spoiled identity*. New York: Simon and Schuster.

Gutman, H. G. (1976). *The Black family in slavery and freedom: 1750–1925*. New York: Random House.

Hagen, K. A., & Myers, B. (2003). The effects of secrecy and social support on behavioral problems in children of incarcerated women. *Journal of Child and Family Studies, 12*, 229–242.

Haignere, C. S., Freudenberg, N., Silver, D. R., Maslanka, H., & Kelley, J. T. (1997). One method for assessing HIV/AIDS Peer-Education Programs. *Journal of Adolescent Health, 21*(2), 76–79.

Hamilton, S. F., & Hamilton, M. A. (Eds.). (2004). *The youth development handbook: Coming of age in American communities*. Thousand Oaks, CA: Sage.

Johnson, E. I., & Waldfogel, J. (2004). Children of incarcerated parents: Multiple risks and children's living arrangements. In M. Patillo, D. Weiman & B. Western (Eds.), *Imprisoning America: The social effects of mass incarceration*. New York: Russell Sage Foundation.

Kaplan, L. J. (1984). *Adolescence: The farewell to childhood.* New York: Simon & Schuster.

Lan, C. (1997). *Monkey bridge.* New York: Penguin.

Leadbeater, B. J. R., & Way, N. (1996a). Family relationships. In B. J. R. Leadbeater & N. Way (Eds.), *Urban girls: Resisting stereotypes, creating illusions* (pp. 83–84). New York: New York University Press.

Leadbeater, B. J. R., & Way, N. (1996b). Introduction. In B. J. R. Leadbeater & N. Way (Eds.), *Urban girls: Resisting stereotypes, creating identities* (pp. 1–12). New York: New York University Press.

Luthar, S. S. (1999). *Poverty and children's adjustment.* Thousand Oaks, California: Sage Publications.

McGowan, B. G., & Blumenthal, K. L. (1978). *Why punish the children?* San Francisco: National Council on Crime and Delinquency.

Merriam, S. B. (1988). *Case study research in education: A qualitative approach.* San Francisco, CA: Jossey - Bass

Mumola, C. J. (2000). *Incarcerated parents and their children.* U.S. Department of Justice.

National Research Council, & Institute of Medicine. (2002). *Community programs to promote youth development.* Washington DC: Board on Children, Youth, and Families, Division of Behavioral and Social Sciences and Education National Academy Press.

Nelson, H. L. (1999). Always connect: Toward parental ethics of divorce. In J. E. Hanigsberg & S. Ruddick (Eds.), *Mother troubles* (pp. 117–138). Boston: Beacon.

Oldfather, P. (1995). Songs "Come back most to them." Students' experiences as researchers. *Theory into practice, 34*(2), 131–137.

Osborne Association. (1993a). *How can I help? Working with children of incarcerated parents* (Vol. 1). New York: Osborne Association.

Osborne Association. (1993b). *How can I help?: Working with children of incarcerated parents* (Vol. 1). New York: Osborne Association.

Parke, R. D., & Clarke-Stewart, K. A. (2003). The effects of parental incarceration on children: Perspectives, promises, and policies. In J. Travis & M. Waul (Eds.), *Prisoners once removed: The impact of incarceration and reentry on children, families, and communities* (pp. 189–232). Washington DC: The Urban Institute Press.

Perkins, D. F., Borden, L. M., Keith, J. G., Hoppe-Rooney, T. L., & Villarruel, F. A. (2003). Community youth development: Partnership creating a positive world. In F. A. Villarruel, D. F. Perkins, L. M. Borden, & J. G. Keith (Eds.), *Community youth development: Programs, policies, and practices.* Thousand Oaks, CA: Sage.

Phelan, P., Davidson, A. L., & Yu, C. H. (1998). *Adolescents' worlds: Negotiating family, peers, and school.* New York: Teachers College Press.

Phillips, S. D., Burns, B. J., Wagner, H. R., Kramaer, T. L., & Robbins, J. M. (2002). Parental incaraceration among adolescents receiving mental health services. *Journal of Child and Family Studies, 11*(4), 385–399.

Pittman, K., & Cahill, M. (1992). *Youth and caring.* Washington, DC: Center for Youth Development Policy and Research.

Pittman, K., Martin, S., & Williams, A. (2007, July). *Core principles for engaging young people in community change.* Washington D.C.: The Forum for Youth Investment, Impact Strategies Inc.

Rahman, M. A., & Fals-Borda, O. (1991). A self-review of PAR. In O. Fals-Borda & M. Rahman (Eds.), *Action and knowledge: Breaking the monopolicy with participatory action research* (pp. 24–34). New York: Apex Press.

Reed, D. F., & Reed, E. L. (2004). Mothers in prison and their children. In B. R. Price & N. J. Sokoloff (Eds.), *The criminal justice system and women: Offenders, prisoners, victims, & workers* (pp. 261–274). New York: McGraw Hill.

Reinharz, S. (1992). *Feminist methods in social research.* New York: Oxford University Press.

Roberts, D. (1995). Racism and patriarchy in the meaning of motherhood. In M. A. Fineman & I. Karpin (Eds.), *Mothers in law: feminist theory and the legal regulation of motherhood* (pp. 224–249). New York: Columbia University Press.

Roth, J., Brooks-Gunn, J., Murray, L., & Foster, W. (1998). Promoting healthy adolescents: Synthesis of youth development program evaluations. *Journal of Research on Adolescence, 8*(4), 423–459.

Schirmer, S., Nellis, A., & Mauer, M. (February 2009). *Incarcerated parents and their children.* Washington D.C.: The Sentencing Project.

Seltzer, V. C. (1989). *The psychosocial worlds of the adolescent: Public and private.* New York John Wiley & Sons.

Shaffer, D. R. (2000). *Social and personality development* (Fourth ed.). Belmont, CA: Wadsworth.

Sokatch, A. (2005, April 14). *A qualitative investigation into peer influence on college going decisions of low income urban youth.* Paper presented at the American Educational Research Association, Montreal Canada.

Stack, C. B. (1974). *All our kin: Strategies for survival in a Black community.* New York: Harper & Row.

Stake, R. E. (2000). Case Studies. In N. K. Denzin & Y. S. Lincoln (Eds.), *Handbook of qualitative research* (pp. 435–454). Thousand Oaks, CA: Sage.

Tierney, W. G., & Colyar, J. E. (2005). The role of peer groups in college preparation programs. In W. G. Tierney, Z. Corwin, B. & J. E. Colyar (Eds.), *Preparing for college: Nine elements of effective outreach.* Albany: State University of New York.

Travis, J., & Waul, M. (2003). Prisoners once removed: The children and families of prisoners. In J. Travis & M. Waul (Eds.), *Prisoners once removed: The impact of incarceration and reentry on children, families, and communities* (pp. 1–29). Washington DC: The Urban Institute Press.

Villarruel, F. A., Perkins, D. F., Border, L. M., & Keither, J. G. (Eds.). (2003). *Community youth development: Programs, policies, and practices.* Thousand Oaks, CA: Sage.

Ward, J. V. (1996). Raising resisters: The role of truth telling in the psychological development of African American girls. In B. J. R. Leadbeater & N. Way (Eds.), *Urban girls: Resisting stereotypes, creating identities* (pp. 89–99). New York New York University Press.

Weis, L., & Fine, M. (2000). Construction sites: An introduction. In L. Weis & M. Fine (Eds.), *Construction sites: Excavating race, class, and gender among urban youth.* New York: Teachers College.

Wolf, A. E. (1991). *Get out of my life but first could you drive me and Cheryl to the mall?: A parent's guide to the new teenager.* New York: Farrar Straus Giroux.

ADDITIONAL RESOURCES

The Web site of the National Resource Center on Children and Families of the Incarcerated at Families and Connections Network. http://fcnetwork.org.

Osborne Association. (1993a). *How can I help? Working with children of incarcerated parents* (Vol. 1). New York: Osborne Association.

Environmental Considerations

5

The Effects of Incarceration on Neighborhoods and Communities

HE LEN CHUNG
DANIEL McFADDEN

INTRODUCTION

In the United States, the significant increase in imprisonment during the last twenty years has far outpaced research on the effects of incarceration on communities and the children residing in them (Lynch & Sabol, 2004b; Rose & Clear, 2004). The common belief is that incarceration promotes community health, organization, and functioning through crime reduction. Indeed, the U.S. Department of Justice initiated its "Operation Weed and Seed" approach based on the idea that "weeding out" violent offenders is an important step toward neighborhood restoration and maintaining the safety of families and children (U.S. Department of Justice, 2004). To date, however, much more theoretical than empirical work has explored the effects of imprisonment on communities, and many researchers argue that we are not yet in a position to determine whether additional expansion of prison capacity is warranted (Spelman, 2000).

Typical studies have focused on the direct effects of imprisonment on individuals (e.g., psychological health, recidivism) and families (e.g., parenting, family structure) rather than the impact of incarceration on the overall health and functioning of a community. Of critical importance is to understand whether (and how) the process of incarceration can change communities for the better or worse. Addressing this question has significant implications for the development of children living in these areas, as the quality of important social influences in their lives— adult role models, peer groups, schools—is shaped by the neighborhood in which they reside (see Leventhal & Brooks-Gunn, 2004). Community-level influences are thought to be especially salient for child development because compared to adolescents and adults who may leave their neighborhoods to attend school or work, children are more restricted in their mobility (Sampson, 1999). As such, the neighborhood provides as well as organizes opportunities for activities and social interactions. The primary goal of this chapter is to provide a theoretical framework and review research aimed at understanding the effects of incarceration on communities, and ultimately child development. Specifically, the chapter discusses theories from the fields of criminology, sociology, and developmental psychology to highlight the complex direct and indirect effects that mass incarceration can have on communities and the development of children growing up in them.

DISTRIBUTION OF INCARCERATION ACROSS COMMUNITIES

According to a recent study conducted by the Pew Public Safety Performance Project, more than one in every 100 adults is now confined in an American jail or prison (The Pew Charitable Trusts, 2008). At the start of the year, more than 2.3 million adults were being held by the American penal system, nearly 1 million more adults than any other country (China was second with 1.5 million). For some groups, the figures are even more sobering. It is well known, for example, that imprisonment disproportionately affects ethnic minority groups, particularly young Black men (see Huizinga, Thornberry, Knight, & Lovegrove, 2007). The 2008 Pew Project found that a startling one in nine Black males between the ages of 20 and 34 is behind bars (for men in general in that age group, the figure is one in 30). Moreover, the lifetime probabilities of spending time in prison are 16 per 100 for Hispanic males and 28.5 per 100 for Black males, about three and six times higher, respectively, than for White males (Bonczar & Beck, 1997).

Although discussions of disproportionate confinement tend to focus on gender and ethnicity, it is important to note that increasing imprisonment rates have also disproportionately affected certain communities.

Lynch and Sabol (2004a) recently summarized evidence that incarceration is highly clustered in a small number of geographic spaces. One study in Tallahassee, Florida, for example, revealed that a high concentration of offenders were released to only a few neighborhoods (Clear, Rose, Waring, & Scully, 2003). The authors (2001) also found extreme concentrations of offenders within neighborhoods in Ohio. Based on one-day incarceration rates of Ohio's prisons on July 1, 2000, they found that about 10,000 offenders (20%) were sentenced in Cuyahoga County and 20% of the County's prisoners came from only 3% of the 1,539 census block groups in Cuyahoga County (primarily within the City of Cleveland). In a different study, the researchers found similar patterns of clustering in Baltimore City (Lynch & Sabol, 2004b). According to admissions to the Maryland Department of Corrections between 1987 and 1992, 5% of the neighborhoods accounted for 25% of the admissions in Baltimore, 10% of the neighborhoods accounted for 40% of admissions, and 25% of the neighborhoods accounted for 65% of admissions. In general, depending on the size of the neighborhood and the method of counting, studies have estimated that up to 25% of adult male residents in certain neighborhoods are locked up on any given day (Mauer, 2000).

Given evidence that the process of incarceration and reentry is clustered in certain geographic areas, it is important to understand how mass imprisonment can affect the well-being of these communities. Removing (and eventually returning) large proportions of young men and women from their homes and neighborhoods has significant consequences not only for the individuals, but for the families and communities that will eventually try to reabsorb them post-incarceration. To understand the complex influences of incarceration on community- and individual-level outcomes, two frameworks are important to review: (1) frameworks for explaining community-level effects on child development, and (2) frameworks for understanding the effects of mass incarceration on communities.

PATHWAYS OF COMMUNITY EFFECTS ON CHILD DEVELOPMENT

During the last 50 years, interest in studying the community as a context for child development has been shaped by concerns about the increasing concentration of poverty in urban areas (Jencks & Mayers, 1990;

Wilson, 1987). Indeed, research indicates that neighborhoods characterized by weak structural factors (e.g., concentrated poverty, residential instability) are likely to be the same communities that show high rates of criminal offending and imprisonment (Sampson, Raudenbush, & Earls, 1997). In addition, children who live in these high-risk communities are more likely to report poor developmental outcomes such as low academic achievement, low educational attainment, and early sexual activity (see Leventhal & Brooks-Gunn, 2000). To explain how neighborhood effects are transmitted to children and adolescents, Leventhal and Brooks-Gunn (2004) describe three complementary models: (1) norms and collective efficacy, (2) institutional resources, and (3) relationships and ties.

The norms and collective efficacy model draws heavily from social disorganization theory, which focuses on group adaptations to social processes such as shifting patterns of economic growth or decline (see Bursik, 1988; Sampson, 1986; Shaw & McKay, 1942/1969). According to social disorganization theory, some communities are unable to effectively self-regulate due to the damaging effects of certain environmental and structural characteristics like concentrated poverty. As a result, individuals' ties to each other and to the community weaken and the community structure is unable to maintain effective social controls. Indeed, a number of social organizational factors predict youth deviance and other behavior problems. Among the community-level organizational factors are neighborhood disorder (e.g., Chung & Steinberg, 2006), weak social connections within the neighborhood (e.g., Rountree & Warner, 1999), low levels of informal social control (the extent to which residents help each other to regulate the behavior of youths in the neighborhood, e.g., Elliott et al., 1996), and low levels of collective efficacy (a combination of informal social control and social connections, e.g., Sampson et al., 1997). Examples of questions that assess informal social control include "Would neighbors try to stop a breaking and entering?" and "Would neighbors stop teenagers from shouting at night?" Given the model's emphasis on establishing community-level norms and social controls, the link between neighborhood disadvantage and individual adjustment is thought to be largely mediated by peer group norms and behavior (e.g., deviant attitudes and delinquent activity).

The institutional resources model highlights community-level resources—schools, health and social services, recreational and social programs, and employment—that could influence well-being (Leventhal & Brooks-Gunn, 2000). The specific focus is on the resources and opportunities to which children theoretically have access, i.e., quantity, quality, diversity, and affordability of resources. Although work in this area is limited, especially in contrast to studies on social disorganization, research suggests that schools are an important vehicle through which neighborhood effects can operate on developmental outcomes, particularly academic achievement (see Jencks & Mayers, 1990). In addition, high-quality after-school and youth development programs such as Boys and Girls Clubs can promote positive adjustment and mental health, especially among low-income children (Durlak & Weissberg, 2007; Mahoney, Larson, & Eccles, 2005). Finally, the institutional resources perspective considers the supply of job prospects, access to employment (including transportation), and children's own expectations about available opportunities. Indeed, youth who live in disadvantaged neighborhoods are keenly aware that they face obstacles and barriers to success, such as the lack of good jobs (e.g., MacLeod, 1987). In addition, a recent study of juvenile offenders revealed that youths' perceptions of opportunities in their neighborhood (regarding school and employment) help to explain the effects of neighborhood socioeconomic status on educational outcomes (Chung, Steinberg, & Mulvey, 2009). Specifically, youth who perceived more opportunities in their communities reported higher grades and stronger attachments to school and their teachers.

The relationships and ties model suggests that neighborhood effects are transmitted to children through parental relationships (e.g., supervision practices) and characteristics of the home environment (e.g., level of economic hardship). This model is based on developmental-ecological frameworks, which stress the importance of the family system, particularly parent-child relationships, in mediating the effects of neighborhood functioning (Gorman-Smith, Tolan, & Henry, 2000). The frameworks highlight the influence of an "outer" system (e.g., the neighborhood) on an "inner" system (e.g., the family) such that community characteristics act as ecological determinants to "frame" the developmental influence of more proximal systems. A growing body of research indicates that neighborhood conditions—mainly poverty, danger, and violence—are associated with several parenting behaviors—supervision and monitoring, warmth, and hostility—and subsequent child development (e.g., Klebanov, Brooks-Gunn, & Duncan, 1994). In addition, there is now compelling evidence that neighborhood structural factors, particularly socioeconomic status (SES), are linked to parents' physical and mental health. For example, experimental studies demonstrate that low-income parents report improved health outcomes after moving from high- to low- poverty neighborhoods (e.g., Leventhal & Brooks-Gunn, 2003, see Leventhal & Brooks-Gunn, 2004, for a review).

The three models—norms and collective efficacy, institutional resources, and relationships and ties—are meant to be complementary, not conflicting. Depending on the outcome or developmental period, one model may be more relevant than others for explaining outcomes. With respect to developmental differences, community-level institutional resources may play an equally important role during childhood and adolescence, but the specific resource of most significance may differ for the two age groups. For example, relationship mechanisms might be more relevant for children than adolescents because family systems and parents may exert a greater influence during this period. In contrast, community norms and processes may be more relevant for adolescents than children because of the growing influence of peer groups during this period. With respect to developmental outcomes, norms and collective efficacy processes may be most salient for studying low-SES-delinquency associations; institutional resources mechanisms may be most relevant for understanding high-SES-achievement links, and relationship pathways may be most important for examining SES-sexual outcome associations (Leventhal & Brooks-Gunn, 2004).

EFFECTS OF MASS INCARCERATION ON COMMUNITIES

Theories that try to explain the impact of incarceration on communities have considered both negative and positive effects. In general, studies have examined these effects in one of two ways—as direct influences on social control mechanisms, or as indirect influences transmitted through systems such as the family. To date, however, research in both of these areas remains limited.

Positive Effects of Incarceration

Effects on Crime

The argument that imprisonment improves neighborhood functioning is intuitively appealing and straightforward. The prevailing assumption until recently was that incarceration not only benefitted the individual offender—by reducing the likelihood of recidivism—but also the community he or she left behind (Lynch & Sabol, 2004a). Specifically, the residents would feel safer and less victimized after criminals, especially those who were responsible for violent acts, were taken out of the neighborhood. Moreover, the community as a whole would experience less crime. Sometimes, the benefits could be felt even closer to home. For instance, removing an abusing spouse from the house could improve the functioning of the remaining parent, children, and other family members (Lynch & Sabol, 2001). Ultimately, the primary assumed benefit of incarceration was crime reduction through deterrence or incapacitation.

Currently, no definitive evidence indicates that incarceration leads to crime reductions in affected communities (Lynch and Sabol, 2004a). As such, researchers are cautious about overgeneralizing the deterrent effects of imprisonment (Lynch & Sabol, 2004a; Nagin, 1998). Nagin argues that the deterrent effect depends on the social context in which it is applied, and that deterrence will not occur in the absence of stigmatization. He focuses on the stigma that imprisonment brings to the offender's family and community, and asserts that attachments to the labor force, family, and community make individuals vulnerable to informal sanctions from these groups; deterrence is likely to be particularly strong for individuals with meaningful attachments to these institutions. Thus, Nagin devalues the role of incarceration (in and of itself) for crime reduction and stresses the significance of less coercive forms of social control associated with imprisonment.

Effects on Informal Social Control

Building upon the social disorganization framework, Lynch and Sabol (2004b) have tried to explain how incarceration might lead to reductions in crime. As described earlier, social disorganization theory posits that weak neighborhood structural characteristics (e.g., concentrated poverty) interfere with a community's ability to develop and maintain effective social controls. In their model, Lynch and Sabol suggest that the willingness of community residents to engage in informal social control is determined by the (1) extent to which they have positive attitudes toward and feel as if they belong to the neighborhood (community solidarity), and (2) amount of interaction they have with their neighbors (neighboring). High levels of interaction among neighbors on a regular basis lay the foundation for the more "specific mobilization of these networks for activities such as informal social control" (p.139). Without the foundation of persistent patterns of interaction and community solidarity, residents will be much less likely to enforce community-level norms. According to Lynch and Sabol (2004b), high levels of incarceration are expected to reduce crime and encourage the types of interactions that build shared norms and solidarity, which then promote informal social control.

Lynch and Sabol (2004b) used four data sources to examine associations in their proposed model. The first data were collected in 1982 and 1994 for a study on crime and social organization in Baltimore (Taylor, 2001). The data included aggregate community-level measures of the demographic and socio-demographic features of 277 neighborhoods, along with their crime rates and interviews with residents about community cohesiveness, attachment, participation, and experiences with self-protection and crime. Lynch and Sabol supplemented these data with the second data source, census data, to assess the social and economic characteristics of the census tracts that make up the Taylor neighborhoods. The third data source, Baltimore City police data, indicated arrests made by the police in 1987 and 1992 and the offenses recorded, including the address where they occurred. The researchers geo-coded street addresses into longitude and latitude coordinates and then used the coordinates to compute counts of events that occurred within neighborhoods. The Maryland Department of Public Safety provided the final set of data (Gowen, 2000). These data included all of the admissions to and releases from prison in Baltimore City and Baltimore County between 1982 and 2000. As with the police data, street addresses were geo-coded and linked with the appropriate neighborhood. In sum, Lynch and Sabol used census data for 1980 and 1990 to develop measures of residential poverty, residential mobility, and other characteristics. Prison admission rates were used to assess incarceration. Finally, Taylor's (2001) interview data were used to create measures of community solidarity, neighboring, participation in voluntary associations, and informal social control.

Data analyses revealed that incarceration had positive effects on informal social control in the neighborhoods studied, and at the same time had negative influences on the social processes on which informal social control depends. As incarceration increased, residents were more willing to engage in informal social control, but they reported weaker feelings of attachment to their communities; they were also not influenced to change either their neighboring activities or their levels of participation in voluntary associations. These results suggest that the effects of incarceration on communities involve a complex set of processes. Although supporting the notion that incarceration can benefit communities, the findings suggest that high levels of incarceration can undermine the ability of neighborhoods to carry out their social control functions. The results, however, are tentative, and Lynch and Sabol stress the importance of replicating study findings outside of Baltimore and with a larger number of communities.

Negative Effects of Incarceration

There are various pathways and mechanisms by which incarceration can adversely affect communities, and ultimately child development. This section organizes research findings according to the three models outlined by Leventhal and Brooks-Gunn (2004) to explain how neighborhood effects are transmitted to children and adolescents.

Implications for the Norms and Collective Efficacy Model

As described earlier, the norms and collective efficacy model draws heavily from social disorganization theory. Rose and Clear (1998) have expanded Bursik and Grasmick's (1993) General Systems Model (GSM) to elucidate how incarceration can adversely affect less coercive institutions of social control. According to the GSM, community disorganization leads to crime principally through the variables mobility, heterogeneity, and SES. Specifically, these variables can inhibit or promote interaction in communities that allow residents to set and realize collective goals. To elaborate the GSM, Rose and Clear assert that incarceration will introduce a pattern of "coercive" mobility into communities, and this pattern will undermine the achievement of less coercive institutions of informal social control. The researchers posit a feedback loop in which the use of imprisonment at time one results in greater mobility and heterogeneity at time two. Thus, in contrast to Lynch and Sabol's (2004b) model of positive effects, Rose and Clear speculate that coercive mobility can disrupt social networks, thereby inhibiting informal social control.

As noted earlier, Lynch and Sabol (2004b) found that high levels of incarceration undermined the ability of communities to perform their social control functions. In an earlier study, Lynch, Sabol, and Shelly (2002) also found that increases in incarceration are associated with less community solidarity and decreases in voluntary associations. In general, however, empirical evidence that imprisonment can inhibit social control mechanisms in communities is limited, uneven, and incomplete (Lynch & Sabol, 2004a).

Despite limited research on informal social control, previous studies indicate that incarceration can disrupt interpersonal networks in communities. Clear, Rose, and Ryder (2001), for example, have argued that the aggregate effect of these disruptions is a reduction in the capacity of social supports for everyone concerned. The authors conducted a series of individual and group interviews with a sample of 39 Tallahassee, Florida, residents (including ex-offenders) living in two high-incarceration communities. Study participants readily identified a number of ways that incarceration affects their neighborhoods, from community identity to tangible community assets such as economic activity. In terms of interpersonal networks, respondents reported that when ex-offenders return home, neighbors are welcoming but cautious, and often fearful. Relationships with neighbors can become strained—especially if offenders' families isolate from the larger community—and neighborhood networks can be completely severed if ex-offenders move in with extended family members or move to a different environment. Participants also described restricted public social interaction because of police surveillance, and they expressed regret about the way that high levels of incarceration lead to secondary community problems. Clear et al. note that the stigma of incarceration is frequently transferred to the community, such that the community loses its reputation as a good place to live and do business. The net result is that these locations become defined as "problem" places and positive social organization becomes an uphill battle.

Implications for the Institutional Resources Model

As described earlier, the institutional resources model highlights community-level resources—schools, health and social services, recreational and social programs, and employment—that could influence well-being. Not surprisingly, communities with high imprisonment rates dedicate a large proportion of their economic resources to incarceration expenses. In addition, the increasing number of inmates being housed in centers that are funded by the community translates to an increased monetary burden on the community.

States spent near a total of $50 billion on corrections in 2007, a significant increase from the $12 billion spent on corrections in 1987 (The Pew Charitable Trusts, 2008). By 2011, expenditures are expected to reach around $75 billion. On average, state governments spend more than $22,000 per year to house one inmate, and rising rates of incarceration mean rising costs (Lewis, Garfinkel, & Gao, 2007). Unfortunately, the increased economic burden may necessitate a shifting of fiscal resources, which can lead to deficits in areas that focus on child development issues. Developmental areas, such as education and after-school programming, may see reductions in fiscal allocations as they become reduced priorities (Jacobson, 2005). In the 2006 fiscal year, corrections saw a 9.8% jump in growth rate and outpaced increases in spending for community programs related to education (The Pew Charitable Trusts, 2008). The implication is that rising imprisonment rates could translate to programming deficits for children at the community level. As more and more individuals leave the workforce and are put behind bars, government funds must be reallocated to account for the increased responsibilities of prisons. The finite pool of community resources becomes disproportionately funneled in an attempt to match the growth of the penal system's economic demands. Unfortunately, the extra funding needed to shoulder the increasing fiscal burden is likely redirected from community-level programs that target child and youth development. Thus, communities with high incarceration rates are in danger of unintentionally weakening or eliminating some of their child-focused programs in place of supporting prison maintenance and (in many cases) expansion.

A growing body of research indicates that child-focused community programs like Big Brothers Big Sisters can promote positive psychosocial outcomes for children and adolescents (see National Research Council, 2002, for a review). Especially in high-incarceration communities, child-focused programs can provide invaluable developmental supports. Youth in these communities are likely to have weakened social and economic support, in general, as adult role models and family wage earners are more likely to be put behind bars. This thinning of adult resources for children, typically assumed as a standard in most communities, empha-sizes the importance of having access to high-quality community-level programs. The children of incarcerated parents, for example, may not be able to afford and gain access to private programs, due to the fam-ily's loss of income from a primary wage earner. Unfortunately, children in some neighborhoods are "more likely to know someone involved in the criminal justice system than to know someone who is employed in a profession such as law or medicine" (Case & Katz, 1991). Particularly in high-incarceration neighborhoods, community programs can support child development via access to adult role models and activities aimed at promoting healthy psychosocial adjustment.

Increases in incarceration rates—700% between 1970 and 2005 (Shivy et al., 2007)—often translate to declines in the number of viable men and women in the work force. As more and more young people are imprisoned, the total number of workers "in their prime" dwindles, and the community is dealt an indelible blow. Senior senator Charles Schumer reports that in the state of New York, a black man in his twenties without a high school diploma is more likely to be in jail than working (Wright, 2007). This staggering statistic can spell economic disaster for communities with increasing incarceration rates. Not only is the community forced to shoulder the fiscal responsibility of more incarcerated individuals, but it loses workers during what is likely to be their prime years of production (Chung, Little, & Steinberg, 2005). Indeed, the span between 18 and 25 years of age is precisely the time when most people gain the level of education and training needed to achieve their future achievements (William T. Grant Foundation Commission on Work, Family, and Citizenship, 1988). Moreover, the elevated rate of residents out of the workforce and imprisoned may translate to a reduction in community-level productivity. Unfortunately, when an individual is incarcerated, the community is likely to pay for it twofold.

Although findings suggest that incarceration can negatively affect economic institutions in communities, it is unclear if incarceration is the primary cause. A number of studies have already documented adverse effects on the labor force attachments of incarcerated individuals. Most of these studies, however, were conducted with the individual as the unit of analysis. In contrast, theories that link imprisonment to disrupted community-level processes assume neighborhoods and families as the unit of analysis. At the individual level, it is well-established that ex-offenders often battle social stigma, institutional marginalization, and economic disenfranchisement when reentering the community workforce (Peck & Theodore, 2008). For example, the federal government (and most states) prohibits ex-offenders from accessing funds allocated for public aid or financial assistance for educational purposes (Harrison & Schehr, 2004). This type of regulation, unfortunately, likely hinders individual progress in the areas of schooling, workforce development, and gainful employment. In one study, researchers found that formerly incarcerated fathers earned 28% less annually than fathers who were never incarcerated (Lewis et al., 2007). In addition, previously incarcerated fathers were almost 50% less likely to be working during the week prior to their study interview and worked fewer weeks per year (and hours per week) than fathers who had never been incarcerated. Estimates suggest that the income of recently released individuals often falls below the Henderson poverty line, indicating that these individuals do not achieve an adequate standard of living (Shinkfield, Shinkfield, & Graffam, 2009).

There is also evidence to suggest that the negative effects of incarceration on labor force participation and income are more pronounced for some groups of individuals and certain communities. With respect to individuals, the effects may be the greatest for those who have the lowest risk of imprisonment, i.e., higher-income offenders. Kling (1999), for example, found that incarceration has more pronounced negative effects on earnings among white-collar offenders than among drug or federal violent offenders. Waldfogel (1994) also found that negative effects on income and employment are most significant for white-collar offenses such as fraud. Finally, Lott's (1992) research revealed that the negative effects of imprisonment are most pronounced for individuals with higher incomes prior to their incarceration. With respect to communities, Lynch and Sabol (2003) found that imprisonment affects economic institutions in predominantly black, but not white, areas. Specifically, data analyses revealed that higher rates of incarceration are more likely to affect the rates of labor force participation (assessed at the county level) among blacks than whites. Given such limited research, however, additional studies on the effects of incarceration on economic institutions are needed.

Implications for the Relationships and Ties Model

As described earlier, the relationships and ties model suggests that neighborhood effects are transmitted to children through parental relationships and characteristics of the home environment. Weak neighborhood structural factors, particularly concentrated poverty, can hinder the development of effective parenting behaviors and also have deleterious effects on parents' physical and mental health (see Leventhal & Brooks-Gunn, 2004).

In the context of the relationships and ties model, incarceration may have indirect effects on child development via its impact on the financial capacity of the neighborhood. To the extent that imprisonment reduces the socioeconomic status of a community, it has the potential to impact the adjustment of children living in the community. Clear et al. (2001) found that a significant concern among residents in high-incarceration communities is that incarceration adversely affects the economic capacity of the neighborhood. At the family level, those who lose a breadwinner will ultimately struggle to compensate for the loss. Families are likely to struggle not only from the lost income while someone is incarcerated, but from the financial drain of supporting an ex-offender post-release. At the community level, local businesses experience financial losses when ex-offenders fail as employees. Residents may also be wary about doing business with ex-offenders, and companies could lose existing and potential customers. Unfortunately, the financial strains are particularly salient because it is difficult for low-resource neighborhoods (and the families who live there) to absorb additional deficits.

CONCLUSIONS

As the rate of incarceration has increased in the United States, the consequences of imprisonment have disproportionately affected certain communities, especially those in low-resource areas. Understanding how the process of incarceration can change communities for the better or worse has significant implications for child development, as the quality of important social influences in youths' lives—adult role models, peer groups, schools—is shaped by the neighborhoods in which they reside (see Leventhal & Brooks-Gunn, 2004). Although empirical research is limited, two lines of inquiry help to shed light on the consequences of incarceration for communities and the children living in them: (1) the effects of mass imprisonment on community functioning, and (2) community-level effects on child development.

Preliminary evidence indicates that mass incarceration can undermine a community's ability to establish informal social control, maintain labor force participation, and sustain economic resources that support child development. Specifically, the process of removing and eventually returning so many individuals from a given area can make it difficult for residents to build attitudes and social networks that promote informal social control (e.g., orientation toward collective community action and youth development). In addition, rising incarceration rates translate to more money being spent to imprison individuals and less money being available for child-focused, community-based programs. High incarceration areas also contend with stigma and the concerns of wary outsiders (and residents), which can interfere with the community's ability to attract good businesses, employees, and customers.

Children living in communities that struggle to establish informal social control as well as institutional and economic resources are at increased risk for a number of negative psychosocial outcomes. Most research has focused on antisocial behavior and related externalizing issues, but community-level problems have also been linked to educational failure, internalizing symptoms (e.g., depression), early sexual behavior, and low aspirations and expectations for future success (see Leventhal & Brooks-Gunn, 2004). Thus, although incarceration may result in positive outcomes for an individual child—for example, if an abusive parent is removed from the home—the process of mass incarceration can adversely affect child development to the extent that it interferes with the development of strong community-level social processes and the acquisition (and effective use) of economic resources.

To promote child development in high-incarceration areas, researchers recommend a comprehensive programmatic response. The response targets issues that can affect offenders and their communities during imprisonment as well as throughout the challenging reintegration process. According to Clear et al. (2001), the following recommendations can minimize the disruptions that can result from incarceration, and ultimately improve the health and functioning of the community and its residents. This section does not address specific recommendations to support family or parent-child relationships, as these issues are discussed elsewhere in the text.

1. Provide Transitional Housing

This accommodation would alleviate the immediate need that ex-offenders have a place to stay, and prevent individuals from going to the streets or shelters. It would also relieve the burden that families sometimes experience when they house ex-offenders. Transitional housing, with support staff to assist with the reintegration process, could function as a service center that facilitates the process of obtaining identification papers, employment, clothing, and other items and resources. Housing ex-offenders together may also streamline services, as parolees tend to be in the same situation, often monitored for substance abuse and visited regularly at home by parole officers.

2. Modify Rules Associated with Obtaining a Lease

The inability of many ex-offenders to obtain a lease often forces them into transient living situations. Upon checking an applicant's background, most property owners will automatically reject parolees and ex-convicts. One solution is for real estate companies and property managers to register as a specific vendor to the state's Department of Corrections. This status gives them referrals of recent parolees looking for housing in exchange for an agreement to rent exclusively to ex-offenders. For example, in an effort to reverse the trend of mass incarceration in Colorado, 13 landlords are registered vendors of the Department of Corrections and the landlords own a total of 27 eligible homes across the state (LaRocque, 2009).

3. Reduce Initial Financial Pressures Upon Release

This can be accomplished by assisting with the fees imposed by the criminal justice system (e.g., supervision fees) and providing short-term financial assistance to pay for needs such as security deposits, first months' rent, initiation of utilities, and obtaining other basic living necessities. This type of financial assistance may help to reduce the incentive to participate in illegal activities to access money quickly.

4. Assist in Obtaining and Retaining Employment

This type of assistance would help to alleviate the financial strain ex-offenders experience and the financial burden often absorbed by families. The assistance would also likely reduce the stigma associated with incarceration and unemployment. Assistance might include

    a. programs to help ex-offenders become self-employed;
    b. employer-education programs to promote the hiring of ex-offenders;
    c. incenting employers to hire ex-offenders through a program of government bonding to reduce the risk assumed by potential employers; and
    d. encouraging employers to provide full-time employment and benefits.

5. Make Education, Training, and Legal Assistance Available

Education and training are the foundation of quality employment. Ex-offenders who have trouble getting and keeping good jobs should have access to vocational training. Individuals also need basic information about legal issues and assistance in solving legal problems, restoring their civil rights, and closing out any pending criminal cases and legal obligations.

6. Match Ex-Offender to Community Mentors

Community mentors can serve as contacts, advisors, and support for returning offenders and even take part in the transition planning process. They can help ex-offenders with basic life skills (e.g., opening a checking account), as well as serve as advocates. The mentor system can apply to families as well, with families "adopting" other families for support.

7. Involve Ex-Offenders in Neighborhood Projects

Ex-offenders can play a positive role in a large range of neighborhood activities, from neighborhood reclamation projects to organized sports programs. These types of efforts would place ex-offenders in productive contact with fellow residents in activities that can lead to the overall improvement of the community. In addition to promoting neighborhood development, the interactions may contribute to enhanced social organization among residents.

8. Develop Awareness Programs to Reduce Stigma

De-stigmatizing individuals and communities is likely to help reduce the pressures experienced by ex-offenders who are trying to make a new start post-release. In addition, an improved understanding of the needs and challenges facing ex-offenders may enhance the quality of community life by countering some of the unintended consequences of incarceration. Program targets might include

   a.   probation officers, to assist in the reintegration process;
   b.   police, to help alleviate difficult tensions in the community;
   c.   educators, who can discuss issues regarding reintegration with increasing levels of knowledge and sensitivity;
   d.   employers, who may be fearful of hiring ex-offenders or lack knowledge in working with them; and
   e.   community at large, to promote tolerance and strengthen interpersonal networks with returning offenders and other residents.

9. Provide Services at a Neighborhood-Based Center

This type of center could promote access to important services for returning offenders and their families, and enable services to be tailored to the specific needs of the community. By locating multiple services in a central location, the center would promote integration and the maintenance of informal networks. It could involve neighborhood groups such as neighborhood associations in the design and delivery of service. The center could also play a key role in transferring resources from the society at large to the community by serving as the site through which financial and institutional resources are funneled into the neighborhood.

10. Provide Services through Partnerships of Public and Private Sources

Human service organizations, both public and private nonprofits, can organize partnerships to create and focus their work in high-incarceration communities. In addition, private, for-profit organizations can contribute to the public services programmatically and financially. This type of concentrated effort would leverage the resources of both public and private interested organizations and direct them toward community-based strategies that might include

   a. social service provider-neighborhood partnerships to coordinate and intensify local service delivery;
   b. police-resident group partnerships to engage in problem-solving strategies and to provide individuals and families with support they need;
   c. public-private partnerships to create new jobs for residents; and
   d. expert-citizen group partnerships to help resident groups develop new project ideas and write grant proposals.

In discussing and trying to implement such programmatic recommendations, three issues are important to consider. First, the needs of individual offenders must be balanced with the interests of public safety. Individuals (and communities) will differ dramatically in their interest and willingness to change, and implementing certain programs with "hard-to-reach" ex-offenders is likely to engender public safety concerns. Second, strength-versus deficit-based approaches to program development are likely to yield successful outcomes. Multisystemic therapy (MST), for example, targets individual-, family-, and community-level strengths as levers of change (Henggeler, 1999). MST was developed to treat serious antisocial behavior among children and adolescents and has shown impressive outcomes for families living in low-income, low-resource communities (see Huey & Henggeler, 2001). Finally, additional research is required to understand the complex effects of incarceration on community, families, and ultimately child development. Given that incarceration is clustered in certain geographic spaces, it is critical to understand how the process changes communities for the better or worse. Addressing this question has significant implications for the development of children living in these areas, as the quality of important social influences in their lives—adult role models, peer groups, schools—is shaped by the neighborhood in which they reside.

REFERENCES

Bonczar, T. P., & Beck, A. (1997). *Lifetime likelihood of going to state or federal prison.* Washington DC: U.S. Department of Justice, Bureau of Justice Statistics.

Bursik, R. J., Jr. (1988). Social disorganization and theories of crime and delinquency: Problems and prospects. *Criminology, 26,* 519–551.

Case, A. C., & Katz, L. F. (1991). *The company you keep: The effects of family and neighborhood on disadvantaged youths.* Cambridge, MA: National Bureau of Economic Research.

Chung, H. L., Little, M., & Steinberg, L. (2005). The transition to adulthood for adolescents in the juvenile justice system: A developmental perspective. In D. W. Osgood, E. M. Foster, C. Flanagan, & G. R. Ruth (Eds.), *On your own without a net: The transition to adulthood for vulnerable populations* (pp. 68–91). Chicago: The University of Chicago Press.

Chung, H. L., & Steinberg, L. (2006). Relations between neighborhood factors, parenting behaviors, peer deviance, and delinquency among serious juvenile offenders. *Developmental Psychology, 42,* 319–331.

Chung, H. L., Steinberg, L., & Mulvey, E. P. (2009). Neighborhood affluence and school outcomes among adolescent offenders: The motivating function of beliefs about success. Unpublished Manuscript.

Clear, T. R., Rose, D. R., & Ryder, J. A. (2001). Incarceration and the community: The problem of removing and returning offenders. *Crime & Delinquency, 47,* 335–351.

Clear, T. R., Rose, D. R., Waring, E., & Scully, K. (2003). Coercive mobility and crime: A preliminary examination of concentrated incarceration and social disorganization. *Justice Quarterly, 20,* 33–64.

Durlak, J. A., & Weissberg, R. P. (2007). *The impact of after-school programs that promote personal and social skills.* Chicago: Collaborative for Academic, Social, and Emotional Learning.

Elliott, D. S., Wilson, W. J., Huizinga, D., Sampson, R. J., Elliott, A., & Ranking, D. (1996). The effects of neighborhood disadvantage on adolescent development. *Journal of Research in Crime and Delinquency, 33,* 389–426.

Gorman-Smith, D., Tolan, P. H., & Henry, D. B. (2000). A developmental-ecological model of the relation of family functioning to patterns of delinquency. *Journal of Quantitative Criminology, 16,* 169–198.

Gowen, R. (2000). *Admissions from and releases to Baltimore County from Maryland state correctional facilities.* Baltimore: Maryland Department of Public Safety and Correctional Services.

Harrison, B., & Schehr, R. C. (2004). Offenders and post-release jobs: Variables influencing success and failure. *Journal of Offender Rehabilitation, 39,* 35–68.

Henggeler, S. W. (1999). Multisystemic therapy: An overview of clinical procedures, outcomes, and policy implications. *Child Psychology and Psychiatry Review, 4,* 2–10.

Huey, S. J., Jr., & Henggeler, S. W. (2001). Effective community-based interventions for antisocial and delinquent adolescents. In J. N. Hughes & A. M. La Greca (Eds.), *Handbook of psychological services for children and adolescents.* (pp. 301–322). New York: Oxford University Press.

Huizinga, D., Thornberry, T., Knight, K., & Lovegrove, P. (2007). *Disproportionate minority contact in the juvenile justice system: A study of differential minority arrest/ referral to court in three cities.* Washington DC: U.S. Department of Justice.

Jacobson, M. (2005). *Downsizing prisons: How to reduce crime and end mass incarceration.* New York: New York University Press.

Jencks, C., & Mayers, S. E. (1990). The social consequences of growing up in a poor neighborhood. In L. E. Lynn, Jr. & M. McGreary (Eds.), *Inner-city poverty in the United States.* Washington DC: National Academy Press.

Klebanov, P. K., Brooks-Gunn, J., & Duncan, G. J. (1994). Does neighborhood and family poverty affect mothers' parenting, mental health, and social support? *Journal of Marriage and the Family, 56,* 441–455.

Kling, J. (1999). *The effect of prison sentence length on the subsequent employment and earnings of criminal defendants.* Woodrow Wilson School Discussion Papers in Economics, No. 208. Princeton, NJ: Princeton University Press.

LaRocque, T. (2009, January 11). From the big house to a rental home [Electronic Version]. Retrieved April 10, 2009, from Denverpost.com.

Leventhal, T., & Brooks-Gunn, J. (2000). The neighborhoods they live in: The effects of neighborhood residence on child and adolescent outcomes. *Psychological Bulletin, 126,* 309–337.

Leventhal, T., & Brooks-Gunn, J. (2003). Moving to opportunity: An experimental study of neighborhood effects on mental health. *American Journal of Public Health, 93,* 1576–1582.

Leventhal, T., & Brooks-Gunn, J. (2004). Diversity in developmental trajectories across adolescence: Neighborhood influences. In R. Lerner & L. Steinberg (Eds.), *Handbook of Adolescent Psychology* (2nd ed., pp. 451-486). Hoboken, NJ: John Wiley & Sons.

Lewis, C. E., Garfinkel, I., & Gao, Q. (2007). Incarceration and unwed fathers in fragile families. *Journal of Sociology & Social Welfare, 34,* 77–94.

Lott, J. R. (1992). Do we punish high-income criminals too heavily? *Economic Inquiry, 30,* 538–608.

Lynch, J. P., & Sabol, W. J. (2001). *Crime, coercion, and communities: The effects of arrest and incarceration policies on informal social control in neighborhoods (Final Report).* Washington DC: National Institute of Justice.

Lynch, J. P., & Sabol, W. J. (2004a). Assessing the effects of mass incarceration of informal social control in communities. *Criminology & Public Policy, 3,* 267–294.

Lynch, J. P., & Sabol, W. J. (2004b). Effects of incarceration on informal social control in communities. In M. Patillo, D. Weiman, & B. Western (Eds.), *Imprisoning America: The social effects of mass incarceration.* New York: Russell Sage Foundation.

Lynch, J. P., Sabol, W. J., & Shelly, M. (2002). *Crime, coercion and community: The effects of arrest and incarceration policies on informal social control in neighborhoods. Unpublished Manuscript.*

MacLeod, J. (1987). *Ain't no makin' it: Leveled aspirations in a low-income neighborhood.* Boulder, CO: Westview Press.

Mahoney, J. L., Larson, R. W., & Eccles, J. S. (Eds.). (2005). *Organized activities as contexts of development: Extracurricular activities, after-school and community programs.* Mahwah, NJ: Erlbaum.

Mauer, M. (2000). *Race to incarcerate.* Washington, DC: The Prison Project.

Nagin, D. (1998). Criminal deterrence research at the outset of the twenty-first century. In M. Tonry (Ed.), *Crime and Justice: A Review of Research.* Chicago: University of Chicago Press.

National Research Council. (2002). *Community programs to promote youth development.* Washington D.C.: National Academy Press.

Peck, J., & Theodore, N. (2008). Carceral Chicago: Making the ex-offender employability crisis. *International Journal of Urban & Regional Research, 32,* 251–281.

Rose, D. R., & Clear, T. R. (1998). Incarceration, social capital, and crime: Implications for social disorganization theory. *Criminology, 36,* 441–480.

Rose, D. R., & Clear, T. R. (2004). Incarceration, reentry and social capital: Social networks in the balance. In J. Travis & M. Waul (Eds.), *Prisoners once removed: The impact of incarceration and reentry on children, families, and communities.* Washington DC: Urban Institute Press.

Rountree, P. W., & Warner, B. D. (1999). Social ties and crime: Is the relationship gendered? *Criminology, 37,* 789–813.

Sabol, W. J., & Lynch, J. P. (2003). Assessing the longer-run consequences of incarceration: Effects on families and employment. In D. Hawkins, J. Samuel L. Myers & R. Stone (Eds.), *Crime Control and Social Justice: The Delicate Balance.* Westport, CT: Greenwood Press.

Sampson, R. J. (1986). Crime in cities: The effects of formal and informal social control. In J. Albert J. Reiss & M. Tonry (Eds.), *Communities and crime.* Chicago: University of Chicago Press.

Sampson, R. J. (1999). What 'community' supplies. In R. F. Ferguson & W. T. Dickens (Eds.), *Urban problems and community development* (pp. 241–292). Washington, DC: Brookings Institution Press.

Sampson, R. J., Raudenbush, S. W., & Earls, F. (1997). Neighborhoods and violent crime: A multilevel study of collective efficacy. *Science, 277,* 918–924.

Shaw, C., & McKay, H. (1942/1969). *Juvenile delinquency and urban areas.* Chicago: University of Chicago Press. (Original work published in 1942).

Shinkfield, A. J., Shinkfield, A. J., & Graffam, J. (2009). Community reintegration of ex-prisoners: Type and degree of change in variables influencing successful reintegration. *International Journal of Offender Therapy and Comparative Criminology, 53,* 29–42.

Shivy, V. A., Wu, J. J., Moon, A. E., Mann, S. C., Holland, J. G., & Eacho, C. (2007). Ex-offenders reentering the workforce. *Journal of Counseling Psychology, 54,* 466–473.

Spelman, W. (2000). What recent studies do (and don't) tell us about imprisonment and crime. In M. Tonry (Ed.), *Crime and Justice: A Review of Research* (Vol. 27). Chicago: University of Chicago.

Taylor, R. B. (2001). *Breaking Away from Broken Windows*. Boulder, CO: Westview Press.

The Pew Charitable Trusts. (2008). *One in 100: Behind bars in America 2008*. Washington DC: Author.

U.S. Department of Justice. (2004). *The Weed and Seed Strategy*. Washington DC: U.S. Department of Justice, Office of Justice Programs.

Waldfogel, J. (1994). The effect of criminal conviction on income and the trust reported in the workmen. *Journal of Human Resources, 29,* 62–81.

William T. Grant Foundation Commission on Work, Family, and Citizenship. (1988). *The forgotten half: None-college-bound youth in America*. Washington DC: William T. Grant Foundation.

Wilson, W. J. (1987). *The truly disadvantaged: The inner-city, the underclass, and public policy*. Chicago: University of Chicago Press.

Wright, J. (2007). Crisis: Black Male Unemployment. *New York Amsterdam News*, p. 2.

ADDITIONAL RESOURCES

1. www.communityscience.com

   Since 1997, Community Science has provided an integrated approach to building the capacity of organizations and institutions, helping to develop healthy, just, and equitable communities. The primary objective of the organization is to develop the knowledge necessary to address social problems in a way that benefits all communities. Its services include research and evaluation services, capacity-building products and services, and initiative management and support.

2. http://www.ojp.usdoj.gov/ccdo/programs/reentry.html

   The mission of the Community Capacity Development Office (CCDO) is to promote comprehensive strategies to reduce crime and revitalize communities. CCDO helps communities help themselves, enabling them to reduce violent and drug crime, strengthen community capacity to increase the quality of life, and promote long-term community health and resilience.

3. http://www.urban.org/center/jpc/index.cfm

   The Justice Policy Center (JPC) carries out nonpartisan research to inform the national dialogue on crime, justice, and community safety. JPC researchers collaborate with practitioners, public officials, and community groups to make the center's research useful not only to decision makers and agencies in the justice system but also to the neighborhoods and communities harmed by crime and disorder.

4. http://www.reentrymediaoutreach.org/index.html

   The Reentry National Media Outreach Campaign is designed to support the work of community and faith-based organizations through offering media resources that will facilitate community discussion and decision making about solution-based reentry programs. Based on the belief that diverse media play an essential role in motivating and mobilizing community action, the campaign aims to expand public awareness and work in partnership with local organizations and initiatives to foster public safety and support healthy communities.

6

Living Arrangements of Children of Incarcerated Parents: The Roles of Stability, Embeddedness, Gender, and Race/Ethnicity

HOLLY FOSTER

MASS IMPRISONMENT AND CHILDREN

Mass imprisonment, or the rapid increase in incarceration since the mid-1970s, has uniquely shaped the contemporary American social context in comparison to other Western industrialized nations (Garland, 2001; West & Sabol, 2008). The rapid increase in imprisonment emerged from a series of policies accruing over time beginning with "the war on drugs," or particularly punitive policies aimed at drug crimes, through determinate or fixed sentencing guidelines, as well as "truth-in-sentencing" policies or longer sentences served among those incarcerated (Mauer, 2001). A further defining feature of mass imprisonment is its socio-demographic concentration by race/ethnicity, with African American males being disproportionately likely to experience imprisonment, especially if they have lower levels of education

Support for this research from the Race and Ethnic Studies Institute and the Mexican-American Latino Research Center at Texas A&M University, and permission from the Texas Department of Health and Human Services to analyze data gathered for the former Texas Commission on Alcohol and Drug Abuse are very much appreciated.

(Garland, 2001; Pettit & Western, 2004). Rates of imprisonment of men and women in American society more broadly are also unequal by race and ethnicity with the highest rates found among African Americans, followed by Hispanics and Whites (Glaze & Maruschak, 2008). As most incarcerated adults are parents (Mumola, 2000; Glaze & Maruschak, 2008), minority children are therefore also disproportionately affected. In fact, African American children are most likely to have a parent in prison (7.5%), followed by Hispanic children (2.3%) and white children (1%) (Western, Pattillo, & Weiman, 2004; see also Mumola, 2000; Glaze & Maruschak, 2008). In further illustration of these disparities, estimates show that by the time the child turns 14, among children born in 1990 the cumulative risk of parental imprisonment is 25.1–28.4% for African American children and 3.6–4.2% for white children, or 6.8 times more likely in the former group (Wildeman, in press). As the number of children under age 18 with parents in prison has increased from 1991–2007 (Glaze & Maruschak, 2008), the developmental implications of parental incarceration for children remains a pressing issue for practitioners, policymakers, and researchers attending to child well-being.

Among the intergenerational consequences of parental incarceration for children are elevated levels of behavior problems (e.g., antisocial behavior problems and delinquency, anxiety/depression), the social exclusion or disconnection of youth from societal institutions, and school problems (Foster & Hagan, 2007; Hagan & Dinovitzer, 1999; Murray & Farrington, 2005; Murray & Farrington, 2008a; Murray & Farrington, 2008b; Trice & Brewster, 2004; Stanton, 1980; Travis & Waul, 2003). Parental incarceration has further consequences for child living arrangements, as is the focus here (Enos, 2001; Murray, 2007; Johnson & Waldfogel, 2004). This chapter has two main sections: the first reviews literature on child living arrangements prior to and during parental incarceration with particular attention to parental gender and race/ethnicity, and the second section presents new research on how living arrangements influence parental expectations of living with their children upon release from prison. Findings are presented from a Texas data set with information on children of both incarcerated mothers and fathers from African-American, Hispanic, and non-Hispanic White groups. By discerning factors that may support parental expectations of living with children upon release, both child well-being and successful prisoner reentry into society may be facilitated.

TYPES OF LIVING ARRANGEMENTS, STABILITY, AND CHILD WELL-BEING

Two perspectives on child living arrangements in the broader literature on child well-being are relevant to understanding the influences of parental incarceration on children. One set of studies highlights the influences of types of living arrangements (e.g., with parents, relatives, or non-kin living arrangements) on child outcomes, and another emphasizes stability (e.g., continuity of living with a primary caregiver) in living arrangements.

In their empirical work on the living arrangements of children of incarcerated parents, Johnson and Waldfogel (2004) first review relevant child welfare literature on types of substitute care placements and child outcomes more broadly. They note that a developmental perspective may emphasize the importance of types of care where parental care would be preferable to substitute care for child well-being, all else being equal, due to the potential for continuity in relationships and other daily activities. Their review highlights that mixed empirical results are found on the influences of types of living arrangement on child well-being. Some research shows that children placed in non-relative and relative foster care fare worse in terms of behavior problems than national samples (Berrick, Barth & Needell, 1994). Furthermore, on types of substitute or nonparental care arrangements, mixed findings are evident in the sparse literature considering their influences on child well-being (Johnson & Waldfogel, 2004). In the short term, children placed in kinship care (relatives paid as foster parents) have fewer behavior problems and less grade repetition than those placed in non-relative foster care arrangements (Berrick et al., 1994; Benedict, Zuravin, and Stallings, 1996). However, children placed in kin care had fewer problems prior to placement than did those in non-relative foster care placement; therefore, preexisting differences rather than placement per se may affect child outcomes (Benedict et al., 1996).

However, research on long-term outcomes of children in different substitute care arrangements finds no significant differences in adulthood on educational attainments, income, and housing situations (Benedict et al., 1996; Johnson & Waldfogel, 2004). More recent work similarly supports these mixed results where kinship care is associated with lower levels of adolescent self-reported depressive symptoms than is group home care among a U.S. sample (Perry, 2006), but other work in the Netherlands finds no immediate differences in child functioning, including a total behavior problem index, among children placed in kinship compared to non-relative foster care (Strijker, Zandberg, & van der Muelen, 2003). These mixed findings for child well-being may be explained in part by the benefit of more stability in relationships yielded by placement in kinship than non-relative care arrangements (Benedict et al., 1996), but such benefits may be offset by kinship caregiver disadvantages (compared to non-kin caregivers), including lower levels of education, access to fewer supportive services, lower income, and health disadvantages (Berrick et al., 1994). Johnson and Waldfogel (2004) conclude that regarding children's outcomes, challenges remain in establishing causal effects in these studies on the relative effects of kinship and non-kinship care environments, and "there does not appear to be a clear hierarchy with regard to substitute care arrangements" (p. 102).

Instead of emphasizing the influences of types of living arrangements, a broader interdisciplinary literature on children and family structure is yielding consensus on the dimension of stability in living arrangements as more directly promotive of child well-being across a range of outcomes and samples (Fomby & Cherlin, 2007). The "instability hypothesis" posits that multiple transitions in family structure may lead to worse outcomes for children compared to stable two-parent families and possibly stable, single-parent families (Fomby & Cherlin, 2007). Research finds that family instability or "turbulence" is consistently associated with behavior problems (Ackerman, Kogos, Youngstrom, Schoff, & Izard, 1999; Foster, Nagin, Hagan, Angold, & Costello, In Press; Capaldi & Patterson, 1991; Fergusson, Diamond, & Horwood, 1986; Kurdek, Fine, & Sinclair, 1995; Moore, Vandivere, & Ehrle, 2000; Thornberry, Smith, Rivera, Huizinga, & Stouthamer-Loeber, 1999; Juby & Farrington, 2001; Najman et al., 1997). Social stress is emphasized in instability perspectives given the demands involved with multiple transitions, including the demands of disruption and readjustment.

Although some work on family structure supports that children living in single-parent families fare worse than those living with two parents (McLanahan & Sandefur 1994), other work finds that stable single-parent homes protect against child misbehavior (Hao & Xie, 2002; Juby & Farrington, 2001; Najman et al., 1997; Pagani, Boulerice, & Tremblay, 1997). Cavanagh and Huston (2006) found the influence of being born into a single parent family at birth on observer-reported antisocial behavior was contingent on levels of family instability: children in stable single-parent homes fared better than those experiencing multiple family transitions. Recent studies strengthen the support for a causal role of family instability and change on child antisocial behavior problems by taking into account social selection factors. Hao and Xie (2002) use fixed effects models (which eliminate the effects of time-invariant unobserved family and child characteristics contributing to the "endogeneity" or potential self-selection into family structures), and Fomby and Cherlin (2007) operationalize an extensive set of maternal characteristics to show that family instability and change effects on child behavior problems are not solely a function of preexisting factors. Thus, children facing multiple disruptions should be more at risk for antisocial behaviors. The role of incarceration in relation to stability of child living arrangements is next examined.

Incarceration and Stability in Child Living Arrangements

Results from a longitudinal epidemiological community study of adolescents finds a unique influence of parental criminal justice system involvement on facilitating family instability and other parental problems (i.e., substance abuse, mental health problems, and low education) (Phillips, Erklani, Keeler, Costello, & Angold, 2006). Because family instability is a risk factor for child problem outcomes, it may be particularly important for preventive research on children of incarcerated parents to examine what factors are associated with stability in these children's living arrangements.

The importance of stability has been further supported in children's care arrangements during imprisonment. A study of young children of incarcerated mothers, all placed in relative care, and all of whom had their mothers as primary caretakers prior to her imprisonment, found that children's attachment representations to their caregivers were strongly influenced by the stability of child living arrangements during her incarceration (Poehlmann, 2005). Children who experienced stable living circumstances after maternal imprisonment (i.e., lived continuously with one caregiver) were 85 times more likely to form secure attachment representations of caregivers than children in unstable living circumstances (i.e., experienced at least one change in caregiver).

Among children of incarcerated mothers, caregiver stability during maternal incarceration is facilitated by their family relationships (Poehlmann, Shafer, Maes, & Hanneman, 2008). Placement with the father during maternal incarceration facilitates caregiver stability, but more children in the household decreases caregiver stability. Furthermore, a higher quality of the mother's and caregiver's relationship during her imprisonment also facilitated stability in children's living arrangements. Thus, relationship type and quality facilitate children's stable living arrangements during incarceration. Investigated in this chapter is how child embeddedness at the time of arrest or family living arrangements facilitates a different form of stability: the expectation of parents to live with children upon release. Although measuring stability in terms of expectations to live with children upon release may be an optimistic measure as many barriers and challenges upon release will shape parental opportunities for involvement with their children (Hairston, 1991; Nurse, 2002), this expectation nonetheless has policy relevance. These positive attitudes and potential source of stability in children's lives can be structurally supported by programs and policies to further support prisoner family embeddedness, and through supports to translate these expectancies into future co-residence with children where possible.

LIVING ARRANGEMENTS AND "SOCIAL EMBEDDEDNESS"

Granovetter's (1985) concept of social embeddedness facilitates conceptualizing human action within the structure of the social relations within which individuals live. His perspective explains how social relations facilitate economic actions, and has been elaborated in terms of crime, social networks, and resultant unemployment (Hagan, 1993). A further focus on the strengths of family embeddedness and how this is shaped by gender and race/ethnicity can help to explain the social structures within which parental expectations are formed regarding child living arrangements. It is suggested that "parental embeddedness," operationalized here in terms of marital status and number of children, influences "children's embeddedness" or their living arrangements upon parental arrest, as depicted in Figure 6.1. It is further proposed that child embeddedness is also influenced by social structural location measured by parental gender, parental race/ethnicity, and children's gender and age. Children's embeddedness in family relationships at the time of parental arrest is then hypothesized as a mechanism through which socio-demographic factors, including gender and race/ethnicity, are associated with parental expectations to live with their children upon release from prison. The expectation of parents concerning children is conceptualized as a form of stability in relationships that may foster the child's well-being. Thus, structural embeddedness in family relationships should contribute to stability in children's living arrangements.

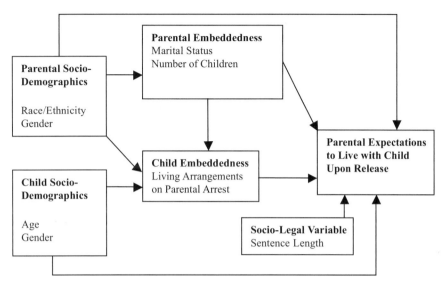

Figure 6.1 Conceptual model of socio-demographic influences on parental expectations to live with children upon release from prison as mediated by structural embeddedness.

Embeddedness, Gender, and Race/Ethnicity

Research to date on incarcerated parents' child living arrangements includes their circumstances before and during imprisonment, with more emphasis on the latter. During parental imprisonment, living arrangements of children often depend upon parental gender (Glaze & Maruschak, 2008; Johnson & Waldfogel, 2004; Johnston, 1995; Mumola, 2000). Children of incarcerated fathers tend to live with their mother or other family member during his incarceration, but children of incarcerated mothers tend to live with relatives (especially grandparents), foster home or agency care, or friends (Glaze & Maruschak, 2008; Johnson & Waldfogel, 2004). Yet little is known about the variety of children's living situations before parental incarceration (Johnson & Waldfogel, 2004; La Vigne, Davies, & Brazzell, 2008). Children living with the incarcerated parent upon arrest may be quite differently affected by parental imprisonment than children living in other situations (Koban, 1983).

More attention is needed to the intersectionality between gender and race/ethnicity in considering parental incarceration effects on living arrangements of children. Work on race/ethnicity highlights potential sources of resilience in minority families in terms of resources from extended family networks. The presence of extensive help systems among

African American families comprised of networks of relatives, friends, and neighbors has been found among middle-class and impoverished families (Jayakody, Chatters, & Taylor, 1993; McAdoo 1980; Stack, 1974; Sudarkasa, 2007). Familism or " . . . a strong identification and attachment of individuals with their families (nuclear and extended), and strong feelings of loyalty, reciprocity, and solidarity among members of the same family" (Sabogal, Marin, Otero-Sabogal, Marin, & Perez-Stable, 1987) is associated with ethnicity. In a comparative analysis, familism scores were higher on two of three dimensions among Hispanics than non-Hispanic Whites (Sabogal et al., 1987).

Because the above familial resources are more often found among minority families than among whites, minority children of incarcerated parents may experience both more embeddedness and higher parental expectations to live with them upon release, a potential source of stability. The potential embeddedness of minority families should not be overlooked, as without these resources the racially disproportionate consequences of mass incarceration may be even more severe. This argument is consistent with recent work by Swisher & Waller (2008) suggesting the importance of considering incarceration effects by race/ethnicity where African American families, for example, due to family features, may show a "greater adaptability of families to incarceration" (p. 1072). In their research, they find that the effects of incarceration are greater in diminishing mother's trust in fathers in terms of caring for young children among White compared to African American and Latino families. Examined next in further detail is the literature on race and ethnic differences in living arrangements of children by gender of the incarcerated parent.

Incarcerated Mothers

Research on race and ethnic variation in the types of care arrangements used by inmate mothers during incarceration highlights their socially structured family embeddedness and underpins a call for further research at the intersection of race and gender. Johnson & Waldfogel's (2004, p. 114) research with national data finds African American and Hispanic women were more likely to have children living in grandparental or relative care than White women during their incarceration. Enos' (2001) review and qualitative research on women finds that African Americans were more likely to rely on grandparents and relatives for child placement during incarceration, and Whites were more likely to rely on husbands and foster care (see also Snell, 1994; Ruiz, 2002). Enos' (2001) qualitative research further found that Hispanic women use both husband and relative care for child living arrangements during incarceration (p.56). Baunach's (1985) research with African American and White incarcerated mothers further found higher non-relative care among the latter group. Bresler and Lewis (1986) also describe differences in family ties from two small studies of African American and White mothers in and after jail. White women in their sample tended to be estranged from their families and rely on boyfriends and friends for assistance on release. Although African American women were less likely to have been married than White women, the former group reports more family contact than the latter. In fact, Lewis and Bresler (1981) found significant racial differences in terms of contact with family during incarceration: 71% of whites reported no contact with family, but 86% of African Americans reported contact with family, as did 61% of other minority women (p. 51). White women also reported their ties with children were tenuous and broken, but Black women were more likely to maintain close contact with children (Bresler & Lewis, 1986). These results suggest differential family embeddedness by race/ethnicity among women.

A majority of female inmates in state (64.3%) and federal (84%) prisons lived with their children prior to incarceration (Mumola, 2000; see also Glaze & Maruschak, 2008). Bloom and Steinhart (1993) found 67% of children lived with their mothers at the time of her arrest. McGowan and Blumenthal (1978) found approximately three quarters of the incarcerated mothers in their national survey were living with one or more children at the time of their arrest. Race and ethnic variation is also apparent. Snell (1994) found 75.5% of African American women were living with children under 18 before entering prison, and slightly lower estimates are found among Hispanics (65.7%) and Whites (68.7%). Lewis and Bresler (1981) found race was a factor in whether a woman had her children with her before being put in jail, with 15% of Whites, 57% of African Americans, and 46.6% of other minority groups residing with the children prior to incarceration. African American children are consistently found to be more likely than White children to have been living with their mother prior to her incarceration (Baunach, 1985; Bresler & Lewis, 1986; Enos, 2001). Ruiz's research (2002, p. 192) also finds both African American (64.7%) and Hispanic (64.1%) mothers more likely to have been living with their minor children at the time of arrest than White mothers (50.8%). Baunach's research at two prisons (1985, p. 33) further uniquely reports significant differences in where children lived prior to maternal incarceration, if not with their mothers. African American children were significantly more likely to have lived with grandparents or other relatives, and Whites were more likely to have lived with their fathers or non-relatives. These patterns suggest that African American children may be differentially affected by maternal incarceration compared to Whites, due to variations in living arrangements at the time of maternal arrest. More research is needed on Hispanic children.

Parental embeddedness is posited to affect children's living arrangements. Because female-headed single-parent families are more prevalent than male-headed ones (Kreider, 2008), marital status may be a less salient predictor of incarcerated mothers' rather than fathers' co-residence with children upon arrest. In fact, the literature on incarcerated parents indicates most of the women who lived with their children lived in single-parent households rather than in two-parent homes (Mumola, 2000; Glaze & Maruschak, 2008). However, the literature also suggests the number of children per household is another component of parental embeddedness that influences children's living arrangements. McGowan and Blumenthal (1993) found that Hispanic and African American incarcerated mothers had higher numbers of children than other racial and ethnic groups. Research with women has found that having more children is associated with a lower likelihood of living with children upon arrest (Glick & Neto, 1977, p. 119) and on release from prison (Koban, 1983). Poehlmann et al. (2008) found higher numbers of children were associated with less caregiver stability during maternal incarceration. The number of children per parent is therefore included in the research that follows as an indicator of adult embeddedness.

Incarcerated Fathers

National research shows that a substantial minority of fathers in prison lived with their children prior to admission (Mumola, 2000), with the most recent state estimates at 42.4% (Glaze & Maruschak, 2008). These estimates are consistent with those from individual studies (Hairston, 1995; see also Murray, 2007). Western et al. (2004, p. 10) found that Hispanic fathers were slightly more likely than White and African American fathers to have been co-resident with children upon their arrest. Ruiz (2002, p. 192) also finds that Hispanic fathers (44.5%), followed by White males (41.5%) were more likely to be living with their minor children before confinement, compared to African American men (39.1%).

Paternal embeddedness (e.g., marital status) influences men's relationships with children. Men who lived with their children prior to arrest tend to live in two-parent rather than single-parent households (Mumola, 2000; Glaze & Maruschak, 2008). A consistent pattern emerges in studies of currently or previously incarcerated fathers, where the child's mother determines whether fathers have relations (e.g., visitation) with their children during imprisonment (Edin et al., 2004; Nurse, 2004). Having a positive relationship with the child's mother facilitates father-child social bonds. Hairston (1995) summarizes prior studies and notes how forms of both child and parental embeddedness matter for fathers in terms of sustaining relationships with children: " . . . fathers who are married to the mothers of their children or who lived with their children prior to imprisonment are more likely to see their children and/or correspond with them during imprisonment than unmarried fathers and those who lived in separate households (p. 36)."

There is little research on paternal embeddedness and its implications for incarcerated father-child relationships along the dimension of race/ethnicity. Nurse's (2002) research with paroled juvenile fathers highlights race and ethnic variation in the centrality of men's family relationships for facilitating relations with children. She finds that African American and Latino fathers are more involved with and saw their children more often than white males (p. 97). Nurse also finds that young Latino paroled fathers were less likely to break up with the mother of their child than were Whites or African Americans. Holt and Miller's research in California (1972) found Mexican-American male inmates were more likely to receive family visits in prison than were Whites or African Americans. Recent work finds Hispanic men are as likely to be living with their children prior to incarceration as are White women (Foster & Hagan, 2009), suggesting race/ethnic and gendered structural circumstances that may affect the influence of parental incarceration on children. Children may therefore be differentially impacted by paternal incarceration due to parental embeddedness, and this may further vary by race/ethnicity. Together, this review underpins two hypotheses:

Hypothesis 1: Women will be more likely to live with their children at the time of arrest than men. Furthermore, children's living arrangements at the time of parental arrest will vary within parental gender by race/ethnicity.

Hypothesis 2: Adult family embeddedness will facilitate children's residence with the incarcerated parent at the time of parental arrest.

The living arrangements of children at the time of parental arrest are posited to influence parental expectancies to live with children upon release as indicated in Figure 6.1. The literature on parental expectations of incarcerated parents is reviewed next.

Family Social Bonds: Expectancies to Live with Children Upon Release

The majority of incarcerated mothers expect to live with or reunite with children upon release from prison, ranging from 61% in Zalba's (1964) study of inmate mothers in California to a high of 88% in Baunach's (1985) study in Kentucky and Washington states (see also Bloom & Steinhart, 1993; McGowan & Blumenthal, 1978). In a comparative study in Kentucky, more women (83.3%) than men (68.4%) expected to reunite with children upon release (Koban, 1983), suggesting a difference by parental gender.

Several studies suggest that child embeddedness or residential arrangements prior to arrest influence parental expectations to live with children upon release from prison. Among women, Hairston (1991) found 83% of women in a small sample of jailed mothers expected to live with their children upon release, and 47% of women who did not live with children prior to arrest expected to live with them upon release. Among both women and men, Koban (1983) finds that living with children prior to incarceration was influential in their plans to reunite with children (180). Lanier (1991) also found in a multivariate analysis that having lived with children before incarceration was positively associated with men's expectation to live with them upon release (1991). Murray (2007) further found that living arrangements prior to imprisonment predicted paternal expectations that their children would visit them in prison. Furthermore, parents co-residing with their children at the time of arrest were significantly more likely to actually receive child visits or have contact with children, which may also be a mechanism through which embeddedness affects expectations (Glaze & Maruschak, 2008; Lanier, 1991; Bloom & Steinhart, 1993).

Although prior research points to the importance of co-residence at the time of arrest for future expectancies, the role of other living situations, such as living with relatives at the time of arrest, or living in foster or other care arrangements, are relatively unexplored. Among women, Bresler and Lewis (1986) found in a small study of African American and White women that if African American children were not living with mother at time of arrest, they were living with relatives and in close contact with their mothers. Therefore, living arrangements involving relatives at the time of arrest may also contribute to positive parental expectations to live with children upon release.

Further work on race/ethnicity within parental gender groups is required to more fully understand expectations to live with children upon release. If minority mothers are more likely to live with their children than White mothers, they may also be more likely than Whites to expect to live with their children on release. Mixed findings have emerged on maternal expectancies by race/ethnicity. Fessler's (1991, p. 146) study of 50 incarcerated women found that both African American and Hispanic mothers were significantly more likely to expect to reunify with children upon release than were White mothers. However, Baunach (1985, p. 45) found no difference between African American and White women by race/ethnicity in whether they planned to live with their children on release. Still, although most (88%) of the incarcerated mothers in that study planned to live with their children upon release, the percentage was higher (about 97%) if they had lived with their child in the past (Baunach 1985, p. 44), suggesting that living arrangements on arrest, or child embeddedness, is influential. Foster & Hagan (2009) found similarities in expectancies of incarcerated mothers to live with their children on release, although they were slightly higher among African American and Hispanic women than White women.

Little research is available on men's expectations regarding living with children upon release by race/ethnicity. Foster & Hagan (2009) found Hispanic fathers were more likely to expect to live with children on release than White or African American fathers, who were similar in their expectancies. Further attitudinal data on men from a voluntary sample of over 800 inmates in New York State comprised of predominantly African Americans and Latinos indicated that 92% of the men wanted to improve their relationship with their children (Mendez, 2000). These results indicate men desire relationships with their children. This sample also reports a high level of embeddedness in family relationships, where 83% of men reported their families supported them and continued to maintain contact, although only 29% were married.

This research together underpins the hypotheses regarding parental expectancies:

Hypothesis 3: Women will be more likely than men to expect to live with children upon release from prison.

Hypothesis 4: Living in parental and relative care arrangements at the time of arrest will be positively associated with parental expectations to live with children upon release.

Hypothesis 5: Racial and ethnic minority parents will be more likely to expect to live with their children upon release than White parents.

Hypothesis 6: For mothers and fathers, race and ethnic differences in expectations to live with their children upon release will be mediated by child and parental embeddedness.

The current chapter elaborates prior findings on expectancies of incarcerated men and women with multivariate analyses with further attention to race and ethnicity and the role of child and parental embeddedness. Hypotheses 1–6 are tested using data from incarcerated women and men in Texas. This data set and the methodology used are next briefly described with additional details in Appendix B. The results of the Texas research constitute the remainder of the chapter.

METHODS

Because prior research has shown differences in children's living arrangements by parental gender (Johnson & Waldfogel, 2004), data on incarcerated mothers and fathers are analyzed separately. Influences of race/ethnicity within gender sub-groups on child living arrangements and parental expectations of living with children upon release from prison are further examined. These analyses involve data on the living arrangements of multiple children per incarcerated parent. Multilevel analyses are appropriate for studying siblings nested in families (Jenkins, Rasbash, & O'Connor, 2003; Krull, 2007). The multilevel models that follow are estimated with HLM 6.02 for incarcerated mothers and fathers (Raudenbush & Bryk, 2002; Raudenbush et al., 2004, p.128).

These analyses use data compiled for the former Texas Commission on Alcohol and Drug Abuse by the Public Policy Research Institute of Texas A&M University through face-to-face interviews with a sample of male and female inmates in 1998–99 (Crouch, Dyer, O'Dell, & McDonald, 1999; Mullings, Pollock, & Crouch, 2002). These data uniquely include where multiple children per household were living prior to parent's incarceration. The sample was drawn from newly arrived inmates to intake facilities for the Texas Department of Criminal Justice Institutional Division and State Jail Division. Virtually all prisoners in Texas pass through these intake facilities, yielding a representative sample. Male respondents were sampled off lists from these facilities and every female prisoner was sampled unless prevented by medical or security concerns. Trained interviewers used a computer-assisted interviewing system to gather data from respondents on the living arrangements, age, and gender of up to 11 of the respondent's children at the time of arrest. Response rates among groups ranged from 73% to 86%. Data are used on 1,813 minor children (age 18 and below) nested in 785 incarcerated mothers and 1,344 minor children in 675 incarcerated fathers. The full sample includes 1,295 men and 1,198 women. Women had on average close to three children, and men had on average two.

The first set of analyses that follow pertain to Hypotheses 1 and 2, and examine children's living arrangements (or child embeddedness) at the time of parental arrest, indicating whether a child lives with his or her reporting incarcerated parent upon arrest; (1) in an "other" care arrangement (e.g., lives on own, lives in system care); (2) lives with other relatives (e.g., grandparents, aunts/uncles); (3) lives with their other parent; or (4) the reference category in the analyses that follow. Multinomial hierarchical generalized linear models (HGLM) are used to investigate whether the log odds of living with the parent at the time of arrest vs. living with the child's other parent will vary randomly for mothers and then for fathers. The second set of analyses predict maternal and paternal expectations to live with their children upon release from prison by testing Hypotheses 3 through 6 with a series of binomial HGLM logit models. Parental embeddedness is measured through the number of children they have and their marital status. Further detail on variable construction is provided in Table 6.1. Detail on both sets of multilevel models employed in this research is provided in Appendix B.

RESULTS

Descriptive statistics on the Texas sample of incarcerated mothers (n = 785) and fathers (n = 675) of minor children are presented in Table 6.1. In brief, 15% of the female sample is Hispanic, 46% are African American, and 39% are non-Hispanic White. In the male sample 28% is Hispanic, 41% are African American, and 30% are non-Hispanic White. Women tend to have shorter average sentence lengths than men. In terms of parental embeddedness, men and women are likely to have several minor children on average, and slightly more men (36%) than women (28%) report being married. In terms of child socio-demographics, information on minor children of incarcerated mothers (n = 1,813) and children of incarcerated fathers (n = 1,344) indicates their average age is almost 9 years among the former group and 8 years among the latter. The majority of children of incarcerated mothers lived with them upon arrest (56%), and a substantial minority of children of incarcerated fathers lived with them upon arrest (41%). Of children of incarcerated fathers, 52% lived with their other parent upon his arrest, in sharp contrast to 18% of children of incarcerated mothers.

The results of the multinomial HGLM logit models are presented in Table 6.2a for incarcerated mothers and in Table 6.2b for incarcerated fathers. The unconditional models (Model 1 of each table) are first presented (Raudenbush & Bryk, 2002). The predicted probabilities derived from the unconditional model lend insight into the other circumstances that children live in at the time of their parent's arrest. Children of incarcerated mothers live in a variety of arrangements upon her arrest, including a .10 probability of living in an "other" arrangement, a .15 probability of living with relatives, and .17 probability of living with their other parent. Children of incarcerated fathers are most likely to be living with their other parent with a predicted probability of .54, followed by rather low probabilities of living with relatives (.05) or in other arrangements (.03). The expected log odds of a child of a "typical" incarcerated mother living with that mother at the time of her arrest is greater than the log odds of living with the child's other parent (b = 1.19, p <.001). This corresponds to a predicted probability of .58 (Raudenbush et al. 2004, p.132). The expected log odds of a child of a "typical" incarcerated father living with that father at the time of his arrest is lower than the log-odds of living with that child's other parent (b = −.34, p < .001), corresponding to a probability of .38. In support of Hypothesis 1, children of incarcerated

Table 6.1

DESCRIPTIVE STATISTICS OF INCARCERATED MOTHERS AND FATHERS AND THEIR MINOR CHILDREN (≤ 18)

	MOTHERS (N = 785) M (SD)	FATHERS (N = 675) M (SD)	Range	VARIABLE DESCRIPTION
Parental Factors				
Parental Expectation to Live with Child Upon Release	.75 (.73)	.56 (.50)	0–1	"Do you expect him/her to live with you when you get out of prison?" 1 = yes; 0 = no.
Hispanic	.15 (.36)	.28 (.45)	0–1	Parental report of race/ethnicity.
African-American	.46 (.50)	.41 (.49)	::	
White	.39 (.49)	.30 (.46)	::	
Married	.28 (.45)	.36 (.48)	0–1	Are you currently married, widowed, divorced, separated, or have you ever been married?
Single	.34 (.47)	.33 (.47)	::	
Separated/ Divorced/ Widowed	.39 (.49)	.31 (.46)	::	
Number of Children	2.72 (1.52)	2.33 (1.59)	1–11 Mothers / 1–16 Fathers	After affirmative response to a question asking whether or not he or she had children, the respondent was asked "if yes, how many?"
Sentence Length	3.29 (4.41)	5.36 (7.72)	.17–50 Mothers / .08–65 Fathers	"How long is your present sentence?" (coded in years)
Child Factors	(n = 1813)	(n = 1344)		
Child Age	8.99 (5.03)	7.94 (5.39)	0–18	Years
Child Gender	.47 (.50)	.49 (.50)	0–1	Female = 1
Lived with Parent Upon Arrest	.56 (.50)	.41 (.49)	0–1	For up to 11 children the parent was asked of each: "was she/he living with you before you were arrested this last time? 1 = yes, 2 = no. If no, the follow up question was asked: "Where was the child living?"
Lived in Other Arrangement Upon Arrest	.10 (.30)	.03 (.17)	::	
Lived with Other Relative Upon Arrest	.15 (.36)	.04 (.20)	::	
Lived with Other Parent Upon Arrest	.18 (.39)	.52 (.50)	::	

mothers are more likely to have been living with them at the time of their arrest than are children of incarcerated fathers.

Child gender, age, and parent race/ethnicity are added in Model 2 of Tables 6.2a and 6.2b. Consistent with Hypothesis 1, as indicated in Column 1 of Table 6.2a, children of African American mothers are more likely (b = .65, p < .001) [or in exponentiated form (e^b) 1.92 times more likely] than Whites to be living with their mothers at the time of her arrest. Furthermore, child socio-demographics are also influential, where older children are less likely to be living with their mothers at the time of her arrest than are younger children (b = −.08, p < .001), and female children are more likely than male children to be doing so (b = .27, p < .05). These patterns hold net of the maternal family embeddedness measures added in Model 3 of Table 6.2a, where the difference in the log odds of living with their mother at the time of her arrest becomes slightly strengthened between children of African American and White mothers (b = .72, p < .001 with a corresponding odds ratio of 2.05). In Hypothesis 2, maternal embeddedness in terms of marital status and number of children is marginally influential. A trend is found where women with more children are less likely (b = −.14, p < .10) to live with their children upon arrest.

Parental race and ethnicity also shapes children of incarcerated father's living circumstances. As indicated in Model 2 of Table 6.2b, children of Hispanic fathers are more likely (b = .62, p < .01) (or 1.86 times more likely) than children of White fathers to be living with him at the time of his arrest. Of this difference, 13% is explained by paternal embeddedness, as seen in Model 3 of Table 6.2b (b = .54, p < .05). Model 3 indicates children of Hispanic fathers are 1.71 times more likely than Whites to be living with him at the time of his arrest. Consistent with Hypothesis 2, parental embeddedness also matters: married men are more likely (b = 2.10, p < .001) by eight times than single men to be living with their children at the time of their arrest. Child socio-demographics are also influential, where older children are less likely to be living with their fathers at the time of his arrest compared to living with their other parent (b = −.06, p < .001), but are more likely to be living with relatives than with their other parent (b = .09, p < .01).

The results of population average HGLM logit models of parent's expectations to live with children upon release are presented in Models 1–4 of Table 6.3 for incarcerated mothers and in Models 5–8 for incarcerated fathers. The unconditional models show a clear gender difference in this expectancy. The predicted probability of the average

Table 6.2a

HGLM MULTINOMIAL LOGISTIC REGRESSION MODEL OF MINOR CHILDREN'S STRUCTURAL LIVING ARRANGEMENTS UPON MATERNAL ARREST [b/(sb)[e]]

	MODEL 1			MODEL 2			MODEL 3		
	Mother[a]	Other	Relatives	Mother[a]	Other	Relatives	Mother[a]	Other	Relatives
Intercept	1.19***(.10)	−.58***(.12)	−.18(.12)	.73***(.16)	−.71***(.20)	−.44*(.19)	.74**(.26)	−.27(.34)	.12(.28)
Age				−.08***(.02)	.02(.02)	−.02(.02)	−.08***(.02)	.03(.02)	−.01(.02)
Gender[b]				.27*(.13)	.18(.18)	.31†(.16)	.28*(.13)	.19(.18)	.34*(.17)
Hispanic[c]				.36(.31)	−.33(.35)	.09(.34)	.47(.32)	−.44(.37)	.12(.34)
African-American				.65**(.22)	.17(.27)	.26(.25)	.72***(.23)	−.15(.32)	.08(.26)
Married[d]							.34(.28)	−.51(.35)	−.41(.31)
Sep./Div./Wid.							−.28(.26)	−.65†(.34)	−.82**(.28)
# of children							−.14†(.08)	.12(.09)	−.07(.09)
U_0(1)	2.50			2.64			2.64		
Chi-Square	1562.24*** 784df			1565.61*** 782df			1545.07*** 779df		

†p < .10, * p < .05, ** p < .01, *** p < .001 (two-tailed tests); Ref. [a]Live with other parent, [b]Female = 1; Male = 0; [c]Whites, [d]Single; [e]Robust Std. Errors.

Table 6.2b

HGLM MULTINOMIAL LOGISTIC REGRESSION MODEL OF MINOR CHILDREN'S STRUCTURAL LIVING ARRANGEMENTS UPON PATERNAL ARREST [b/(sb)e]

	MODEL 1			MODEL 2			MODEL 3		
	Father[a]	Other	Relatives	Father[a]	Other	Relatives	Father[a]	Other	Relatives
Intercept	-.34*** (.09)	-2.91*** (.21)	-2.47*** (.18)	-.45* (.18)	-2.90*** (.41)	-3.08*** (.39)	-1.31** (.26)	-3.29 (.56)	-2.58*** (.51)
Age				-.07*** (.01)	.02 (.05)	-.07* (.03)	-.06*** (.02)	.01 (.05)	.09** (.03)
Gender[b]				-.09 (.12)	.31 (.31)	.35 (.30)	-.12 (.13)	.30 (.32)	.36 (.30)
Hispanic[c]				.62* (.24)	-.47 (.53)	.53 (.51)	.54* (.24)	-.58 (.56)	.56 (.50)
African-American				-.17 (.21)	.22 (.49)	.31 (.42)	.11 (.23)	-.33 (.48)	.21 (.49)
Married[d]							2.10*** (.23)	.67 (.58)	-.74 (.58)
Sep./Div./Wid.							-.09 (.26)	.29 (.55)	-.62 (.49)
# of children							-.10† (.05)	.10 (.07)	-.11 (.09)
U0(1)	1.96			1.95			1.71		
Chi-Square	1145.15*** 674df			1107.33*** 672df			945.77*** 669df		

†p < .10, * p < .05, ** p < .01, *** p < .001 (two-tailed tests); Ref. [a]Live with other parent, [b]Female = 1; Male = 0; [c]Whites, [d]Single; [e]Robust Std. Errors.

Table 6.3

POPULATION AVERAGE MODELS: HGLM LOGISTIC REGRESSION OF INCARCERATED MOTHER'S AND FATHER'S EXPECTANCIES OF LIVING WITH THEIR CHILD UPON RELEASE ON PREDICTORS [b(sb)ᵈ]

	INCARCERATED MOTHERS				INCARCERATED FATHERS			
	1	2	3	4	5	6	7	8
Intercept	1.14***(.07)	1.00***(.11)	.22(.17)	.11(.23)	.25***(.08)	.05(.14)	-1.06***(.20)	-1.32***(.23)
Child Age		-.07***(.01)	-.05***(.01)	-.05***(.01)		-.11***(.01)	-.11***(.01)	-.11***(.01)
Gender		-.03(.09)	-.14(.09)	-.14(.09)		-.31***(.10)	-.39*(.15)	-.39*(.12)
Hispanicᵃ		.30(.22)	.14(.23)	.31(.21)		.80***(.19)	.69***(.24)	.80***(.22)
African-American		.32*(.15)	.19(.16)	.30(.18)		.31†(.17)	.57*(.22)	.75***(.21)
Child Living Arrangement Upon Parental Arrest								
Incarcerated Parentᶜ			2.53***(.19)	2.58***(.18)			3.22***(.20)	3.15***(.21)
With relative			.20(.19)	.20(.19)			1.07***(.35)	1.06***(.29)
With other			-.92***(.22)	-.88***(.22)			-1.18*(.55)	-1.15*(.47)
Parental Embeddedness								
Marriedᵇ				.10(.21)				.49*(.23)
Separated/Divorced/Widowed				.08(.19)				.23(.23)
Number of children				-.14**(.04)				-.15**(.05)
Socio-Legal Factor								
Sentence Length				-.04*(.02)				.01(.01)
U₀₍₁₎	2.20	2.23	2.40	2.40	1.80	1.67	1.85	1.84
Chi-Square	1310.04*** 784df	1286.08*** 782df	1002.68*** 782df	975.35*** 778df	1134.27*** 674df	1032.04*** 672df	832.62*** 672df	821.35*** 668df

Reference Groups: ᵃWhites ᵇSingle ᶜLived with other parental figure ᵈRobust Std. Errors. †p < .10, *p < .05, **p < .01, ***p < .001 (two-tailed tests) incarcerated mother of expecting to live with her child upon release is .76. This probability derived for incarcerated fathers is .56. These results support Hypothesis 3 regarding gendered expectancies.

Race and ethnic variation within gender in expectations to live with children upon release are also supported. As indicated in Model 2 of Table 6.3, African American women are more likely to expect to live with their child upon release compared to Whites (b = .32, p < .05), consistent with Hypothesis 5; however, this coefficient is reduced to nonsignificance in Model 3 (b = .19, p > .10) when differences in children's living arrangements upon arrest are taken into account. This mediation effect is consistent with Hypothesis 6. Net of children's living arrangements upon arrest, there are no differences among women in expecting to live with their children upon release from prison. Child embeddedness is influential on maternal expectations consistent with Hypothesis 4. As indicated in Model 3, children who were living with their mother at the time of her arrest are almost 13 times more likely (b = 2.53, p < .001) to be expected to live with their mothers upon her release than those living with their other parent. Children living in relative care arrangements (b = .20, p > .10) do not differ from children living with their other parent in terms of maternal expectations to live with their child upon release. However, living in other care arrangements at the time of maternal arrest reduces maternal expectations of living with mothers upon her release (b = −.92, p < .001). The influence of children's structural embeddedness on maternal expectancies holds net of maternal embeddedness and sentence length in Model 4. Mothers with more children (b = −.14, p < .01) are less likely to expect to live with their children upon release, as are mothers with longer sentences (b = −.04, p < .05).

Regarding men, the results in Model 6 of Table 6.3 indicate that Hispanics are twice as likely (b = .80, p < .001) as Whites to expect to live with their children upon release from prison, consistent with Hypothesis 5. This difference is in part explained by children's living arrangements at the time of paternal arrest, added in Model 7 (to b = .69, p < .01). This partial mediation by child embeddedness is supportive of Hypothesis 6 as also found with mothers. Furthermore, once differences in children's structural embeddedness are taken into account, African American men become more likely than Whites (by almost two times) to expect to live with their children upon release (b = .57, p < .01). Thus, minority men are more likely than Whites to expect to live with their children on release once differences in child living arrangements on arrest are taken into account. This finding supports Hypothesis 5. Children who lived with their incarcerated parent at the time of his arrest are 25 times more likely (b = 3.22, p < .001) than those living with their other parent to be expected by fathers to live with them upon release from prison. However, variety in living arrangements also matters. Children who live with relatives rather than their other parent are three times more likely to be expected to live with their fathers upon release (b = 1.07, p < .001). However, as was the case with mothers, children living in other care arrangements rather than living with their other parent at the time of paternal arrest are less likely to be expected to live with the father upon release (b = −1.18, p < .05).

Turning to Model 8, racial and ethnic differences in paternal expectancies to live with children are strengthened when paternal embeddedness is taken into account. Suppression effects are revealed in Model 8 when paternal marital status and number of children are taken into account. The coefficient for African American compared to White men increases by almost one third (from b = .57, p < .01 to b = .75, p < .001) and by 16% for Hispanic men (b = .69, p < .01 to b = .80, p < .001). Again these results support Hypothesis 5. These results further show the structural basis of paternal expectancies. Married men are 1.63 times more likely (b = .49, p < .05) to expect to live with their children upon release, and like women, those with more children are less likely to expect to live with them on release (b = −.15, p < .01). However, in contrast to women, sentence length has no significant influence on paternal expectancies.

DISCUSSION/CONCLUSIONS

Mass incarceration has intergenerational consequences for children (Hagan & Dinovitzer, 1999; Murray & Farrington, 2008b), and given socio-demographic patterns of imprisonment, disproportionately affects minority children. This chapter finds African American mothers were more likely than White mothers to be living with their children at the time of arrest and Hispanic fathers were more likely to be living with their children upon arrest than were White or African American fathers (Baunach, 1985; Bresler & Lewis, 1986; Enos, 2001; Foster & Hagan, 2009; Ruiz, 2002; Western et al., 2004). These results suggest that minority children of incarcerated parents are differentially embedded in family relationships than are Whites, with a higher likelihood of living with parents upon arrest among the former group, which may serve as a source of resilience in coping with mass incarceration. The findings in this chapter further support the conceptual model in Figure 6.1, where both child embeddedness and parental embeddedness facilitate parental expectancies to live with children upon release from prison. This expectancy is conceptualized as a form of stability in children's lives if they were living with the parent at the time of arrest.

African American women were more likely than Whites to expect to live with their children upon release from prison in multivariate analyses building on the findings of Foster and Hagan (2009). However, once differential living arrangements at the time of arrest were taken into account, these racial differences in expectations were statistically explained, yielding no significant racial or ethnic differences among women in expectancies to live with children upon release from prison. These results shed light on the mixed results evident in prior work (Baunach, 1985; Fessler, 1991). Race and ethnic differences among women in expectations to live with children upon release from prison are initially found, however; these differences are due to differential living arrangements of children at the time of maternal arrest. Once these differences are taken into account statistically, differences in maternal expectancies by race/ethnicity are explained so that no differences are found among women in terms of expectancies to live with children on release. In general, expectancies of women to live with children on release are high, corresponding to a predicted probability of .76 in keeping with prior research (Zalba, 1964; Baunach, 1985; Koban, 1983; Hairston, 1991).

Turning to men, very little research has examined expectations to live with children upon release by race/ethnicity. The predicted probability of expecting to live with children upon release for fathers is .56. However, this chapter additionally revealed that Hispanic and African American fathers are more likely than White fathers to expect to live with their children upon release once differences in marital status (parental embeddedness) and child living arrangements (child embeddedness) are taken into account. These results expand the findings of Foster and Hagan (2009) on the higher expectations of Hispanic men to live with their children on release from prison by further finding with multivariate analyses the higher expectancies of both Hispanic and African American men compared to White men. Thus, minority men are more likely than White men to expect to live with their children once structural embeddedness has been taken into account. These results suggest that factors that support paternal embeddedness will also support paternal expectancies to live with children on release. Prevention efforts that build on men's positive expectations regarding children (Mendez, 2002) may encourage social bonding between men and their children. This bonding may also serve as a source of stability in children's lives, which has been linked to child well-being. A recent study found familial support (26%) and seeing children (9%) were identified a few months after release by returning male prisoners as the "most" important thing that had kept them out of prison (Visher & Courtney, 2006, p.7). Thus, efforts to facilitate bonds among fathers and children may be beneficial for both.

Information on multiple children of incarcerated parents in Texas were analyzed in this chapter using multilevel modeling techniques and taking into account variation in child living arrangements and parental expectancies regarding living with each child. Children's gender and age were taken into account as well. Thus, the modeling strategy captures the possibility that children in the same family may live in different living arrangements during parental incarceration and may be differentially expected to live with parents upon release. These findings encourage future research that takes into account both parent and child factors in understanding how incarceration affects children, and research designs that gather further information on multiple children per incarcerated parent. Future research should also develop more detailed measures of parental and child embeddedness, including living in multigenerational families and types of extended family ties, to further identify factors that facilitate parental expectations to live with their children upon release from prison. In addition, longitudinal research is needed to examine how parental expectations in living with their children translate into actual living arrangements regarding those children after release from prison. Finally, research and policies pertaining to children of incarcerated parents' living arrangements should be sensitive to variability found at the intersection of race/ethnicity and parental gender.

CHAPTER SUMMARY

This chapter examined living arrangements as one area of children's lives affected by parental incarceration. Racial and ethnic disparities are found in the contemporary context of mass imprisonment in American society, with parental imprisonment disproportionately concentrated among minority children. It is argued in this chapter that the impact of mass incarceration on minority children would be even greater if not for family embeddedness that facilitates stability in children's living arrangements. The expectation of incarcerated parents concerning living with children upon release was conceptualized as a form of stability. It was hypothesized that structural embeddedness in family relationships will contribute to stability in children's living arrangements. Because instability in living arrangements is associated with problem child psychological outcomes, factors that facilitate stability in lives of children will inform prevention and intervention initiatives.

Results from a diverse Texas data set of incarcerated men and women showed that African American children are more likely than Whites to live with their mothers at the time of arrest, a form of child embeddedness. Furthermore, African American women are more likely than White women to expect to live with their children upon release from prison; however, these differences are explained by child living arrangements upon arrest. Those mothers who lived with their children at the time of their arrest are more likely to expect to live with them upon release from prison. Children of Hispanic incarcerated fathers are more likely to live with them upon arrest than are children of White and African American fathers. However, both African American and Hispanic men are more likely than Whites to expect to live with their children upon release once child and parental embeddedness are taken into account. Although alternatives to incarceration should be explored, it is essential that supports to stability in family relationships are provided to foster this protective resource for child well-being.

REFERENCES

Ackerman, B. P., Kogos, J., Youngstrom, E., Schoff, K., & Izard, C. (1999). Family Instability and the Problem Behaviors of Children from Economically Disadvantaged Families. *Developmental Psychology* 35: 258–268.

Baunach, P. J. (1985). *Mothers in prison.* New Brunswick, NJ: Transaction.

Benedict, M. I., Zuravin, S., & Stallings, R.Y. (1996). Adult functioning of children who lived in kin versus nonrelative family foster homes. *Child Welfare, 75,* 529–549.

Berrick, J. D., Barth, R. P., & Needell, B. (1994). A comparison of kinship foster homes and foster family homes: Implications for kinship foster care as family preservation. *Children and Youth Services Review, 16,* 33–63.

Bloom, B. & Steinhart, D. (1993). *Why punish the children? A reappraisal of incarcerated mothers in America.* San Francisco, CA: National Council on Crime and Delinquency.

Bresler, L. & Lewis, D. K. (1986). Black and White women prisoners: Differences in family ties and their programmatic implications. *The Prison Journal, 63,* 116–123.

Capaldi, D. M. & Patterson, G. R. (1991). Relation of parental transitions to boys' adjustment problems: I. A linear hypothesis. II. Mothers at risk for transitions and unskilled parenting. *Developmental Psychology, 27,* 489–304.

Cavanagh, S. E. & Huston, A. C. (2006). Family Instability and Children's Early Problem Behavior. *Social Forces, 85,* 551–581.

Crouch, B., Dyer, J. A., O'Dell, L. L., & McDonald, D. K. (1999). Methodology used in the 1998 Survey of Texas Prison Inmates male and female institutional division. The Texas Commission on Drug and Alcohol Abuse. Public Policy Research Institute, Texas A&M University, College Station, TX.

Edin, K., Nelson, T. J., & Paranal, R. (2004). Fatherhood and incarceration as potential turning points in the criminal careers of unskilled men. In M. Patillo, D. Weiman, & B. Western (Eds.), *Imprisoning America: The social effects of mass incarceration,* (pp. 46–75). New York: Russell Sage Foundation.

Enos, S. (2001). *Mothering from the inside: Parenting in a women's prison.* Albany, NY: State University of New York Press.

Fergusson, D. M., Diamond, M. E., & Horwood, L.J. (1986). Childhood family placement history and behavior problems in 6-year-old children. *Journal of Child Psychiatry, 27,* 213–226.

Fessler, S. R. (1991). *Mothers in the correctional system: Separation from children and reunification after incarceration.* Unpublished PhD Dissertation, State University of New York. Albany: NY.

Fomby, P. & A. J. Cherlin. (2007). Family Instability and Child Well-being. *American Sociological Review, 72,* 181–204.

Foster, H. & J. Hagan. (2007). Incarceration and intergenerational social exclusion. *Social Problems, 54,* 399–433.

Foster, H. & J. Hagan. (2009). The Mass Incarceration of Parents in America: Issues of Collateral Damage to Children and Prisoner Re-entry. *Annals of the American Academy of Political and Social Sciences, 623,* 179–194.

Foster, H., Nagin, D., Hagan, J., Angold, A., Costello, E. J. In Press. Specifying Criminogenic Strains: Stress Dynamics and Conduct Disorder Trajectories. *Deviant Behavior.*

Garland, D. (2001). Introduction: The meaning of mass imprisonment. In D. Garland (Ed.), *Mass imprisonment: Social causes and consequences,* (pp. 1–3). Thousand Oaks, CA: Sage.

Glaze, L. E. & Maruschak, L. M. (2008). *Parents in Prison and Their Minor Children.* U.S. Department of Justice, Washington DC, #NCJ 222984.

Glick, R. M. & Neto, V.V. (1977). *National Study of Women's Correctional Programs.* Washington DC: U.S. Department of Justice.

Granovetter, M. (1985). Economic action and social structure: The problem embeddedness. *American Journal of Sociology, 91,* 481–510.

Hagan, J. (1993). The social embeddedness of crime and unemployment. *Criminology, 31,* 465–491.

Hagan, J. & Coleman, J. P. (2001). Returning captives of the American war on drugs: Issues of community and family reentry. *Crime and Delinquency, 47,* 352–367.

Hagan, J. & Dinovitzer, R. (1999). Collateral consequences of imprisonment for children, communities, and prisoners. *Crime & Justice, 26,* 121–162.

Hairston, C. F. (1991). Mothers in jail: Parent-child separation and jail visitation. *Affilia, 6,* 9–27.

Hairston, C. F. (1995). Fathers in prison. In K. Gabel & D. Johnston (Eds.), *Children of incarcerated parents,* (pp. 31–40). New York: Lexington Books.

Hairston, C. F. (2003). Prisoners and their families: Parenting issues during incarceration. In J. Travis & M. Waul (Eds.), *Prisoners once removed: The impact of incarceration and reentry on children, families, and communities,* (pp. 259–282). Washington DC: Urban Institute Press.

Hao, L. & Xie, G. (2002). The Complexity and Endogeneity of Family Structure in Explaining Children's Misbehavior. *Social Science Research, 31,* 1–28.

Holt, N. & D. Miller. (1972). *Explorations in inmate-family relationships.* Research Report #46. Research Division, Department of Correction, State of California.

Jenkins, J. M., Rasbash, J., & O'Connor, T. G. (2003). The role of shared family context in differential parenting. *Developmental Psychology, 39,* 99–113.

Jayakody, R., Chatters, L. M., & Taylor, R. J. (1993). Family support to single and married African American mothers: The provision of financial, emotional, and child care assistance. *Journal of Marriage and the Family, 55,* 261–276.

Johnson, E. I. & J. Waldfogel. (2004). Children of incarcerated parents: Multiple risks and children's living arrangements. In M. Patillo, D. Weiman, & B. Western (Eds.), *Imprisoning America: The social effects of mass incarceration* (pp. 97–131). New York: Russell Sage Foundation.

Johnston, D. (1995). The care and placement of prisoners' children. In K. Gabel & D. Johnston, (Eds). *Children of Incarcerated Parents* (pp.103–123). New York: Lexington Books.

Juby, H. & Farrington, D. P. (2001). Disentangling the link between disrupted families and delinquency. *British Journal of Criminology, 41,* 22–40.

Koban, L. A. (1983). Parents in prison: A comparative analysis of the effects of incarceration on the families of men and women. *Research in Law, Deviance and Social Control, 5,* 171–183.

Kreider, R. M. (2008). *Living arrangements of children: 2004.* Current Population Reports. #P70-114. U.S. Department of Commerce, U.S. Census Bureau.

Krull, J.L. (2007). Using multilevel analyses with sibling data to increase analytic power: An illustration and simulation study. *Developmental Psychology, 43,* 602–619.

Kurdek, L., Fine, M.A. & Sinclair, R.J. (1995). School adjustment in sixth graders: Parenting transitions, family climate, and peer norm effects. *Child Development, 66,* 430–445.

Lanier, C.S. (1991). Dimensions of father-child interaction in a New York state prison population. *Journal of Offender Rehabilitation, 16,* 27–72.

La Vigne, N. G., Davies, E., & Brazzell, D. (2008). *Broken bonds: Understanding and addressing the needs of children with incarcerated parents.* Washington DC: Urban Institute.

Lewis, D. K. & Bresler, L. (1981). *Is there a way out? A community study of women in the San Francisco county jail.* San Francisco, CA: Unitarian Universalist Service Committee.

Mauer, M. (2001). The causes and consequences of prison growth in the United States. In D. Garland (Ed.), *Mass imprisonment: Social causes and consequences,* (pp. 4–14). Thousand Oaks, CA: Sage.

McAdoo, H.P. (1980). Black mothers and the extended family support network. In L.F. Rodgers-Rose (Ed.), *The Black Woman,* (pp. 125–144). Newbury Park: Sage.

McGowan, B. G. & Blumenthal, K.L. (1978). *Why punish the children? A study of children of women prisoners.* Hackensack, NJ: National Council on Crime and Delinquency.

McLanahan, S. & Sandefur, G. (1994). *Growing up with a Single Parent: What Hurts, What Helps?* Cambridge, MA: Harvard University Press.

Mendez, G. A., Jr. (2000). Incarcerated African American men and their children: A case study. *Annals of the American Association of Political and Social Sciences, 569,* 86–101.

Moore, K. A., Vandivere, S., & Ehrle, J. (2000). Turbulence and Child Well-Being. Assessing the New Federalism Report B–16 (Series B). Washington DC: Child Trends and the Urban Institute. http://www.urban.org/UploadedPDF/anf_b16.pdf, retrieved November 8, 2005.

Mumola, C. J. (2000). Incarcerated parents and their children. Bureau of Justice Statistics Special Report. U.S. Department of Justice, Office of Justice Programs. Washington DC, #NCJ182335.

Mullings, J. L., Pollock, J. & Crouch, B. M. (2002). Drugs and criminality: Results from the Texas Women Inmates Study. *Women & Criminal Justice, 13,* 69–95.

Murray, J. (2007). The cycle of punishment: Social exclusion of prisoners and their children. *Criminology & Criminal Justice, 1,* 55–81.

Murray, J. & Farrington, D.P. (2005). Parental imprisonment: Effects on boys' antisocial behavior and delinquency through the life-course. *Journal of Child Psychology and Psychiatry, 46,* 1269–1278.

Murray, J. & Farrington, D. P. (2008a). Parental imprisonment: Long-lasting effects on boys' internalizing problems through the life course. *Development and Psychopathology, 20,* 273–290.

Murray, J. & Farrington, D. P. (2008b). The Effects of Parental Imprisonment on Children. Crime & Justice, 37, 133–206.

Najman, J. M., Behrens, B. C., Andersen, M., Bor, W., O'Callaghan, M., & Williams, G.M. (1997). Impact of Family Type and Quality on Child Behavior Problems: A Longitudinal Study. *Journal of the American Academy of Child and Adolescent Psychiatry, 36,* 1357–1365.

Nurse, A. M. (2002). *Fatherhood arrested: Parenting from within the juvenile justice system.* Nashville, TN.: Vanderbilt University Press.

Nurse, A. M. (2004). Returning to strangers: Newly paroled young fathers and their children. In M. Patillo, D. Weiman, & B. Western (Eds.) *Imprisoning America: The social effects of mass incarceration,* (pp. 76–96). New York: Russell Sage Foundation.

Pagani, L., Boulerice, B., & Tremblay, R.E. (1997). The Influence of Poverty on Children's Classroom Placement and Behavior Problems. Pp. 311–339 in *Consequences of Growing Up Poor,* edited by G. J. Duncan & J. Brooks-Gunn. New York: Russell Sage Foundation.

Perry, B.L. (2006). Understanding Social Network Disruption: The Case of Youth in Foster Care. *Social Problems, 53,* 371–391.

Pettit, B. & Western, B. (2004). Mass imprisonment and the life course: Race and class inequality in U.S. incarceration. *American Sociological Review, 69,* 151–169.

Phillips, S. D., Erklani, A., Keeler, G. P., Costello, E. J., & Angold, A. (2006). Disentangling the risks: Parent criminal justice involvement and children's exposure to family risks. *Criminology & Public Policy, 5,* 677–702.

Poehlmann, J. (2005a). Representations of Attachment Relationships in Children of Incarcerated Mothers. *Child Development, 76,* 679–696.

Poehlmann, J., Shlafer, R. J., Maes, E., & Hanneman, A. (2008). Factors associated with young children's opportunities for maintaining family relationships during maternal incarceration. *Family Relations, 57,* 267–280.

Raudenbush, S. W. & Bryk, A. S. (2002). *Hierarchical Linear Models: Applications and data analysis methods, second edition.* Thousand Oaks, CA: Sage.

Raudenbush, S., Bryk, A., Cheong, Y. F., Congdon, R., & du Toit, M. (2004). *HLM 6: Hierarchical linear & nonlinear modeling.* Lincolnwood, Illinois: Scientific Software International.

Ruiz, D. S. (2002). The increase in incarcerations among women and its impact on the grandmother caregiver: Some racial considerations. *Journal of Sociology and Social Welfare, 29,* 3.

Sabogal, F., Marin, G., Otero-Sabogal, R., VanOss Marin, B., & Perez-Stable, E. J. (1987). Hispanic Familism and Acculturation : What Changes and What Doesn't ? *Hispanic Journal of Behavioral Sciences, 9,* 397–412.

Snell, T. L. (1994). *Women in prison.* Bureau of Justice Statistics, Special Report. U.S. Department of Justice. Washington DC, # NCJ 145321.

Stack, C.B. (1974). *All Our Kin: Strategies for Survival in a Black Community.* New York: Harper & Row.

Stanton, A. M. (1980). *When Mothers Go To Jail.* Lexington, MA: Lexington Books.

Strijker, J., Zanberg, T., & van der Meulen, B.F. (2003). Kinship foster care and foster care in the Netherlands. *Children and Youth Services Review, 25,* 843–862.

Sudarkasa, N. (2007). African American Female-Headed Households: Some neglected dimensions. In H.P. McAdoo (Ed.) Black Families: Fourth Edition, (pp. 172–183). Thousand Oaks: Sage.

Swisher, R. & Waller, M. (2008). Confining fatherhood: Incarceration and paternal involvement among nonresident White, African American, and Latino fathers. *Journal of Family Issues, 29,* 1067–1088.

Thornberry, T. P., Smith, C. A., Rivera, C., Huizinga, D., & Stouthamer-Loeber, M. (1999). *Family Disruption and Delinquency* U.S. Department of Justice, Office of Justice Programs, Office of Juvenile Justice and Delinquency Prevention, # NCJ 178285.

Travis, J. & Waul, M. (2003). *Prisoners once removed: The impact of incarceration and reentry on children, families, and communities.* Washington DC: Urban Institute Press.

Trice, A. D. & Brewster, J. (2004). The effects of maternal incarceration on adolescent children. *Journal of Police and Criminal Psychology, 19,* 27–35.

Visher, C. A. & Courtney, M. E. (2006). *Cleveland Prisoners' Experiences Returning Home.* Washington DC; Urban Institute Press.

West, H. C. & Sabol, W. J. (2008). *Prisoners in 2007.* Bureau of Justice Statistics, U.S. Department of Justice, Washington DC, #NCJ 224280.

Western, B., M. Pattillo, & Weiman, D. (2004). Introduction. In M. Patillo, D. Weiman, & B. Western (Eds.) *Imprisoning America: The social effects of mass incarceration* (pp. 1–18). New York: Russell Sage Foundation.

Wildeman, C. In press. Parental incarceration, the prison boom, and the concentration of childhood disadvantage. *Demography.*

Zalba, S. R. (1964). *Women prisoners and their families.* Los Angeles, CA: Delmar.

ADDITIONAL RESOURCES

Comfort, Megan. (2008). *Doing time together: Love and family in the shadow of the prison.* Chicago: University of Chicago Press.

Enos, S. (2001). *Mothering from the inside: Parenting in a women's prison.* Albany, NY: State University of New York Press.

Johnson, E. I. & J. Waldfogel. (2004). Children of incarcerated parents: Multiple risks and children's living arrangements. In M. Patillo, D. Weiman, & B. Western (Eds.), *Imprisoning America: The social effects of mass incarceration* (pp. 97–131). New York: Russell Sage Foundation.

Nurse, A. M. (2002). *Fatherhood arrested: Parenting from within the juvenile justice system.* Nashville, TN.: Vanderbilt University Press.

Travis, J. & Waul, M. (2003). *Prisoners once removed: The impact of incarceration and reentry on children, families, and communities.* Washington D.C.: Urban Institute Press.

Parenting from Prison

PART IV

7

Building Partnerships to Strengthen Families: Intervention Programs and Recommendations

KRISTINA TOTH
KERRY KAZURA

Parental incarceration is a dynamic experience that impacts children's lives to varying degrees across their lifespan. Although there is little research on the impact of children's visitations to prison or on children's perceptions of relationships with their incarcerated parents (Arditti, Lambert-Shute, Joest, 2003; Hairston, 2007; Kazura, Baber & Temke, 1999), some conclusions can be drawn. For example, the degree to which parental incarceration affects children is likely to fluctuate depending upon whether or not the child lived with the parent prior to incarceration, if the child's mother versus father was incarcerated, the age and gender of the child, the type of alternative care the child receives, whether the child has opportunities to visit the incarcerated parent, and the quality of those visits.

Programs that aid children with incarcerated parents have adopted a wide range of formats that have been delivered by a variety of agencies: family support providers, state agencies, and community- and faith-based organizations (Parke, Clark-Stewart, 2003). Many intervention programs are either volunteer- or community-based services that struggle for funding and often do not last beyond a few years. Interventions often are developed based on anecdotal evidence, and evaluations of programs' effectiveness are rare; this has resulted in a lack of best-practice policies and inconsistencies from one program to the next.

This chapter highlights the importance of visitation for children, barriers that prevent visitation, and model intervention programs including the Family Connections Center. We will conclude with a study on program evaluation and recommendations for creating similar programs.

PARENT-CHILD SEPARATION AND THE IMPORTANCE OF VISITATION

The existing literature on child outcomes for having an incarcerated parent suggests that children are at risk for both emotional and behavioral difficulties; these can lead to future problems such as cognitive delays, delinquency, anxiety, post-traumatic stress disorder, and depression (Hagen, Myers, & Mackintosh, 2005; Murray, Janson, & Farrington, 2007). Fristsch and Burkhead (1981) found that 67% of the incarcerated parents (fathers and mothers) reported that their children had behavior problems stemming from the beginning of the parent's incarceration. Both incarcerated mothers and fathers listed the same number of problems per child; however, the types of behaviors they reported were different. Incarcerated fathers reported that their children had problems related to substance abuse and aggression, and incarcerated mothers reported issues associated with emotional problems such as withdrawal, fearfulness, and excessive crying (Fristsch & Burkhead,1981). It is difficult to determine whether these results were due to children experiencing the incarceration of a father versus a mother, or if they were due to differential perceptions of the parent. Differences associated with children's genders were not reported, and outcome differences for daughters and sons are largely overlooked in the literature.

Regardless of this lack of knowledge, prolonged absence of a parent from the home caused by incarceration not only threatens family cohesion, but also puts excessive strain on parent-child relationships (Hairston, Rollin, & Jo, 2004). Attachment between parent and child is therefore threatened due to this separation (Bowlby, 1983). A secure attachment creates an enduring bond between parent and child that can provide the children with long-lasting protective factors and is associated with resilience (Bowlby, 1983). By contrast, children with insecure attachment relationships with their parent(s) often develop an increased sensitivity to later separations and have difficulty with emotional closeness. If the parent-child relationship is threatened, the child is at risk for negative reactions leading to poor social choices in the future.

Children of incarcerated parents are particularly vulnerable for insecure attachments due to the trauma surrounding the parent-child separation. Often children are subject to witnessing the arrest of their parent followed by a long absence prior to visitation (Johnston, 1995). Poehlmann (2005) conducted one of the first studies of parent-child attachment on this population. Her findings suggest that the majority of the children in this study had insecure attachment relationships with both their incarcerated mothers and their caregivers. Young children were at higher risk for insecure attachment than older children. An argument could be made that younger children do not have the opportunity to form an attachment relationship (insecure or secure) with their incarcerated parent due to the lack of interaction over time that is required to form this relationship. This is especially true for the father-child relationship because incarcerated fathers are less likely than incarcerated mothers to live with their children prior to arrest. Without intervention, children's reactions to the separation with their incarcerated parent can result in increased aggressive behavior, substance abuse, sexual experimentation, and incarceration (Nesmith & Ruhland, 2008; Reed & Reed, 1997).

Parent-child visitation where positive adult-child interaction can take place is a critical intervention following forced separations, such as those that occur when a parent is incarcerated (Kazura, Baber, & Temke, 1999). Review of the current child welfare literature supports the importance of frequent, regular parent-child visitation following separation when visitation is deemed to be in the best interest of the child. Researchers and clinicians (Johnston, 1995; Osborne Association, 1993; Snyder, Carlo, Mullins, 2001) agree that visitation between incarcerated parents and their children is important to combat childhood risk factors. Visits allow children to express their emotions regarding the separation, which they may not be allowed to do elsewhere. Visitation during incarceration allows parents and children to rebuild their relationships and allows the family to reunite more successfully when the parent is released (Hairston, 2007). Therefore, visits in correctional facilities deserve support and examination. Synder, Carlo, & Mullins (2001) reported that mothers who participated in a special visitation program demonstrated better attitudes and reported an increase in the quality of their relationship with their children. Such programs can maintain parent-child relationships during the physical separation, which in turn has important implications for custody upon release and/or providing financial support. Incarcerated parents' participation in family programs has been suggested to lower recidivism rates, which can benefit children by having their parents in their daily lives.

BARRIERS REGARDING VISITATION

Unfortunately, many facilities do not accommodate children's needs during visitation (Hairston, 2007). Most prison visiting areas have large, undecorated rooms with adult-size furniture. Johnston (1995) observed that in crowded visiting rooms, parents were reluctant to pursue children who ran around, for fear they would lose their seats. Therefore, many children remained unsupervised, did not interact with the incarcerated parent, and caused additional distractions for other families. Kazura (2001) found that incarcerated mothers and fathers felt discouraged during visitations in a cafeteria setting, where the lack of toys and opportunities for typical parent-child interactions hinders families from reconnecting. In maximum-security facilities, visitation conditions can be worse, as noted by Comfort (2003). Visitors reported that the waiting area felt like a holding tank, and did not wish to subject their children to the cramped and unclean visitation area and rigid rules. In general, parents found visitations with young children emotionally and physically draining with the long waiting lines, frisk searches, and lack of privacy.

In addition to potential inhospitable visitation spaces, the incarceration of the mother versus father is particularly disruptive and destructive to families, and creates challenges for child visitation (Bloom & Steinhart, 1993; Couturier, 1995). Mothers are likely to have more children than male inmates, and are more likely to have had their children living with them at the time of arrest and incarceration. Mothers are also less likely to have a partner or spouse who will care for their children and bring them to visit during the mothers' imprisonment. In a national study on incarcerated mothers (Bloom & Steinhart, 1993), children's fathers provided care for only 17% of the children, while 65% of the children were placed with another relative, most frequently with the maternal grandmother. Women often are disadvantaged by dependence on relatives and others caring for their children. Incarcerated men generally can depend on the mother of their children to bring them to visit; however, fathers are much less likely to provide the same support for mother-child visitation, often citing work demands and inconvenient visiting hours. In one study (Koban, 1983), mothers brought children of 70% of incarcerated fathers to visit, but fathers brought only 19% of incarcerated mothers' children to visit them. Hairston (2007) reported on data from the Survey of Inmates in State and Federal Correctional Facilities, designed by the Bureau of Justice Statistics. Data was collected on 12,663 prisoners across the United States. Half of the inmates with children reported that they had not seen their children since their incarceration, and children who lived with the parent prior to incarceration were most likely to visit. In addition, most correctional institutions themselves are unable to provide assistance to these families to increase the likelihood of visits (Arditti, Lambert-Shute, & Joest, 2003).

Establishing family services in prisons and jails is a controversial issue (Tweksbury & DeMichele, 2005). Many corrections professionals and community leaders view family relationships as a distraction that interferes with inmates' rehabilitation. Prison administrators must weigh the benefits of the visits (i.e., improved inmate behavior) and the reality of security issues (i.e., families bringing in contraband) with budget constraints. Therefore, administrators face many logistic and financial hurdles when attempting to create and oversee visitation programs. These challenges have resulted in little consistency in visitation policies across prison facilities, even within the same state. In addition, many citizens resent money being spent on people who have violated societal laws. However, without necessary intervention at the family level, the offender may return to a dysfunctional system, increasing the likelihood of reoffending, and creating a cycle of intergenerational criminal behavior. These obstacles leave many children with incarcerated parents with feelings of isolation, frustration, and helplessness, and incarcerated parents worry about being replaced in their children's lives (Hairston, 2001).

In sum, there are many hardships placed on family members that create challenges for children to visit. Some of these include the travel distance from a home to a prison, financial burdens, caregiver work schedules, and inconvenient and/or inadequate visitation programs and policies (Hairston, 2007; Nesmith & Ruhland, 2008; Tewksbury & DeMichele, 2005). Many family members report that visiting at the facility is stressful and the lack of privacy is mentally draining. Caregivers are often concerned about bringing children into a prison facility and how it impacts them psychologically (Kazura & Toth, 2004). These problems are compounded by the lack of community resources available to address the needs of the families of incarcerated parents. Without a link such as family resource centers between community-based services and the criminal-justice system (Kazura, 2001), the few family support services available in communities may be ineffective in facilitating positive family function for this population.

CHILD VISITATION PROGRAMS

The literature reviewed suggests that by addressing these barriers and providing services to incarcerated parents, their children and their families would help to rehabilitate the offender, support the family during the period of prison separation and reunification, and break the cycle of crime (Arditti, 2005). It further appears that a multi-system approach that takes into consideration all family members, the correctional facility and staff, and the community context will be most effective.

Despite the barriers associated with child visitation, a number of correctional facilities across the United States have created programs and play areas for children and their incarcerated parents. Common features across many of these programs are extended visits, flexible scheduling, and planned parent-child activities to strengthen these relationships. Many programs require incarcerated parents to participate in parenting programs, and to meet certain criterion such as good behavior prior to specialized visitation. The following highlights a few organizations that have created child visitation programs, and many have supporting programs for other family members as well. Although this is not an exhaustive list of the available programs, it is a good representation of the vital work many caring professionals are conducting.

Center for Children of Incarcerated Parents (CCIP)

Founded in 1989 by Denise Johnston and Katherine Gabel, CCIP is located in Eagle Rock, CA. CCIP has many projects and services to support families of inmates in the state of California. Some therapeutic services that CCIP provides are the Early Therapeutic Intervention Project, the Therapeutic Intervention Project, the Attachments Project, and the Developmental Education and Enhancement Project (CCIP, 2001). These programs offer services respectively to children and caregivers, support programs for mothers with infants, residential treatment settings, and mentoring for children of inmates. The Attachment Project is offered in four female correctional facilities and focuses on building trust and affection between incarcerated mothers and their children. CCIP provides inmates with curriculum manuals that cover a broad variety of topics, including parent education for prisoners, parent empowerment, family life education, and effects of trauma and violence on children.

Children's Justice Alliance

Founded in 2004 in Portland, Oregon, the Children's Justice Alliance strives to improve outcomes for children of incarcerated parents. It provides families and inmates with a visiting center called The Center of Family Success. The center is a community resource facility that offers families support such as parent education, GED and basic adult education, addiction support groups, parent/child literacy connections, and anger management groups (Children's Justice Alliance, 2005). Other programs offer parents the opportunity to gain experience in parenting skills, strengthen relationships with children, gain decision-making skills, and apply acquired parenting skills (Eddy et al., 2008).

Families in Crisis, Inc.

Founded in 1977, this Connecticut agency strives to provide meaningful opportunities for change by promoting active parenting (Families in Crisis, Inc., 2009). Family time and visitations are offered to inmates, as well as parent education classes, inmate support groups, occasional extended visits, and home-based services to family members. The Family Ties program supports children of incarcerated parents and offers family counseling, peer support groups, educational support, positive social connections with parents, and mentoring opportunities. Families in Crisis, Inc. also offers support to fathers to move out of poverty and become an influential parent upon release.

Friends Outside National Organization

The Friends Outside Organization was founded by Rosemary Goodenough in California in 1955. This organization primarily values family unification and inmates' successful reentry into the community. Friends Outside parenting programs are offered in every California state prison in order for inmates to parent more effectively upon their release (Friends Outside National Organization, 2007). Visitor's centers are located on prison grounds, and provide parents with children's activities for better engagement, a sheltered place to meet with families, support pre- and post-visits, and transportation for visitors to and from the center. Several programs are offered to build parent-child relationships, increase literacy in children, and create awareness for parents.

Parents and Children Together, Inc. (PACT)

PACT is a nonprofit organization started in Fort Worth, Texas, in 1984 that works to maintain strong and healthy family relationships for incarcerated parents (PACT, 2009). PACT offers community networks and referral services to inmates as well as family support groups, a hospitality house for visiting family members, parenting education classes, and life skills classes. PACT offers a volunteer mentor program for parents and a support group for young children of incarcerated parents. This group is called SKI—or Support Group for Kids with Incarcerated Parents—and is provided to elementary schools.

The Osborne Association

Founded in 1931 by Thomas Osborne, the Osborne Association administration office is located in Bronx, New York. Osborne has several programs designed to reconnect families and strengthen relationships. Its three main programs are Family Works, the Family Resource Center, and Family Ties (The Osborne Association, 2008). Family Works is located in Sing Sing and Woodbourne Correctional facilities, and provides supervised child-focused play spaces for children and parents. Family Works offers inmates parenting courses, counseling leading up to release, and resources for incarcerated fathers. The Family Resource Center services families with a parent in the New York state prisons. It offers a hotline, information workshops, group discussions of family reunification, treatment, family services, peer advocacy, referrals for education, and support groups for families. Family Ties is run in Albion Prison and offers parenting services, structured mother-child visits, and reunification services to mothers.

There are too few support programs helping children and families of inmates. Fortunately, many of the programs that are in existence appear to be of a high quality. However, most organizations do not have the resources to formally evaluate the effectiveness of their programs (i.e., child outcomes, long-term parenting behavior). Program facilitators are left with trial-and-error approaches for creating, modifying, and implementing services. Policies are created based on anecdotal information, which has lead to a lack of consistency in services provided and possibility negative impact outcomes (Parke & Clarke-Stewart, 2003). One program that sets itself apart from others is the Family Connections Center; it was created using evidence-based research and programs, and staff members have been collecting evaluation data since its inception (Kazura et al., 1999).

HISTORY OF THE FAMILY CONNECTIONS CENTER

The Family Connections Center was founded in 1998 and has provided an exciting example of how an alliance of three organizations achieved goals to which all had aspired, but were beyond the reach of any organization working in isolation (Kazura, et al., 1999). Because of the high incidence of incarceration and the family issues associated with incarceration, a partnership was created among the New Hampshire Department of Corrections, University of New Hampshire's (UNH) Department of Family Studies, and UNH Cooperative Extension. From this partnership the Family Connections Center was created at the Lakes Region Correctional Facility. It offers parenting classes, life skills seminars, recorded books on tape for children of incarcerated parents, parenting support groups, and supervised visitation for incarcerated parents and their children. Programming objectives were to strengthen at-risk families and improve the healthy development of children with incarcerated parents through a family-centered, strength-based approach. The principal objective was the acquisition of positive family and relationship skills to increase protective factors and decrease risk factors in families with an incarcerated parent. Individuals from each organization committed to a long-term relationship involving programming, evaluation, and research to help families. The Department of Family Studies provided the researchers to direct the project, guide staff training, provide clinical guidance (for children and parents), and conduct evaluations of all programs. Cooperative Extension provided educators to implement education and training programs. The Lakes Region Correctional Facility housed the Family Connections Center and contributed to the Center's operational costs.

At the start of our programming the prison population at the Laconia facility was approximately 500 (450 men and 50 women). Kazura (2000) reported that 73% of the prison inmates were parents (or stepparents), and 58% receive visits from their children. Currently the facility only houses male inmates. The following discussion will address both men and women's experience at the Family Connection Center (FCC).

Parent-Child Visitation and Intervention Program

A section of the FCC was renovated to create developmentally appropriate spaces for supervised visits between incarcerated parents and their children. A playroom was designed for parents to interact with their infants, toddlers, preschoolers, and/or young elementary school children. A recreation or living room was created for parents to interact with their children who were school-age and adolescents. One-way mirrors were installed in each of these rooms so staff members could unobtrusively observe the parent-child interactions from an observation booth. In the last few years an outdoor play space has been created as well.

Incarcerated parents who have completed the parenting education program, attended four sessions of a parenting support group, and continue to attend a support group, can participate in supervised visitations with their children. The incarcerated parents and their children visit for approximately two hours at a time. The caregivers who transport children were asked to wait either in a waiting room or given a beeper and encouraged to take some time for themselves while the incarcerated parent and child reconnected with each other. This allowed for the child to be the focus of the visit. Young children could choose to play with age-appropriate toys and art materials, and older children could receive help with their homework and listen to music with their parent. Once a visit was completed, staff members provided feedback to the parents regarding their parenting behaviors and challenges they experienced. When necessary, staff members provided suggestions and helped parents to plan for their next visit to strengthen the parent-child relationship.

FAMILY CONNECTIONS CENTER CASE STUDIES

The following are four case studies of incarcerated mothers and fathers who participated in the Family Connections visitation program. Their experiences represent common themes seen in many of the families in our programs (Kazura & Toth, 2004).

Mr. G

Mr. G had been to prison before, and he said he knew he would come back. This time, his new girlfriend was pregnant and he stated that he wanted this to be his last time. Mr. G volunteered to take a parenting education class at the FCC, even though he had already attended a mandatory parenting class during his first prison bid.

While in the FCC parenting education class, Mr. G found out that his girlfriend was having twins. Mr. G felt lucky that his girlfriend was committed to him and their children. Once the babies were born, Mr. G visited with his girlfriend and babies almost every week in the regular prison visiting room. The visiting room was the prison's dining hall. It consisted of hard tables and stools bolted to floor. Although it did have toys and a floor mat to play on, the room echoed and was extremely loud when twenty or more people were visiting. Once Mr. G was eligible, he applied for and received FCC visits. Mr. G visited with both babies for an hour and half every week. Dad learned to change diapers, two at a time, which he was not permitted to do at the regular prison visiting room. He learned to give bottles to his newborns and then learned to spoon feed his children. After the babies were eight months old, the visits decreased to one week with one child, the next week with the other child, and the third week with both. This gave both mom and dad time to spend individually with each child and still gave mom some respite time while dad spent an hour and a half chasing twins around, getting a small taste of what mom was experiencing every day, all day.

The twins visited Dad on their first birthday. Staff members received authorization to bring a small cake into the FCC. Dad was able to give his children their first taste of cake. Photos were taken and the pictures were emailed to mom. During another visit when the children were about 14 months old, they starting banging their sippy cups on the heater in the visiting room. When Dad immediately asked them to stop, they just laughed and banged more. Dad paused, then repeated his request and ultimately took the sippy cups away while explaining to them that they needed to listen to Daddy. After the visit, Mr. G told staff that he hesitated to discipline his twins because he did not want the visit to turn "bad" and did not want them to leave crying. Mr. G said he remembered discussions in the parenting class that centered around disciplining children even when you do not want to because it teaches children right from wrong. Mr. G said he also knew that a staff member was watching and that inspired him to do what was right. The twins did not cry, Dad started a new activity, and he said he had a great visit.

Mr. G and his twins visited a total of 59 times at FCC. Mr. G contacted the FCC staff two and a half years after leaving prison and living in the community. He stated that he, his girlfriend, and his twins are doing great and are looking to buy a house.

Mr. R

Mr. R was happily married when his past caught up with him. His new bride and infant visited him regularly in county jail, but it was difficult to connect with his baby through the Plexiglas separating him from his family. When Mr. R was sentenced to state prison, the visits stopped. As Mr. R's marriage started unraveling, he tried desperately to get visits with his child, to no avail. When Mr. R was transferred to Lacoina prison facility he learned about the FCC. Mr. R attended an 18-hour parenting education class, 27 seminars, and 151 support group sessions. FCC staff encouraged Mr. R to continue writing to his child even though he never received a reply. Mr. R applied for the FCC visits and did not receive a reply from his child's mother. After three years, Mr. R's aunt was allowed to bring his daughter to the regular visiting room, and then shortly after that he was able to visit at the FCC.

When Mr. R had his first visit at the FCC, his child did not cry when his aunt left them alone, which is what he had feared. Instead, his daughter was curious about the new play area. They played with a tea set and then they went outside to throw a ball. Eight months after leaving prison, Mr. R said one of his favorite memories is of that first visit with his daughter.

Mr. R only had four visits at the Family Connections Center, but he said that they were incredibly helpful to him and his daughter's relationship. When Mr. R went home, his ex-wife would only allow supervised visitation with his daughter, but upon seeing how comfortable their daughter was with Mr. R, that stipulation was lifted. Mr. R now goes to his child's house two or three times a week to read to her, and he has visitation with her every weekend. Mr. R said that the program visits and the parenting programs at FCC made his transition back into his child's life much easier.

Ms. B

Ms. B was a mother of three children; a boy aged 9, a girl aged 3, and an infant son, born while she was incarcerated. Ms. B was the sole caregiver of her children until she was incarcerated due to a heroin addiction. Ms. B became involved in the FCC and immediately took the parenting education class. On completion she applied for FCC visits with her children. Due to the age of her young son, she was eligible to have weekly visits with the infant and visits every other week with the older two children. After the sixth week of visiting with her infant son, Ms. B shared with the staff that up until that point when she called home to talk to her children, she had to remind herself to ask about her infant son. After spending only three days in the hospital with him at his birth, he did not seem like her child. Ms. B stated he seemed like someone else's cute little boy that she held when her two other children visited. Ms. B said that after having these weekly visits in which she was able to rock and feed her son, change his diaper, and experience mothering, she started to automatically ask how the baby was doing when she called home. Ms. B stated "I never thought I would crave anything more than heroin; now I crave my kids."

Mr. M

Mr. M was anxious prior to his first visits alone with his six-month-old daughter. He had never spent time alone with an infant. Over the course of his first six visits his anxiety had visibly lessened. Of particular note was the fact that on his sixth visit he changed his daughter's diaper for the first time. He had had regular prison visits with her and his partner in the dining hall. Until his first FCC visit, Mr. M had managed to avoid changing his daughter's diaper.

During this visit, his daughter became fussy and Mr. M decided a diaper change was necessary. His anxiety became obvious as he placed her on the changing table and picked her up several times before committing to his decision. Mr. M had great difficulty getting her pants off. He listened while staff explained the proper way to clean and diaper a baby girl. He put on a new diaper and then her clothes. Staff praised the good job. As he carried his daughter back to the playroom it looked like he floated a little with the increase in his confidence. From that point on, Mr. M's interaction with his daughter became more animated. He lifted her into the air and down toward the floor to pick up toys. Mr. M held her and kissed her. When the child's mother returned he proudly told her about changing the baby. She was pleased and it appeared Mr. M's confidence as a father and his attachment to his daughter was strengthened that day.

These are just some of the stories of the lives that the FCC staff have impacted in positive ways over the past 10 years. Many parents have worked hard to regain the trust of their children's caregivers to regain contact and eventually visitations with their children. Children have taken their first steps, had their first birthday cake, and completed homework assignments within the prison walls. This type of narrative information is what many family practitioners are forced to rely on for examining the effectiveness of their programs.

Historically, the New Hampshire Department of Corrections (NH DOC) has had similar issues regarding data collection on program effectiveness, especially programs associated with family reunification. Some good NH DOC programs have been discontinued during state budget crunches due to a lack of data to demonstrate the program outcomes. Fortunately, when the FCC was founded, due to progressive thinkers in NH DOC and UNH, this information has been gathered for almost 10 years. Although over 1,000 inmates have gone through the parenting education class offered by the Family Connections Center, that number was drastically reduced when it came to incarcerated parents who had visits at the center. Deterrents were distance of families from the prison, cost of and lack of transportation, and a lack of interest on the part of the caregivers. However, 228 incarcerated parents had 1,979 program visits at the Family Connections Center over the last 10 years. Data for the study described below came from the 101 incarcerated parents who provided consent to share their information.

VISITATION STUDY

A total of 101 incarcerated parents (74 fathers, 27 mothers) with an age range from 18 to 48 (M = 31.04, SD = 6.77) gave consent to use observational data recorded during their first and third visits with their children. Of the inmates, 89 were Caucasian, three were African-American, five were Hispanic/Latino, and four listed themselves as other. Of these inmates, 24 were married at the time of the visits (17 fathers, 7 mothers). The number of children inmates had ranged from zero to six (M = 1.96, SD = 1.06), and the ages of the children that came to the facility for visits ranged from less than a year old to 17 years old (M = 6.38, SD = 4.18). The number of visits ranged from one to 47 (M = 7.86, SD = 8.33). The time between visits ranged from one day to over a year (M = 40.19, SD = 72.35).

A pretest/posttest design was implemented for evaluation of the FCC visitation program. The parenting style rating scale (Cowan & Cowen, 1988) was used to collect information on parent's interaction with their children. This information allowed staff to employ a parenting skill training method. From the information gathered, staff met with the parent immediately after the visit to discuss the skills they demonstrated and techniques for overcoming challenges. The Parenting Style rating scale was developed to assess parents' behaviors with their children during visits to a laboratory playroom (Cowan & Cowan, 1988). The rating scale was designed so that staff could describe a parent's interaction style during the time of the visits. A subset of these behaviors was used for the current study (note: some behaviors were very similar and staff reported difficulty distinguishing them). The behaviors were confidence, respect for child's autonomy, limit setting, expressiveness, maturity demands, clarity of language, responsiveness, sadness, pleasure, and anxiety. For each of the behaviors, staff members evaluated the typical level of the behavior that a parent displayed during the visit. Due to the low number of inmates with more than three visits, only the first and third visit data was examined to detect change over time. The Parenting Style Rating was chosen because it has been able to pick up intervention effects as much as two years after the intervention (Cowan, Cohn, Cowan, & Pearson, 1996).

RESULTS

The Reliable Change Index (RCI) was calculated for each of the observation variables for mothers and fathers using Jacobson and Truax's (1991) method. The RCI was calculated by subtracting pretest scores from posttest scores and then dividing by the standard error of difference between the two test scores. If these scores were greater that 1.96 or smaller than −1.96, then the change was large enough to be reliable (Asscher, Dekovic, Prinzie, & Hermanns, 2008). Table 7.1 lists the totals and percentages of cases that improved, stayed the same, or deteriorated. Improvement was considered when there was an increase in positive parenting behaviors (i.e., confidence, responsiveness) or a decrease in behaviors that could interfere with parenting (i.e., anxiety, sadness). Chi-square tests were conducted on the frequency scores to determine if there were any differences between mothers and fathers in the percentage of cases that improved, stayed the same, or deteriorated. No differences were found between mothers and fathers.

Next, correlations were conducted between the length of time between visits and the rate of change scores. For fathers, length of time and the rate of reliable change across visits for clarity of language demonstrated a negative correlation $r(48) = -.33$, $p < .05$. For mothers, length of time was

Table 7.1

	TOTALS AND PERCENTAGES FOR MOTHERS' AND FATHERS' RELIABLE CHANGE SCORES					
RATE OF CHANGE POSTTEST						
	IMPROVEMENT		**NO CHANGE**		**DETERIORATION**	
Outcome/Parent	*N*	%	*N*	%	*N*	%
Confidence						
Fathers	14	27	35	67	3	6
Mothers	8	35	13	56	2	9
Respect Autonomy						
Fathers	11	22	34	70	4	8
Mothers	1	23	14	64	3	13
Limit Setting						
Fathers	10	21	33	69	5	10
Mothers	7	32	11	50	4	18
Expressiveness						
Fathers	9	18	36	71	6	11
Mothers	8	35	13	56	2	9
Maturity Demands						
Fathers	11	23	34	72	2	4
Mothers	6	27	13	59	3	13
Precision						
Fathers	10	21	33	69	5	10
Mothers	6	27	15	68	1	5
Responsiveness						
Fathers	9	18	39	76	3	6
Mothers	6	26	15	65	2	9
Sadness						
Fathers	7	13	41	79	4	8
Mothers	4	17	17	74	2	9
Pleasure						
Fathers	3	6	46	88	3	6
Mothers	2	9	21	79	0	0
Anxiety						
Fathers	17	35	30	57	4	8
Mothers	9	39	12	52	2	9

Note: For each variable, scores are for participants with complete pretest and posttest data.

negatively correlated with rate of change in confidence $r(22) = -.47$, p < .05, negatively correlated with rate of change for pleasure $r(22) = -.58$, p < .01, and positively correlated with anxiety $r(22) = .66$, p < .01 and sadness $r(22) = .58$, p < .01, suggesting that longer time periods between visits had more negative associations with mothers' versus fathers' rate of reliable change.

Finally, we examined whether or not the initial level of parental behaviors (i.e., pretest scores) was related to the degree of reliable change for each variable (Asscher et al., 2008). In order to achieve this, we created three groups: 1) parents who demonstrated no change across all parenting behaviors ($n = 21$); 2) parents who demonstrated reliable positive change for one behavior ($n = 12$); and 3) parents who demonstrated positive change in two or more behaviors ($n = 41$) at posttest. A MANCOVA was conducted using the pretest scores as dependent variables by reliable change grouping scores (no change, some change, change on two of more variables). The covariate variables were parental age, parental gender, and marital status. The MANCOVA revealed a significant main effect for the reliable change grouping variable, Wilks' $\Lambda = .41$, $F(22, 72) = 2.28$, $p < .01$ $\eta^2 = .36$. For the univariate analyses, significant differences emerged for the following dependent variables: confidence $F(2,50) = 10.55$, $p < .01$, autonomy $F(2,50) = 3.86$, $p < .05$, limit setting $F(2,50) = 6.78$, $p < .01$, expressiveness $F(2,50) = 5.29$, $p < .01$, responsiveness $F(2,50) = 3.86$, $p < .05$, precision of language $F(2,50) = 9.89$, $p < .01$, sadness $F(2,50) = 3.77$, $p < .05$, and anxiety $F(2,50) = 3.22$, $p < .05$.

When pretest mean scores were examined, the group who changes on two or more variables had the lowest mean scores for each of the positive parenting behaviors (see Table 7.2). This group also received the highest scores for displays of sadness ($M = 1.63$, $SD = .99$), and anxiety ($M = 2.16$, $SD = .74$), and the lowest on confidence ($M = 3.23$, $SD = .56$). Conversely, the group that has no change from pretest to posttest demonstrated the lowest level of sadness ($M = 1.00$, $SD = .00$).

DISCUSSION OF RESULTS

Researchers have stated for years that little data is available regarding children visitation programs in prison and the lack of empirical evidence of program effectiveness. This study adds to the growing body of literature demonstrating the importance of such programs. These results suggest that the greatest percentages of improvement for both mothers and fathers were for reducing anxiety behaviors and increasing levels

Table 7.2

PRETEST SCORES MEANS AND STANDARD DEVIATIONS BY CHANGE GROUPS

Outcome/Group	Mean	Std. Deviation
Confidence		
No Change	3.76	.43
Change on 1 Variable	4.00	.00
Change on 2 or more Variables	3.23	.56
Respect Autonomy		
No Change	3.76	.43
Change on 1 Variable	4.00	.00
Change on 2 or more Variables	3.43	.56
Limit Setting		
No Change	3.76	.43
Change on 1 Variable	4.00	.00
Change on 2 or more Variables	3.40	.49
Expressiveness		
No Change	3.84	.37
Change on 1 Variable	3.87	.35
Change on 2 or more Variables	3.40	.62
Maturity Demands		
No Change	3.69	.48
Change on 1 Variable	3.87	.35
Change on 2 or more Variables	3.43	.50
Precision		
No Change	3.76	.43
Change on 1 Variable	4.00	.00
Change on 2 or more Variables	3.33	.54
Responsiveness		
No Change	3.84	.37
Change on 1 Variable	4.00	.00
Change on 2 or more Variables	3.60	.49
Sadness		
No Change	1.00	.00
Change on 1 Variable	1.25	.70
Change on 2 or more Variables	1.63	.99
Anxiety		
No Change	1.53	.77
Change on 1 Variable	1.50	1.06
Change on 2 or more Variables	2.16	.74

of confidence. For fathers, respect for autonomy and expectations for maturity also increased. For mothers, limit setting and expressiveness were the behaviors most likely to go up. For both mothers and fathers, pleasure stayed consistently high across all visits. When the length of time between visits was examined, some interesting differences between mothers and fathers resulted. For fathers, longer time between visits did not seem to impact their parenting behaviors much. Only clarity of language decreased, suggesting that fathers who rarely see their children have more difficulty communicating with them in developmentally appropriate ways. For mothers, the associations were more severe. Length of time was associated with lower levels of confidence and pleasure, and higher levels of sadness and anxiety. These results suggest that length of time between visits is an important component for mother-child visitation, and if too much time lapses, this relationship could be further at-risk. These findings are consistent with the Poehlmann (2005) study that suggested the number of visits and length of time between visits are related to attachment security for incarcerated mothers and their children.

Next we examined the difference between parents who did not change pretest to posttest, parents who changed a little, and parents who changed on many items. It is important to note that the highest at-risk group (i.e., the group with the poorest parenting behaviors pretest), which represented 55% of the participants, made the greatest improvement from visit one to visit three. Not only did this group score lower on the pretest parenting behaviors, they had the lowest mean scores for confidence and the highest for sadness and anxiety, suggesting that they understood that they needed to change and used the resources that were available to them to improve their parenting skills. These findings provide support for the effectiveness of the visitation program for improving parent-child interactions for our high-risk group. The group who improved on one behavior had the highest pretest parenting scores, suggesting that this group already had effective parenting skills and were fine-tuning their behavior. The last group demonstrated no positive changes from pretest to posttest, and may pose the greatest challenge to service providers. At pretest, these parents had average parent behavior scores and the lowest scores for sadness. Possibly they represent a "good enough" ideology of parenting and were not motivated to improve their behaviors with their children. Clearly more data need to be collected regarding this and similar programs to further tease out the intricacies of program effectiveness on different populations.

RECOMMENDATIONS AND CONCLUSIONS

From these findings and the daily experiences of FCC staff and administers, a number of recommendations can be made to child welfare and social work professionals and family educators creating intervention programs in correctional facilities. One of the most important and resilient pieces of the FCC program has been the partnership between the Department of Corrections (DOC) and the University of New Hampshire (UNH)(Kazura, Temke, Toth, Hunter, 2002). Community partnerships can provide training to programming staff and help overcome hurdles that may be difficult for DOC staff to solve on their own. For example, over the past 10 years UNH and other community partners have acted as the fiscal agents for the FCC. Having community partners act as fiscal agents has helped sustain staff and programs during state budget crunches. Community partners often have support systems in place to submit and implement grants in a timely manner that often are not readily available to DOC staff. When forming a partnership with multiple organizations it is important to develop a memorandum of understanding that outlines each organizations' roles and responsibilities during the development and implementation of the programs. This will strengthen the commitment of each organization and improve the likelihood of successful programs.

Another recommendation to family educators is to respect the mission of the DOC and recognize that security comes first. Family support programming is important, but cannot be facilitated without the support of security staff. Corrections officers are in charge of getting inmates from their units to the program. Correctional officers may be either implicitly or explicitly resistant to programs providing support to inmates and their families. They can easily make or break a program. For example, if corrections officers are not willing to provide security to family events, then those events cannot take place. Having DOC personnel committed to the importance of incarcerated family issues can stop similar situations from happening. FCC administrators achieved officers' support by having planning meetings with all the correctional officers and other prison program facilitators to educate them on the importance of family programs and to receive their feedback on potential challenges and problem-solving strategies.

Along with involving DOC staff in program development, it is also important to encourage the involvement of incarcerated parents at each stage. At FCC, staff conducted focus groups with inmates to discover their challenges regarding child visitation and the types of programs that they needed (Kazura et al., 1999; Kazura 2001). Inmates built and decorated the play spaces. They painted murals on the walls, and landscaped the outdoor space. Inmates created some of our databases, such as the FCC library database. Incarcerated parents provided clerical work, and were encouraged to provide feedback to staff regarding the programs. At the same time a mission statement was created for the center and provided consistent information regarding rules and responsibilities for participants in the programs. Few exceptions have been allowed in the rules; what cannot be done for everyone should not be done for anyone. However, every effort has been made toward fairness; when incarcerated parents were eligible for FCC visits, staff screened the family situation carefully to make sure that visits would be in the best interest of the child. If there were conflicts between the child's caregiver and the inmate, staff worked with the caregiver to provide information regarding the facility and program; often, compromises could be reached. Program facilitators should provide services to the caregiver as well. In the last two years, in large part due to a federal grant from Healthy Marriage and Responsible Fatherhood, FCC was able to actively involve the partner/caregiver in some of the programs. It now offers caregiver support groups, relationship classes, and marriage and family therapy to inmates and their partners. That was the missing link for the FCC and on our list of goals from the beginning.

Finally, the continual program evaluation is vital. FCC consistently conducted exit interviews to both incarcerated parents and their children's caregivers to see what worked and what did not work. Program administrators researched family programs nationwide and attended conferences in search of research-based materials to improve services. Having a research and evaluation component for each program was very helpful in creating a strong, respectable program with a positive reputation in the state. Data has been helpful when applying for grants and reporting to the corrections administration to demonstrate effectiveness. Keeping track of the numbers of participants, their demographic information, and progress through each of the programs has been very helpful for reporting to local and state politicians with interests in families with incarcerated parents. Creating an empirical underpinning for family programs and policies will result in consistencies across state agencies and reliable recommendations.

CHAPTER SUMMARY

Currently there is little understanding about the effects of parental incarceration on children's development. We know even less about how these effects might vary based on age or sex of the child, the family configuration, or which parent is incarcerated. Information is needed about what factors might mitigate the effects of parental incarceration and what might be the most effective interventions for children at various age levels. What we do know is that most incarcerated parents want more contact with their children (Hairston, 2007). Parenting programs can increase parental confidence, provide new skills for parenting from a distance, and strengthen parent-child attachment relationships. Therefore, prison visitation policies and spaces need to become more child-friendly to increase the desirability for caregivers to encourage and support children's visitation in prison facilities.

Family programs are low-cost interventions that improve offender rehabilitation and can reduce the incidence of criminal behavior for children of incarcerated parents. Programs that help parents reconnect with their children, improve their parenting skills, and provide services to other family members help incarcerated parents transition back into the community and reunite with their children successfully. When appropriate, it is critical for family practitioners to maintain their commitments to policies and programs that promote progress in suspended relationships and allow parents to contribute to their children lives, regardless of incarceration. Taken together, the information provided here is a springboard for continued examination of the issues associated with children's visitation programs and the long-term developmental adjustment provided by these programs.

REFERENCES

Arditti, J. A. (2005). Families and incarceration: An ecological approach. *Families in Society: Journal of Contemporary Social Services, 86*(2), 251–260.

Arditti, J. A., Lambert-Shute, J., & Joest, K. (2003). Saturday morning at the jail: Implications of incarceration for families and children. *Family Relations, 52*(3), 195–204.

Asscher, J. J., Deković, M., Prinzie, P., & Hermanns, J. M. A. (2008). Assessing Change in Families Following the Home-Start Program: Clinical Significance and Predictors of Change. *Family Relations, 57*, 351–364

Bloom, B. & Steinhart, D. (1993). *Why punish the children: A reappraisal of the children of incarcerated mothers in America.* San Francisco: National Council on Crime & Delinquency.

Bowlby, J. (1983). *Attachment and loss.* New York: Basic Books.

Breier, A., Kelsoe, J. R., Kirwin, P. D., Beller, Wolkowitz, O. M., & Pickar, D. (1988). Early parental loss and development of adult psychology. *Archives of General Psychiatry, 45,* 9987–9993.

Center for Children of Incarcerated Parents. (2001). *CCIP Educational Projects.* Retrieved March 10, 2009, from http://e-ccip.org/services.html

Children's Justice Alliance. (2005). *Our programs: Services for children and families.* Retrieved March 12, 2009, from http://www.childrensjusticealliance.org/programs.htm

Comfort, M. (2003). In the tube at San Quentin: The secondary prisonization of women visitation inmates. *Journal of Contemporary Ethnography, 32,* 77–107.

Couturier, L. C. (December, 1995). Families in peril: Inmates benefit from family services programs. *Corrections Today* 102–107.

Cowan, P. A., Cowan, C. P. (1988). *Schoolchildren and their families project description of parenting style ratings.* Unpublished manuscript.

Cowan, P. A., Cohn, D. A., Cowan, C. P., & Pearson, J. L. (1996). Parents' Attachment Histories and Children's Externalizing and Internalizing Behaviors: Exploring Family Systems Models of Linkage. *Journal of Consulting and Clinical Psychology, 64,* 53–63.

Eddy, J. M., Martinez, C., Schiffmann, T., Newton, R., Olin, L., Leve, L., Foney, D., & Wu Shortt, J. (2008). Development of a multisystemic parent management training intervention for incarcerated parents, their children and families, *Clinical Psychologist, 12,* 86–98.

Families In Crisis, Inc. (2009). *Families in Crisis, Inc.: support programs and services.* Retrieved March 3, 2009, from http://www.familiesincrisis.org/fic-services/51?task=view

Friends Outside National Organization. (2007). *Friends Outside: Programs.* Retrieved March 20, 2009, from http://www.friendsoutside.org/programs.html

Fritsch, T. A., & Burkhead, J. D. (1981). Behavioral reactions of children to parental absence due to imprisonment. *Family Relations, 30*(1), 83–88.

Hagen, K. A., Myers, B. J., & MacKintosh, V.H. (2005). Hope, social support, and behavioral problems in at-risk children. *American Journal of Orthopsychiatry, 75,* 211–219.

Hairston, C. F. (2007). *Focus on children with incarcerated parents: An overview of the research literature.* Baltimore, MD: The Annie E. Casey Foundation.

Hairston, C. F. (2001). Fathers in prison: Responsible fatherhood and responsible public policies. *Marriage & Family Review, 32*(3), 111–135.

Hairston, C. F. (1998). The forgotten parent: Understanding the forces that influence incarcerated fathers' relationships with their children. *Child Welfare Journal, 77*(5), 617–637.

Hairston, J. Rollin, and H. Jo. Family connections during imprisonment and prisoners' community reentry, *Research brief: Children, families, and the criminal justice system.,* University of Illinois, Chicago (2004).

Jacobson, N. S., & Truax, P. (1991). Clinical significance: A statistical approach to defining meaningful change in psychotherapy research. *Journal of Consulting and Clinical Psychology, 59,* 12–19.

Johnston, D. (1995). Parent-child visits in jails. *Children's Environments, 12,*(1), 25–38.

Kazura, K. (2000). Fathers' qualitative and quantitative involvement: An investigation of attachment, play, and social interactions. *Journal of Men's Studies, 9,* 41–57.

Kazura, K. (2001). Family programming for incarcerated parents: A needs assessment among inmates. *Journal of Offender Rehabilitation, 32*(4), 67–83.

Kazura, K., Baber, K., & Temke, M. (1999). The Family Connection Project: A collaborative approach to supporting families with incarcerated parents. *Family Science Review, 12,* 294–315.

Kazura, K., Temke, M., Toth, K., & Hunter, B. (2002). Building partnerships to address challenging social problems. *Journal of Extension, 40,* 117–121.

Kazura, K., & Toth, K. (2004). Playrooms in prison: Combating risk factors for children of inmates. *Corrections Today, 66* (7) 128–132.

Koban, L. A. (1983). Parents in prison: A comparative analysis of the effects of incarceration on the families of men and women. *Research in Law, Deviance and Social Control, 5,* 171–183.

Masten, A. S. & Coatsworth, J. D. (1998) The development of competence in favorable and unfavorable environments: Lessons from research on successful children. *American Psychologist, 53,* 205–220.

Murray, J., Janson, C.-G., & Farrington, D. P. (2007). Crime in adult offspring of prisoners: A cross-national comparison of two longitudinal samples. *Criminal Justice and Behavior, 34* (1) 133–149.

Nesmith, A., & Ruhland, E. (2008). Children of incarcerated parents: Challenges and resiliency, in their own words. *Children and Youth Services Review, 30,* 1119–1130.

Osborne Association (1993). How can I help? New York: Author.

Oseni, R. J. (2006). Parenting from prison: The experiences of incarcerated African American parents and their families in the state of Louisiana. ProQuest Information & Learning). *Dissertation Abstracts International: Section B: The Sciences and Engineering, 66* (8), 4495–4495.

Parke, R. D., & Clarke-Stewart, K. A. (2003). The effects of parental incarceration on children: Perspectives, promises and policies. In J. Travis & M. Waul (Eds.), *Prisoners once removed* (pp. 189–232). Washington DC: The Urban Institute Press.

Parents and Children Together, Inc. (2009). *Parents and Children Together: Serving children of prisoners for 25 years.* Retrieved March 20, 2009, from http://parentsand-childrentogether.net/default.aspx

Poehlmann, J. (2005). Children's family environments and intellectual outcomes during maternal incarceration. *Journal of Marriage and Family, 67*(5), 1275–1285.

Poehlmann, J. (2005). Representations of attachment relationships in children of incarcerated mothers. *Child Development, 76*(3), 679–696.

Poehlmann, J., Shlafer, R. J., Maes, E., & Hanneman, A. (2008). Factors associated with young children's opportunities for maintaining family relationships during maternal incarceration. *Family Relations, 57*(3), 267–280.

Reed, D. F. & Reed, E. L. (1997). Children of incarcerated parents. *Social Justice, 24,* 152–170.

Schafer, N. E. (1994). Exploring the link between visits and parole success: A survey of prison visitors. *International Journal of Offender Therapy and Comparative Criminology, 38*(1), 17–32.

Snyder, Z. K., Carlo, T. A., & Mullins, M. M. C. (2001). Parenting from prison: An examination of a children's visitation program at a women's correctional facility. *Marriage and Family Review, 32,* 33–61.

Tewksbury, R., & DeMichele, M. (2005). Going to prison: A prison visitation program. *The Prison Journal,* 85(3), 292–310.

The Osborne Association. (2008, Winter). From start to finish: Osborne's prison programs, *Osborne Today* 1–3.

ADDITIONAL RESOURCES

Readings

Bender, J. (2003). *My Dad Is In Jail.* YouthLight Publishing.

Black, C. (1997). My Dad Loves Me, My Dad Has a Disease: A Child's View: Living with Addiction. MAC Publishing.

Black, F. (1998). *A Visit with Daddy.* Las Vegas, NV: Inside-Out Publishing.

Black, F. (1999). *A Visit with Mommy.* Las Vegas, NV: Inside-Out Publishing.

Black, F. (1999). *There Are Some Real Special Kids in Our Class.* Las Vegas, NV: Inside-Out Publishing.

Braman, D. (2004). *Doing Time On The Outside: Incarcerated and family life in urban America.* University of Michigan Press.

Brisson, P. (2004). *Mama Loves Me From Away.* Honesdale, PA: Boyds Mills Press.

Cain, S. and Speed, M. (1999). *Dad's in Prison.* London: A&C Black.

Correctional Education Authority. (1996). *If You Have A Parent In Jail.* Burlington, VT: Flynn School.

Hickman, M. (1990). *When Andy's Father Went to Prison.* Niles, IL: Albert and Whitman Company.

Hodgkins, K. and Bergen, S. (1997). *My Mom Went to Jail.* Madison, WI: The Rainbow Project, Inc.

Jones, D. (1988). *Joey's Visit.* Syracuse, NY: Cornell Cooperative Extension of Onondaga County.

Maury, Inez. (2002). *My Mother and I Are Growing Stronger.* Berkeley, CA: New Seed Press.

Rathbone, C. (2006). *A World Apart.* New York: Random House, Inc.

Stanley, W. (1998). *Life in Prison.* New York: Morrow Junior Books.

Travis, J. (2003). *Prisoners Once Removed: The impact of incarceration and reentry on children, families and communities.* Washington DC: Urban Institute Press.

Van Antwerp, K. (1998). *Can't Come To School My Mom Is In Prison.* CA: Quiet Thunder Publishing.

Walker, J. (2006). *An Inmate's Daughter.* Raven Publishing.

Wittbold, M. (1997). *Let's Talk About When Your Parent is in Jail.* New York: PowerKids Press.

Woodson, J. (2002). *Visiting Day.* New York: Scholastic.

Yaffe, R. and Hoade, L. (2000). *When a Parent Goes To Jail: A Comprehensive Guide for Counseling Children of Incarcerated Parents.* CA: Rayve Productions, Inc.

Web Sites

Action for Prisoner's Families: http://www.prisonersfamilies.org.uk/

Center for Children of Incarcerated Parents (CCIP): http://www.e-ccip.org/index.html

Children's Justice Alliance: http://www.childrensjusticealliance.org/

Families in Crisis, Inc.: http://www.familiesincrisis.org/
Family & Connections Network: http://www.fcnetwork.org/
Friends Outside National Organization: http://www.friendsoutside.org/
National Center on Fathers and Families: http://www.ncoff.gse.upenn.edu/
Osborne Association: http://www.osborneny.org/youth_family_services.htm
PACT (Parents and Children Together, Inc.): http://www.fcnetwork.org/programs/pact.html

Videos

Arkansas Educational Television Network (Producer). (2002). *Mothers in Prison. Children in Crisis.* [Documentary], Available from: www.aetn.org

Barens, E. (Producer). (2001). *A Sentence of Their Own* [Documentary], Available from: www.asentenceoftheirown.com

Brown Hats Productions (Producer). (2003). *Prison Lullabies* [Documentary], Available from: http://www.prisonlullabies.com/

HBO Studio Productions (2005). *Xiara's Song* [Documentary], Available from: hsp@hsptv.com

Luna Productions (Producer). (1999). *The Story of Fathers and Sons* [Television Broadcast]. Available from: www.lunaproductions.com

Oliver, R. P. (Producer). (2009). *The Silent Voice.* [Documentary], Available from: www.gwcinc.com

Petzall, J. & Rogers, D. (Producers), (2002). *When the Bough Breaks-Children of Mothers in Prison* [Documentary], Available from: http://www.filmakers.com/index.php?a=filmDetail&filmID=1052

Strengthening Parent-Child Relationships: Visit Coaching with Children and Their Incarcerated Parents

8

MARTY BEYER
RANDI BLUMENTHAL-GUIGUI
TANYA KRUPAT[1]

Visits between children and their incarcerated parents can be designed to safeguard child well-being, promote a positive identity for a child, and provide continuity of the parent-child relationship or support the beginning of a relationship. This chapter describes visit coaching, an innovative approach to visiting between children and their incarcerated parents, and the therapeutic value of family centers located within prison and jail visiting rooms. Visit coaching and family centers in prisons and jails offer an attachment-based, culturally competent developmental framework to help incarcerated parents and children's caregivers better understand and meet the needs of their children and manage the uncertainties about the future due to incarceration, and to support children in navigating their relationship with their incarcerated parent.

The incarceration of a parent during childhood can have long-lasting effects on self-perception and behaviors that put children at risk (Felitti et. al., 1998). Each risk factor a child is exposed to exponentially increases his or her odds of developing emotional and behavioral difficulties, including withdrawal, aggression, anxiety, depression, poor academic performance, substance abuse, sexual risk taking, and delinquency. Although many children overcome these odds and demonstrate remarkable resiliency, children of incarcerated parents are exposed to a greater total number of risks—parental separation, poverty, mental illness, parental substance abuse, and domestic violence—than other children (Phillips & Gleeson, 2007). Tragically, children of incarcerated parents may end up incarcerated themselves. The isolation children with a parent in prison feel and their lack of access to their parents, rather than "the apple not falling far from the tree," explains the increased risk these children face for negative outcomes.[2]

Many of the risks children face as a result of their parent's incarceration are linked to being unable visit their parent, or when visits are afforded, are linked to the conditions under which the visits must take place. Although each child is affected differently by separation from a parent, three effects of having an incarcerated parent are commonly seen in children. The first is worrying, which may delay the child's development. While other children are progressing in school and social development, the child of an incarcerated parent may be distracted by worrying about their parents' safety and the uncertainty of their parent's return. This worrying is made worse by the child's exposure to media images of the dangers of prisons and jails. Even telephone calls may not mitigate these concerns, as children often need to see for themselves that their parents are being fed and cared for and are not being victimized in jail or prison.

Second, children of incarcerated parents often regress. Regression is a common consequence of trauma, with children's developmental progress halting or sliding backward on developmental steps they were in the process of mastering. For example, young children who have been toilet trained may regress to the diaper stage. For older children, it has been hypothesized that they unconsciously delay milestones until their parent comes home, wishing not to commemorate birthdays, graduations, marriage, and other significant life events without sharing it with their parent. Although not all milestones can be celebrated in jail or prison, visits can go a long way toward helping children enjoy birthdays and other occasions with their incarcerated parent.

Third, children of incarcerated parents are often pushed into adult roles. "Parentification" of children may begin before the parent is incarcerated as a result of substance abuse or being overwhelmed by financial and/or relationship problems. Because of worries and responsibilities they are too young to cope with, these children may be more vulnerable to early problems with substances, school failure, and sexuality. Visiting room regulations exacerbate parentification by reversing the roles between child and incarcerated parent. For example, incarcerated individuals are not allowed to touch money, purchase items from vending machines, or heat up food in the microwaves in visiting rooms; because children are allowed to do these activities, the prison visiting rules require a role reversal between parent and child.

Supportive visiting programs for children of incarcerated parents and family centers inside prison and jail visiting rooms can mitigate these and other negative effects of parental incarceration on children.[3] Programs such as the Bedford Hills Teen and Summer Visiting Programs, New York City child welfare agency's Children of Incarcerated Parents Program, Hour Children's visiting programs, the Osborne Association's Family Ties and FamilyWorks programs, and others around the country support children and their incarcerated parents to have more child-focused, age-appropriate, happier visits and strengthened relationships that benefit the child's development while the parent is in jail or prison, as well as easing the return to the community.

How these programs are designed and offered is as important as what the programs are. A program's underlying beliefs and philosophy will impact its effectiveness. For this reason, the authors want to say a word about language. This article intentionally uses the words "visiting" and "visits," not "visitation," to describe the time that children and their incarcerated parents have together. After decades of working with families in various situations of separation, the authors believe the term "visitation" conveys a legal, formal situation that visit coaching and family centers in jails and prisons are designed to purposely avoid. This has been confirmed for us by children who have told us, "Normal people don't have visitations. They go to visit Grandma or Dad or Uncle." In keeping with feedback from families and the philosophy behind visit coaching and family centers, we believe this shift in language is not merely semantic, but critical to supporting children and their incarcerated parents.

Similarly, it is important to be mindful of the language we use to refer to children's incarcerated parents. Terms that appear frequently in the media such as "inmate," "convict," "offender," and "criminal" are stigmatizing for children who are struggling to figure out who their parent is, to reconcile their complex and often conflicting feelings about the parent, and by association, about themselves. Although with respect to their unlawful behavior, society has designated them as "offenders" and the prison system calls them "inmates," but to their children they are still "Mom" and "Dad," and it is important to honor this relationship and the children's experiences, attachment, and feelings. Saying "Mom," "Dad," "parent who is incarcerated," or a "formerly incarcerated person" is more helpful to children (Ellis, 1994).

This chapter consists of six sections. The first section introduces visiting as an under-utilized therapeutic intervention for children of incarcerated parents. The second section summarizes the challenges of visiting in a correctional setting. The third section presents the attachment and other developmental needs of young children and teenagers who visit their incarcerated parents. In the next two sections, the effectiveness of visit coaching with children and teenagers and their incarcerated parents, and of family centers in jails and prisons is described in detail. The last section provides guidance for implementing visit coaching and family centers in jails and prisons.

VISITING AS AN UNDER-UTILIZED THERAPEUTIC INTERVENTION FOR CHILDREN OF INCARCERATED PARENTS

When children do not live with a parent, visits are essential to maintain their relationship. Visiting as a consequence of parent-child separation is seen as routine in the context of divorce, but less so in the aftermath of a parent's incarceration. The negative assumptions about a parent by virtue of their incarceration often interfere with professionals and others viewing the situation from a child's perspective and a developmental, attachment lens. In addition to the benefits of visiting for children separated from a parent for other reasons, when a parent is incarcerated, visits also allay a child's worries about their parent and can help address the child's feeling of being stigmatized.

The benefits children derive from visiting their incarcerated parent vary depending upon the child's developmental stage, individual family circumstances, and the child's prior relationship with his or her parent. For example, for infants and young children, visits build their attachment to their parent and are essential to establishing a relationship. At this young age, phone calls or letters are not enough to solidify a relationship. For elementary school children, visits make them feel loved, answer questions about the parent's absence and safety, and can also dispel self-blame the child may be burdened with. For teenagers, visits help in their complex process of developing a positive identity and resolving anger and disappointment they feel toward their incarcerated parent.

Visits can be important and valuable whether or not the child lived with the parent prior to incarceration. An assumption is often made that because children with an incarcerated father (less frequently with an incarcerated mother) may not have resided with their parent prior to the parent's incarceration, there was no parent-child relationship worth sustaining or strengthening. Reports from children who have been kept from seeing their parent in prison coupled with descriptions from those who have visited their incarcerated parents attest to the importance of making these child-parent relationships possible. As they get older, children will define their family relationships based on their experiences, and not having been totally separated from a parent—and having opportunities to create memories through visits—will be beneficial. For this reason, visits can be important even if the child and parent have been estranged.

For incarcerated parents, visits with their children are also important. Visits provide opportunities to demonstrate their love for their children, give their children a sense of belonging, be a positive model for their children, explain to their children choices they regret that resulted in incarceration, and participate in their child's education and development. In some prisons and fewer jails, incarcerated parents have completed parenting and other classes that promote self-awareness and growth while in prison and provide the information, motivation, and skills to be outstanding parents to their children despite their limiting circumstances and past behavior. If their children are in foster care, visits are crucial to incarcerated parents retaining parental rights.

Without visit support, incarcerated parents may not know how to prepare for visits and may have difficulty managing their own feelings or responding to the varied needs of their children when they see them. Without support before and after the visit, children may feel confused and rejected despite the incarcerated parent's intention to be loving and build the child's confidence in their relationship. Without support, the caregiver may not know how to help prepare the child or how to interpret and handle the child's reactions to the visit afterwards. If siblings live in different homes but come to the same visit as a family, this can add to the complexity of the situation for the children and their incarcerated parent, as well as the caregivers.[4] In addition, the uncertainties surrounding the next visit and the parent's return to the community can also undermine visits.

Visit coaching provides critical before and after support for all involved with the visit. It is an effective model for maintaining relationships through separation, rebuilding relationships, and for establishing relationships between parents and children who have been estranged.

CHALLENGES OF VISITING IN A CORRECTIONAL SETTING

In contrast to visits between noncustodial parents and their children in the community, visits in jails and prisons present many obstacles to positive interaction. Distance, transportation challenges and cost, facility rules, and concerns of caretakers can all result in infrequent contact, which increases the guilt of the incarcerated parent and makes maintaining the parent-child connection more difficult.

A significant obstacle to visits with incarcerated parents, whether the child is living with a relative or in foster care, is the commonly held view that going to a jail or prison is harmful for the child, and/or seeing a parent whose release date is uncertain would be upsetting to the child. This view may prevent family members, caseworkers, and foster parents from telling children the truth about where their parent is. It is not uncommon for children to be told their parent is at college, away working, in the military, or in the hospital. Although motivated by protective intentions, these lies are often exposed and damage children's trust in their caregivers more than they serve to protect them. Most children eventually discover that their parent is incarcerated, and whether this is immediately or years later, uncovering the lie they were told has greater negative consequences than had they been told the truth. Children may not have the same negative associations with incarceration as adults do; the truth gives them a reality to come to terms with and maintains their trust in those they rely on for their care.

Furthermore, an incarcerated parent's extended absence can affect permanency for the child, but keeping the child and incarcerated parent from visiting is likely to be harmful and is not reasonable, even given the desire of relatives, foster parents, and caseworkers to have stable living arrangements for the child.

Once children know where their parent is and visits are considered, adults may worry about the hardship of a long trip to the prison or jail and the impact on the child of entering the facility through razor wire, metal detectors, and guards who may look like police officers. But children's responses are primarily determined by adult reactions. If the adult behaves as if the visit is an adventure and a wonderful reunion, the child is much less likely to be upset than if the adult's body language and words convey anger, shame, being inconvenienced, and negative views of the prison surroundings. It is crucial for relatives, foster parents, and caseworkers to have support to remember the importance of visits for the child in maintaining their relationship with the incarcerated parent, even though the visit may also stir up feelings in the child that their care-taker will have to manage.

Another major obstacle to visits with incarcerated parents is distance and transportation. Correctional policies in most states do not take into consideration proximity to children and family in prison assignment deci-sions; incarcerated parents are frequently transferred to different pris-ons without prior notice. It is not easy for families to arrange affordable transportation to facilities that are miles away, often in hard-to-reach rural areas. Many families do not have cars and rely on public transpor-tation that does not go to places many prisons are located. Cabs, trains, buses, and airplanes are too expensive for some families. If a caregiver has to pay for transportation per child, they may leave some or all of the children at home. Many foster care systems have not made provisions for paying for transportation by caseworkers or foster parents to jails and prisons. In most households where there is more than one child, man-aging school, medical care, religious life, daily chores, and recreation is so time-consuming that taking a half or full day or more for a visit to a distant jail or prison seems inconceivable.

Another deterrent to visits is the embarrassment of many adult fam-ily members about having a relative in prison. They may be concerned that they will be seen at the prison by people from their community or workplace. The demeaning process of entering the prison may exacer-bate their shame. Both to avoid their embarrassment and protect the child, family members may avoid visiting and may be encouraged to do so by the incarcerated parent, who wants to spare their loved ones the shame. The fear of outstanding warrants for child support or unresolved criminal matters or worries about deportation may also keep family members from visiting, and they may not know how to find out the facil-ity's rules for arranging for another adult to take the child to visit.

Correctional facilities were not set up with children in mind. The fact that most incarcerated people in the United States are also parents (close to 80% of incarcerated women and 66% of incarcerated men are parents) is not reflected in the regulations that govern jails and prisons, including their visiting rooms. This poses challenges for incarcerated parents and others trying to arrange and support positive visits. Every prison has its own set of complicated visit regulations and schedules; although some have certain rules in common, there are enough varia-tions between facilities (even in the same state) that many families have experienced traveling long distances only to be turned away because of their clothing, insufficient ID, arriving on the wrong day, or for other reasons. Especially if family members do not have access to online information, it can be difficult to get the correct telephone number for the facility and to ascertain when visits can occur, what age and how many children are permitted, what documents must be brought to the visit, and what cannot be brought to the visit. Visiting days and hours may vary from facility to facility, even within the same state, and some facilities only offer alternate weekends for visiting based on the first letter of the last name.[5] Having to arrive at the right entry, arriving at the right time, waiting in lines, and being put off by what may be perceived as an unwelcoming attitude by prison staff can also make a relative or foster care worker avoid taking the child to visit their incarcerated parent.

Upon arriving at a prison or jail for a visit, long waits to be "processed" (often outside in inclement weather with no awning or chairs) and poor visiting environments lacking toys and books for children and offering little privacy can result in the parent and children being at their worst during the visit. Relatives may be upset to find themselves visiting with a shackled parent. If the visit is a non-contact visit (common in most jails and many prisons across the country) and has to occur through glass or a wire/gated divider, both the parent and the child may be frustrated by the lack of physical contact and the inadequacy of a telephone for communicating. For young children in particular, these visits may be confusing if they see their own reflection in the glass and difficult because touch and proximity are critical for them to maintain their relationship. The message conveyed by such visits is that their parent is dangerous and is caged like an animal.

Many of the rules within a prison or jail visiting room are also counter to the ways children and families spend time together. For example, sometimes visiting children get to know one another and want to interact during their visits or have their parents meet. In most prisons, this is referred to as "cross-visiting" and is prohibited. Prison rules also ban incarcerated parents from changing their babies' diapers or taking their children to the bathroom, which can be confusing to explain to a young child. Additionally, in visiting rooms that do not have family or children's centers (designated child-friendly play areas), there is often nothing for children to do or anywhere for them to go, and often their caretakers are not permitted to bring even small toys or markers and paper into the visit to entertain them. Children may be required to sit still in adult size metal chairs for long periods of time. Sitting on their incarcerated parent's lap may not be permitted. These are not developmentally-sound expectations and can make the visit an upsetting or frustrating struggle for everyone involved. As a result, the family, parent, and correctional staff may come to the conclusion that visits are not good for children, when in fact it is the inflexible visit rules that are not child-friendly. Visit coaching and family centers are designed to support the parent-child relationship in part by modifying the correctional visiting environment.

Furthermore, older children and teenagers may think visits to a distant prison or jail are too time consuming because they have their own busy lives. They may say they are reluctant to visit or their interest in visiting may be masked by anger at their incarcerated parent. Instead of accepting these ideas at face value or labeling them as teenage "resistance," it is important for adults to discuss the pros and cons of visiting their incarcerated parent with the teenager and come up with visit arrangements (and phone calls and letters to supplement infrequent visits) that respond to the teenager and also meet his or her long-term needs.

> Suzanne, a 14-year-old girl in foster care, was asked by her caseworker if she wanted to visit her incarcerated mother over the coming weekend. She said "No," and the conversation went no further. The caseworker was relieved, as she found the visits to the prison exhausting and upsetting. She did not ask why Suzanne said "No" (which was because on that weekend there was a big party for which she and her friends had been preparing). The caseworker also took this "No" as indicative of Suzanne's future interest in visiting and did not ask again for months. Suzanne wanted to visit her Mom to tell her about the party and catch her up on school and friends, but thought she was only allowed to go when the caseworker brought it up and made arrangements.

Older children or teenagers may be angry or feel awkward visiting with their parent. They may not know what to say or may be afraid of their emotions (anger, rage, sadness, fear). In these situations, a visit coach who functions as a mediator can be helpful, and can point out to adults concerned about the visit that not all valuable contact between a teenager and their incarcerated parent is in the form of "easy visits." Supported visits have therapeutic value for older children and teens, including in situations where the parent and child have been estranged.

Teenagers may want to visit their incarcerated parent, but not know how to set up a visit if their caretaker objects or is unable to accompany them. Although some prisons allow children age 16 and older to visit their parent unaccompanied, or outside organizations may be willing to accompany the child for a visit, many caregivers and teenagers do not know this and it can be difficult to navigate the criminal justice system to discover such information. Even when teenagers can visit unescorted, in many instances they benefit from a visit coach or someone to support them and help them process their feelings before and after the visit.

If children are living with family members, the relationship of the caretaker and the incarcerated parent is a key to visit frequency and satisfaction. If the relative has a positive relationship with the incarcerated parent, they may be much more motivated to bring the child to a jail or prison visit. When children are brought to the visit by an adult with whom the incarcerated parent has a relationship, the nature of the relationship will affect how the parent relates to the children—if the adult is a loved one, the incarcerated parent may be torn over how to divide the visit's precious time; if there is friction between the adult and the incarcerated parent, the visit may be tense or awkward; if the adult is a representative of a foster care agency, the incarcerated parent may have many questions that take up time in the visit. If the child is living with a relative or in a foster home where the incarcerated parent is viewed as a negative influence on the child, the incarcerated parent may be preoccupied by fears the child has been "poisoned" against them. Incarcerated parents may require special support to manage visits with children who are accompanied by relatives who are hostile to them.

If the children are in foster care, visits in jails or prisons can occur through special programs, individual case workers, or the foster parents. Many foster care systems are overwhelmed arranging visits for parents and children in the community and do not have visiting programs for incarcerated parents. Many case workers and foster parents are not trained about the importance of children visiting with their incarcerated parents or provided with guidance for how to arrange such visits. They may believe that until it is certain when the parent will return to the community, it is pointless to "get the child's hopes up" by having a visit. Even when caseworkers and/or foster parents want to support the parent-child relationship, visits may simply seem too challenging and time-consuming given the distance, process, perceptions of prisons and prisoners, and sometimes previous negative experiences.

Correctional Officers assigned to visiting rooms rarely receive training to address these difficult issues. Their priorities and training are in the areas of security, safety, and custody. They are trained to view visitors as potential contraband carriers, including infants. The absence of training about family dynamics, child and youth development, and the attachment needs of children may increase the tension during visits, as officers may misread a family's actions, particularly affection.

THE ATTACHMENT AND OTHER DEVELOPMENTAL NEEDS OF YOUNG CHILDREN AND TEENAGERS VISITING INCARCERATED PARENTS

The trauma of separation from a parent can cause disturbances of emotional regulation, social relationships, attachment, and communication. This may be made worse if the child has experienced other significant losses, abuse, or exposure to violence. Trauma typically slows down development in children and can interfere with all aspects of the child's functioning. Traumatized children often have trouble concentrating in school, are fearful, and may seem emotionally detached. Children who have been separated from their parent often blame themselves and may have trouble forming other relationships. Children need their parents to protect them from harm as well as to ensure a relationship through which they can learn to regulate themselves and form other relationships. Children also look to their parents to teach them values and interpret the world for them. As a result, when the parent and child are separated for long periods, this can be a far more significant loss than for an adult.

"Exposure to trauma . . . interferes with children's normal development of trust and later exploratory behaviors that lead to the development of autonomy" (Osofsky, 2004, pp. 5–6). Disrupted attachment has been linked to irritability, protest, search for missing parents, clinginess to caregivers, diminished appetite or food hoarding, disrupted sleep, and anger. Depending on a child's unique temperament, his or her response to loss can range from defiance to withdrawal. These reactions in the child may wear down the caregiver or foster parent, leading to their emotional withdrawal when the child desperately needs their attentiveness to develop trust.

Reactions to loss, and especially the unique loss of having a parent incarcerated, may significantly interfere with the child's life, although the symptoms of most children of incarcerated parents do not meet the current criteria for Post Traumatic Stress Disorder. The particular nature of children's loss of parents to incarceration—with its stigma, ambiguity, and lack of social support—is also unfortunately little studied and not well understood. Even if they are in a loving home with a relative or foster parent, many children separated from their incarcerated parent need, but do not receive, trauma treatment to support a return to normal development and reduce the likely continuing effects of disrupted attachment, especially fears of abandonment, trust issues, and problems with depression and aggression. The incarcerated parent, families, and foster families also require and often do not receive guidance in responding to children suffering loss.

The child's caregiver and the child's incarcerated parent may overlook the child's feelings because they think the child is too young to be reacting to loss. The incarcerated parent may have so much grief and guilt about not being close to the child that he/she has difficulty being sensitive and responsive to the child. They may have their own trust issues and may not really understand their child's needs. They may minimize the child's feelings because they believe this is the way to teach the child how to be tough to survive in a difficult world. They may simply not know how to respond to their child, and feeling frustrated and helpless, they may shut down.

A further complication incarcerated parents may have is responding to their child's chronological age and/or physical size, rather than understanding their child's attachment and other developmental needs. As discussed above, children with an incarcerated parent may be lagging developmentally or may take on adult roles. Children may appear to be grown, particularly those who move quickly into adult clothing, makeup, and tattoos. The parent may have unrealistic expectations for their children.

> Ms. C is a 23-year-old mother serving a three-year sentence after a drug bust in her apartment. Her mother is caring for her 2-year-old son and 4-year-old daughter, and brought them to visit in prison. This was the first time they had seen their mother in months. Her son sat quietly on his grandmother's lap sucking on a bottle, not making eye contact with his mother, and appeared not to recognize her. Her daughter clung to Ms. C, but when she started doing her daughter's hair, the little girl lashed out at her, crying and asking why she never came home. Ms. C's mother has health problems and looked more worn-out than when they saw each other in court, and Ms. C wished they had more privacy and time for her to show concern for her. At the end of the visit, Ms. C was full of regrets, feeling rejected by her son and awful when her daughter had to be pulled away from her, pleading for her to come home.

No one prepared either Ms. C or her mother for the children's responses to separation from their mother, which could have been predicted given their ages and temperament. Had Ms. C been helped to anticipate their reactions, she would have taken them less personally and been able to respond to her 2-year-old's need for reassurance and her 4-year-old's need for affection and simple explanations of her absence. Both her 2- and 4-year-old also had attachment needs that had to be met in different ways, without Ms. C feeling overwhelmed with sadness that she had to rebuild their relationships. Both children needed to play with their mother, but understandably she got distracted by the 2-year-old's regressed behavior and the 4-year-old's protests; there were no toys or books available to make play easier, nor photographs to provide the children with something concrete and lasting from their mother to take away with them. Preparation and more contact through telephone calls and letters might also have helped Ms. C express compassion for her mother without taking too much time from the visit with the children. Having a visit coach help Ms. C prepare for all of this and help their grandmother support the children would have enhanced their visits.

Teenagers also have attachment and other developmental needs that are difficult for their incarcerated parents to meet during visits. The teenager's love, anger, and uncertainty about their relationship may be hard to decipher because of typical adolescent immature thinking and identity. The teenager may say things without thinking or may minimize his or her risk-taking when the parent inquires about friends, school attendance, or substance use. The parent may worry that the teenager's clothes, hair, or piercings indicate an undesirable identity rather than experimentation. Without preparation, the incarcerated parent may express disapproval rather than support, interest, and praise for the teenager. Wanting to be parental, the parent may anger the teen by giving advice or making punitive comments, which often escalates into an argument as the teenager questions the parent's right to play this role after having abandoned him or her.

> Mr. S is a 30-year-old father who has been incarcerated for 12 years for his involvement at age 17 with a group of friends who severely injured another teenager in a fight. His son, a baby when Mr. S was arrested, is now 14 years old and has been raised by his mother and maternal grandmother. They were angry at Mr. S, had limited transportation, and did not bring his son to the prison more than 100 miles away from where they lived. Over the years, Mr. S wrote letters to his son, which were not answered, and he was not sure they lived at the same address or whether his son got the letters. Mr. S says he has grown up in prison and he is proud of his accomplishments, completing a GED program, becoming a respected leader, and serving as the chaplain's assistant for years. Mr. S has been moved to a prison closer to home, and hopes to be released in the next 18 months. Mr. S's younger

brother is now visiting more, and agreed to contact his son's mother to get permission to bring him on some visits. Mr. S gave a picture of himself and a letter for his son to his brother. He cried when he received his son's picture and a description of his son's school progress and home life.

It is commendable that Mr. S worked so hard to arrange contact with his son. But it is apparent that a visit of a 14-year-old with a father he has not seen since infancy presents many challenges. Mr. S was nervous about the visit, believing his son knew nothing about him except his offense and criticism from his mother and grandmother. He wanted the visit to be the beginning of a wonderful father-son relationship. He hoped he would get released, get a job, begin to support his son, and provide a home for him. He worried because his brother told him his son's grades had been going down, he lived in a high-crime neighborhood with a lot of gangs, and he had not been brought up in the church. He did not know what his son's feelings were about him. Mr. S needed support in separating his ambitious hopes for visits from his son's needs, to figure out how he would respond to his son's views about having a father who loves him and his anger about his father's absence, to spend most of the visit showing an interest in his son's life, and to avoid criticizing his son (or his mother) or putting too much pressure on him to move quickly into a new, close relationship. Having a visit coach help Mr. S prepare and support his son would greatly increase the likelihood of this significant first visit, and those that followed, being a mutually positive experience.

THE EFFECTIVENESS OF VISIT COACHING WITH CHILDREN AND TEENAGERS AND THEIR INCARCERATED PARENT

Visit coaching is an exciting innovation in family visits with children who are separated from their parent. The visit coach actively supports the incarcerated parent to meet their children's unique needs and capitalize on their strengths as a family.

Visit coaching includes

- helping incarcerated parents identify and prepare for their children's feelings and behaviors in visits.
- supporting incarcerated parents to take charge of their visits and plan specifically how they will meet their children's needs.

- helping incarcerated parents identify their strengths in responding to each of their children and their unique relationship despite their separation.

- assisting incarcerated parents in coping with their feelings in order to keep their guilt, sadness, anger, helplessness, and ambivalent or negative relationships with the child's caregiver from undermining positive visits with their children.

- supporting children before and after their visits with their incarcerated parents.

- facilitating co-parenting by helping incarcerated parents, relatives, foster parents, and caseworkers have a shared view of each child's needs and improving communication among these figures in a child's life.

Visit coaching is a valuable service for incarcerated parents because it is a hands-on approach applied directly to their children. Although parenting classes can also address techniques for meeting children's needs and bolster a parent's skills and understanding of their children, visit coaching is more individualized and brings a specific set of strengths-based, child-focused, parent empowerment values to its practice. The two approaches can work together, but unfortunately, parenting classes remain rare in correctional facilities.

Incarcerated parents appreciate having a visit coach provide encouragement before, after, and ideally during visits to build on what they already know. Visit coaches intentionally support parents' own approaches to meeting the unique needs of their children—rather than directing

Table 8.1

BENEFITS OF VISIT COACHING IN JAILS & PRISONS

→ Visit coaching is based on a belief that incarcerated parents can overcome sadness, guilt, and other obstacles to make visits happy for their children.
→ Visit coaching is an important way to reduce the effects of loss and harm of separation on children.
→ Visit coaching encourages the family's cultural preferences in commemorating milestones and other traditions.
→ Through visit coaching, incarcerated parents practice the lifelong habit of asking "What does my child need?" and flexibly adjusting their parenting to meet those needs.

parenting, the coaching is culturally sensitive and builds on the incarcerated parent's strengths. A parent may have changed during the period of incarceration and become more able to appreciate his or her children's needs. Visit coaching is an opportunity for a parent to enlarge their repertoire of enjoyable ways to interact with their children. Visit coaches help incarcerated parents make peace with things they cannot change about their separation from their children so they can have fulfilling visits with them.

Empowering Incarcerated Parents to Plan Their Visits Builds on Their Strengths

Although the regulations of the prison or jail and the unchangeable reality of separation are the framework for visits, it is important for incarcerated parents to view the visit as an experience they can take charge of. The visit coach guides the parent while appreciating the unique ways parents show love for their children. Parents are encouraged to make visits a celebration of the family by doing things they enjoy (both activities from the past and new ones the child is interested in), as well as taking pictures, making a family scrapbook, continuing or creating family rituals, and telling family stories.

Parents are helped to manage competition between the children for the parent's attention in visits. Coaches encourage parents to spend a little special individual time with each child during every visit. Each child has unique needs, and coaches help parents stand in each child's shoes and not take their children's negative behavior personally. By confirming that meeting their children's needs can be frustrating and exhausting, the visit coach gives the parent valuable support.

Visit Coaching to Respond to Children's Reactions

Separation from their incarcerated parents causes a range of feelings and behaviors in children. It is not surprising that many incarcerated parents comment on how different the children seem from when they last saw them. Children who are separated from their parents may be irritable, withdrawn, aggressive, sad, clingy, and emotionally demanding; some show fearfulness and anxiety and have difficulty accepting comforting; others may seek attention and warmth from just about anyone. These behaviors can occur during visits and/or in the child's home and at school. A child's living situation and the degree of support they receive regarding their parent's incarceration significantly impacts a child's response to the separation.

It is normal for a child separated from a parent to have reactions to visits, which are usually not a sign that the visit is harmful or that the prison/jail setting was too upsetting for the child. Incarcerated parents, relatives, foster parents, and caseworkers require support to respond lovingly to children's varied reactions to visits, including being (a) happy and relieved to see his/her incarcerated parent; (b) confused, especially about why the parent has been gone and cannot come home, and sometimes about having "two mommies" or "two daddies;" (c) sad, angry, and feeling out-of-control about being separated from his or her incarcerated parent; (d) guilty that the separation is his or her fault; and (e) worried about whether his or her incarcerated parent is okay. Most children (including older children and teenagers) do not put these feelings into words; instead, their behaviors reflect their feelings. Regression (being babyish, whiney, or scared), numbing feelings, sadness, irritability, overactivity, physical pains, or problems falling asleep are common prior to, during, and following visits. It is not easy to care for a grieving or protesting child during visits. If the child continues to be aggressive or withdrawn, the frustrated parent must be supported not to get overwhelmed by guilt or a sense of powerlessness.

Coaching can relieve children from the painful pressures of choosing loyalties by helping the incarcerated parent and caregiver or foster parent encourage the child to be satisfied in the family he or she lives with while also maintaining a strong relationship with the parent from whom he or she is separated. Without being aware of it, well-intentioned family members and foster parents can contribute to the child's confusion about who to love, who is better, and what to do with negative feelings toward the incarcerated parent, relative, and/or foster parent. It is important not only for the relative or foster parent and incarcerated parent to communicate but for the child to see them interact in a friendly, collaborative way. When visit coaches and incarcerated parents include caregivers or foster parents and caseworkers in exchanges about the children's needs (via telephone and/or letter), everyone has a shared understanding of a child's difficult behaviors and can use the same approaches in managing them. These other adults can then also look for opportunities outside of and in between visits to say positive things about the parent that can affirm the child's positive sense of self.

Supporting Incarcerated Parents to Have a Positive Attitude About Visiting

Visit coaching helps incarcerated parents not get discouraged about how much active parenting time they are missing. They often worry they are losing their children, and feel helpless and hopeless. When they visit with their children, parents may be overwhelmed by their mixed feelings of pleasure, grief, awkwardness, and defensiveness. Separating from their child at the end of the visit is painful. Even though they enjoy their children, visits make most parents feel sad, inadequate, and powerless. Coaches help make the pain of visits tolerable for incarcerated parents so they can remain focused on their children's needs.

Visits may flood parents with anger, sadness, and guilt about separation from their children. The parent benefits from the visit coach's validation of their complicated feelings about visits. But the visit coach's primary goal is to help the parent stand in the child's shoes. Coaches support them to put their own reactions aside in order to concentrate on meeting their child's needs during the visit.

Incarcerated parents are often embarrassed to greet their children wearing prison garb. They are uncomfortable being ordered around by correctional staff in front of their children and they worry about how their children are treated both as they enter the facility and during the visit. It is a very common occurrence to have children witness their incarcerated parent (and sometimes both parents) be chastised in front them by a correctional officer. Coaches guide the incarcerated parent in addressing their concerns, which helps them relax and enables them to concentrate on their children's needs rather than their own worries.

Supporting Incarcerated Parents to Plan Each Visit Around Their Children's Needs

The needs of very young children are different from the needs of elementary school children and teenagers. The needs of children with a strong attachment to their incarcerated parent are different from those without it. Within developmental stages, variations in temperament and coping strategies make every child unique. Although it might be tempting to skip the formal step of planning each visit around the specific needs of each child, it is the key to helping incarcerated parents have positive visits. Visit coaches support parents in attuning to children by emphasizing that reciprocal communication with children builds attachment. Actively anticipating what specifically it would take to make each child happy during the visit may be difficult for incarcerated parents to do on their own. The lasting benefit of visit coaching is the parent saying to himself or herself as the child develops, often years after the initial separation, "What does my child need?"

With teenagers, visit coaches can help incarcerated parents build an enduring positive relationship. Teens are more likely to become successful, independent adults if they are helped to have stable connections. The initial goals of visit coaching with teenagers and their incarcerated parents are to help them enjoy something together and to improve their communication. Most teenagers need praise and positive regard from their parent more than anything else. The coach helps the incarcerated parent appreciate that it is important for the teenager not to feel rejected by the parent's decisions, not to blame himself or herself for the past, and to feel heard and listened to. Teens need to be able to feel safe in expressing their anger, fears, thoughts, dreams, and desires. Incarcerated parents are supported to understand that teenagers struggle with their need to have independence from their family while still feeling loved, accepted, and connected to their parent.

Supporting Children Before and After Their Visits with Their Incarcerated Parents

Incarcerated parents and caregivers are guided by the visit coach in how to help children with their reactions to visits. The incarcerated parent is helped to write letters and have telephone calls that address the child's needs. Caregivers and foster parents are helped to support the child in writing or dictating letters or responding in telephone calls.

Visit coaches can also talk with children individually and/or convene support groups for children of incarcerated parents. Peer support groups where children learn that they are not the only child with an incarcerated parent and receive support for not feeling stigmatized by their parent's situation are important benefits of such groups. There are several examples nationally of such groups and their demonstrated positive effects on children, including the Girls Scouts Behind Bars program (operated in several states), Peanut Butter and Jelly Services' school-based support group (in Albuquerque, New Mexico), and the Osborne Association's Family Ties Program in New York (for more information, see their websites: www.girlscouts.org/program; www.pbjfamilyservices .org; and www.osborneny.org).

Supporting Positive Communication Among Incarcerated Parents, Caregivers, Foster Parents, and Caseworkers

Incarcerated parents, caregivers, and foster parents are guided by the visit coach to develop a shared view of each child's needs and recognize how important it is for them to co-parent successfully. The incarcerated parent is helped to write letters and have telephone conversations with caregivers to achieve this goal.

Depending on distances, visit coaches can also talk with caregivers and foster parents individually and/or convene support groups. The shared experience of a group trip to and from a prison or jail, and facilitated discussions during the ride, can help caregivers and foster parents support the relationship between the child and incarcerated parent. Visit coaches can convene conference calls between incarcerated parents and caregivers to discuss children's needs.

Visit coaching can also help the parent and child prepare for return to the community. Although release may be the moment all have been waiting for, it is also a very stressful time for children, parents, and caregivers. Parole hearings in particular are highly stressful for all, and if parole is denied, disappointment, anger, and sadness can affect visits, telephone calls, and letter writing. Helping parents, children, and their caregivers handle these emotions, as well as having realistic expectations when parents do return can happen through groups as well as during visits before release.

The Effectiveness of Family Centers for Visiting in Jails and Prisons

Family centers embody similar values to visit coaching, aiming to provide a comfortable and child-friendly environment for children and families, which strengthens their relationships during incarceration. A number of correctional facilities across the country offer child-friendly opportunities for children to visit with their incarcerated parent in "children's" or "family" centers. One of the oldest and most well-established of these efforts are the Osborne Association Family Centers in five medium and maximum security correctional facilities for men in New York State. Osborne's family centers vary slightly in size and physical design based on available space and the size of the population at each of the facilities. However, all centers are rooms either inside or adjacent to the visiting halls at the facilities. When walls are built to section off the center they are made out of plexiglass so security staff can monitor interactions in the center while remaining outside. Centers are outfitted with colorful decorations, often painted murals and posters that create a warm, inviting space for children of all ages. Specially shaped tables and different size plastic chairs along with books, toys, arts and crafts, and games are found in all centers. Family centers are open on weekends and holidays during the same hours the visiting halls are open and are staffed by professional staff and incarcerated staff who are graduates of Osborne's parenting program. The family centers are available to children under age 18, and activities are designed to encourage the strengthening of parent-child bonds, improve communications, and provide a forum for parents to help their children build skills from reading and math to creativity and the ability to cooperate and share.

Osborne Family Centers where children and their parents use the child-friendly visiting environment as an opportunity to strengthen their relationships is the most common model for these efforts, but other variations exist. One of these is the Project REACHH (Re-energizing Attachment, Communication, Health, and Happiness) program at the Shelby County Division of Corrections in Memphis, TN. The Project REACHH visiting program takes place on weekday evenings when regular visiting sessions are closed. Children are scheduled to come for specific visiting times. Another key difference between the Osborne Family Center approach and the Project REACHH model is that at Project REACHH visiting sessions only the children and their fathers are allowed to visit together. Caregivers stay in another room where they can talk to each other, receive informative presentations about resources and programs for their children, or just watch TV or read a magazine. The rationale behind the Project REACHH program design is that it affords an opportunity for the incarcerated parent to focus solely on their children and on honing their parenting skills. A program like Project REACHH works well in Memphis because almost everyone incarcerated at the facility comes from the local area, making it possible for caregivers to travel the (on average) less than 30-minute trip during the week to bring their children to see their fathers and still be willing to come out to a visit themselves at another time during the week.

The remarkable children's center at the Bedford Hills Correctional Facility in New York, set up by Sister Elaine Roulet and community volunteers and largely run by incarcerated mothers, has numerous child-friendly programs, funded by the Department of Corrections and administered by Catholic Charities (this noteworthy model for prison visiting is not an Osborne Family Center). The well-equipped playroom is open every day of the year for visits. The children's center also has a summer camp where children spend each day with their mother and stay overnight in nearby volunteer host families. Special buses and volunteers provide transportation for the children, many of whom live an hour or more from the facility. The center also offers a Child Development Associate certificate for incarcerated women, involving course work and supervised work with children in the daycare center; parenting classes and a mother's support group have also been popular in the center.

IMPLEMENTING VISIT COACHING AND FAMILY CENTERS IN JAILS AND PRISONS

Visit Coaching

Implementing visit coaching has the following key components:

- Training for visit coaches in how to
  1 meet individually and in groups with incarcerated parents to help them identify their children's needs and how to meet them during the visit.
  2 meet individually and in groups with incarcerated parents to prepare them for their child's reactions during visits.
  3 support incarcerated parents immediately before, during, and after the visit to meet their children's needs and keep their own feelings from interfering with the visit; visit coaches must be prepared to resist directing visits or telling parents how to parent.
  4 help children prepare for the visit and debrief with them after the visit to help them process their emotions.
  5 support positive communication among incarcerated parents, caregivers, and foster parents and help relatives and foster parents respond to the children's needs before and after visits (including support for letter writing and telephone calls).
- Arranging for toys, books, art supplies, photo albums, a camera, children's music CDs, a portable CD player, snacks, and supplies for birthday parties to be accessible during coached visits in prisons or jails.

- Ongoing supervision for visit coaches.
- Discussions with corrections.

Visit coaches can be trained volunteers as well as a range of paid staff from a variety of organizations.

Ideally, visit coaching is implemented in partnership with a parenting class for incarcerated parents and a child development class or training for correctional officers, focusing on visiting. If these are not available, visit coaches could offer to launch or advise these efforts. Meetings with correctional administrators are important to discuss how visit coaching can reduce the negative impact of incarceration on children and help children and incarcerated parents during visits. Many of the rules that cause a negative visiting experience may never have been viewed from a child's perspective and once seen from the child's shoes, can be changed to implement visit coaching. Visit coaching will improve the visiting room for officers, who are often frustrated by restless or frustrated children running around, yanking at vending machines, or playing at the water fountain, and by parents who may appear passive or authoritarian. The visiting environment, misunderstanding of children's and parent's feelings underneath these behaviors, and the lack of preparation for incarcerated parents, children, caretakers, and correctional officers contribute to visit problems. When toys, books, or games for the children and visit coaching can be provided to the parent, combined with training for the officers, everyone is more satisfied and the child's needs are supported. Such supportive visits can also reduce disciplinary incidents within correctional settings as parents leave visits more satisfied and less frustrated.

Family Centers

Although there are different models of family centers within jails and prisons, core components of effective centers include

- Collaboration between a community or faith-based organization and corrections. When corrections supports child-friendly visiting in principle, the next step is to determine the program design. To do this, the population to be served must be identified and facility capacities must be assessed. The largest cost associated with family centers are the initial set-up expenses, which may include construction, refurbishing, and equipment; after this initial expenditure, family centers are relatively cost-effective to run, particularly when donations are solicited and local groups (churches, businesses, other) take an interest in supporting visiting children.

■ Decisions about who operates the family center will determine staff costs. Programs may be staffed by professionals with a background in social work, education, counseling, recreation, or a related field, volunteers, incarcerated individuals (as is done in New York), and/or college interns (as is done in Memphis) or graduate students. In all instances, comprehensive training, including visit coaching training, should be provided for anyone working in the family center. An offer should be made to provide parenting classes for incarcerated parents at the family center and to provide training for correctional staff on child development and visiting.

When partnerships with corrections support visit coaching and family centers, visiting enhances children's well-being. This does not mean—and this is a frequently expressed concern—that children will view prison or jail as a "nice place" and want to grow up and go there. Even in the most supportive visiting situations, children are aware of the restrictions and punitive aspects of incarceration. Even when young children do not want to leave or say they want to stay with their parent at the end of a visit, it is their parent they do not want to leave, not the prison setting.

CHAPTER SUMMARY

Visits strengthen the attachment between children and their incarcerated parent and reduce the child's worries. Visits help teenagers resolve anger and disappointment toward their incarcerated parent. However, distance, transportation challenges and cost, facility rules, and concerns of caretakers are obstacles to positive visits between children and their incarcerated parents. In addition, incarcerated parents and children's caretakers may not fully appreciate the impact of separation on children and teenagers, resulting in inadequate preparation for visits in jails and prisons. Visit coaching is designed to build on incarcerated parents' strengths, help them identify their children's feelings, and support them to plan how they will meet their children's needs. Visit coaching assists incarcerated parents in coping with their feelings in order to keep their guilt, sadness, anger, helplessness, and ambivalent or negative relationships with the child's caregiver from undermining positive visits with their children. Visit coaching also supports children before and after their visits with their incarcerated parents and facilitates co-parenting by helping incarcerated parents, relatives, foster parents, and caseworkers have a shared view of each child's needs and improving communication among them. Family centers in jails and prisons provide an inviting space for children of all age with books, toys, arts and crafts, and games. Family centers encourage the strengthening of parent-child bonds, improve communication, and support incarcerated parents in actively parenting their children.

Despite their tragically large numbers, children of incarcerated parents remain largely invisible. A casualty of this invisibility is that their relationship with their incarcerated parent does not get supported and children suffer as a result. Visit coaching offers a unique opportunity to support this relationship and in doing so to promote the well-being of children and their healthy futures. Family centers similarly support these outcomes, ensuring that when the parent and children come together on a visit, they do so in a comfortable, developmentally-sound, sensitive environment with trained staff. Together, these child-centered, parent empowerment interventions—if replicated across the country—could go a long way toward safeguarding the futures of children of incarcerated parents.

ENDNOTES

1. In 2000 while working at the Administration for Children's Services (ACS, New York City's child welfare agency), Tanya Krupat launched CHIPP (Children of Incarcerated Parents Program) to provide visits for children in foster care and their parents in jails and prisons in the most child-friendly visiting spaces possible. Ms. Krupat reached out to Marty Beyer, who ACS then hired to provide technical assistance and train staff in more than 25 private foster care agencies in New York City and CHIPP in visit coaching, using her manual published by ACS. Although still lacking research about its effectiveness, visit coaching has been recognized as a promising practice and is being implemented nationally. Randi Blumenthal-Guigui coordinated Memphis Children Locked Out, a community-wide initiative designed to assess and address the needs of Memphis-area children with a parent in prison. Ms. Guigui developed Project REACHH (Re-energizing Attachment, Communication, Health, and Happiness), an innovative visiting program for children in Memphis, Tennessee, whose parents were

incarcerated. Ms. Guigui was also a founding member of the Alliance for Tennessee's Children of Prisoners. Ms. Guigui and Ms. Krupat work at Osborne Association, a New York City-based nonprofit founded in 1931 with a 20-year history of providing innovative prison- and jail-based services to families, including in-prison family centers, parenting education programs, healthy relationships courses, and a visit program that reconnects incarcerated fathers with their children, as well as community services for individuals reentering the community and for their children and families. Osborne coordinates the New York Initiative for Children of Incarcerated Parents to raise awareness about and reform policies and practices that impact the over 200,000 children in NY state whose parents are incarcerated. Ms. Krupat, Ms. Guigui, and Dr. Beyer are collaborating on Osborne's Therapeutic Visit Coaching demonstration project.

2. There is no genetic propensity toward incarceration or criminal involvement, and the statistic often cited that children of incarcerated parents are 5–6 times more likely to become involved in the criminal justice system has been refuted and has no basis in research (Hairston, 2007).
3. Although used interchangeably, jail and prison are distinct entities: a jail holds people charged but not convicted, as well as those with sentences usually of one year or less; a prison holds those convicted and serving longer sentences.
4. The term "caregivers" refers throughout to relatives and non-relatives taking care of children.
5. Because only a limited number of visitors may come at one time, facilities with small visiting rooms and large populations have restricted visit schedules; individuals previously released from prison or those who work in prison may not be allowed to visit or require special permission that is difficult to get.

REFERENCES

Arditti, J. A. (2005). Families and incarceration: An ecological approach. *Families in Society*, 86, 251–258.

Bernstein, N. (2005). *All Alone in the World: Children of the Incarcerated*. New York: New Press.

Beyer, M. (1999). Parent-child visits as an opportunity for change. National Resource Center for Family Centered Practice, *Prevention Report* #1.

Beyer, M. (2004). *Visit Coaching*. New York: ACS.

Beyer, M. (2008). Visit Coaching: Building on Family Strengths to Meet Children's Needs. *Juvenile and Family Court Journal*, 59, 1, 47–60.

Correctional Association Report (2008), Women in Prison Project. www.correctionalassociation.com

Davis, I., Landsverk, J., Newton, R., & Ganger, W. (1996). Parental visiting and foster care reunification. *Children and Youth Services Review*, 18(4/5), 363–382.

Ellis, E. (undated), *Open Letter*. NuLeadership Academy, Medgar Evers College, Brooklyn, New York. *Reconnecting Families* (1996) and *Teaching Family Reunification* (1994). Washington DC: The Child Welfare League of America.

Felitti, V. J. et. al., Relationship of Childhood Abuse and Household Dysfunction to Many of the Leading Causes of Death in Adults: The Adverse Childhood Experiences (ACE) Study. *American Journal of Medicine*, May 1998: 14(4): 245–58.

Haight, W., Kagle, J., & Black, J. (2003). Understanding and supporting parent-child relationships during foster care visits: Attachment theory and research. *Social Work*, 48(2), 195–207.

Haight, W., Mangelsdorf, S., Black, J., Szewczyk, M., Schoppe, S., Gorgio, G., Madrigal, M. & Tata, L. (2005). Enhancing Parent-Child Interaction during Foster Care Visits. *Child Welfare*, July/August.

Hairston, C. F. (2007), *Focus on Children with Incarcerated Parents: An Overview of the Research Literature.* Annie E Casey Foundation.

Hairston, C. F. (2003). Prisoners and Their Families: Parenting Issues During Incarceration. In Travis, J. & Waul, M. (Eds.). *Prisoners Once Removed.* Washington DC: Urban Institute Press.

Hess, P., Mintun, G., Moelhman, A., & Pitts, G. (1992) The Family Connection Center: An innovative visiting program. *Child Welfare*, 71(1), 77–88.

Hess, P. & Proch, K. (1993). Visiting: The heart of reunification. In B. Pine, R. Warsh, and A. Maluccio, (Eds.), *Together again: Family reunification in foster care* (pp. 119–139). Washington DC: Child Welfare League of America.

Kovalesky, A. (2001). Factors affecting mother-child visiting identified by women with histories of substance abuse and child custody loss. *Child Welfare*, 80(6), 749–768.

Kowitz-Margolies, J. & Kraft-Stolar, T. (2005) *When 'Free' Means Losing Your Mother: The Collision of Child Welfare and the Incarceration of Women in New York State.* Unpublished report. Correctional Association of New York, New York.

Krupat, T. (2007). Taking "the Village" Seriously: The Importance of Attachment, Continuity, and Expanded Family Networks for Children and Families in the Child Welfare System. Unpublished manuscript.

The Osborne Association (1994), *How Can I Help?* Booklet series.

Osofsky, J. (2004). *Young Children and Trauma.* New York: Guilford.

Parke, R. D. & Clarke-Stewart, K. A. (2003). The Effects of Incarceration on Children: Perspectives, Promises, and Policies. In Travis, J. & Waul, M. (Eds.), *Prisoners Once Removed.* Washington DC: The Urban Institute Press.

Pavao, J., St. John, M., Cannole, R., Fischer, T., Maluccio, A., & Peining, S. (2007). Sibling Kinnections: A Clinical Visitation Program. *Child Welfare.*

Phillips, S. & Gleeson, J. (2007), *Children, Families and the Criminal Justice System Research Brief,* University of Chicago.

San Francisco Partnership for Incarcerated Parents (October, 2003). *Children of Incarcerated Parents: A Bill of Rights.* Copies available through Friends Outside: (209) 938–0727.

Schirmer, S., Nellis, A., & Mauer, M., (February 2009), *Incarcerated Parents and Their Children: Trends 1991–2007.* The Sentencing Project.

Williams, M. with M. Beyer, "Exploring Options for Better Visiting," *Children's Voice,* Child Welfare League of America, Jan/Feb 2009.

ADDITIONAL RESOURCES

Meek, R. (2007). Parenting education for young fathers in prison. *Child & Family Social Work*, 12(3), 239–247.

Prinsloo, C. (2007). Strengthening the father-child bond: Using groups to improve the fatherhood skills of incarcerated fathers. *Groupwork, 17(3)*, 25–42.

Sandifer, J. L. (2008). Evaluating the efficacy of a parenting program for incarcerated mothers. *The Prison Journal, 88(3)*, 423–445.

Tuerk, E. H. & Loper, A. B. (2006). Contact Between Incarcerated Mothers and Their Children: Assessing Parenting Stress. *Journal of Offender Rehabilitation.43(1)*, 23–43.

Current and Future Directions

PART V

9

Child Welfare Legislation and Policies: Foster Children with a Parent in Prison

ADELA BECKERMAN

INTRODUCTION

The number of children of incarcerated parents (CIP) in foster care almost doubled between 1985 and 2000, from 280,000 to 537,000 (Johnson & Waldfogel, 2002, Swann & Sylvester, 2006). About one third (31%) of this increase has been attributed to growth in the population of incarcerated women alone (Swann & Sylvester, 2006). These children enter foster care through a number of routes (Wright & Seymour, 2000). Some enter foster care prior to their parent's incarceration, following documentation of parental abuse or neglect. Others are placed in foster care following a parent's incarceration or when a relative or friend who has been serving as the child's caretaker during a parent's incarceration can no longer play that role.

Between 4.5% and 6% of the children living in foster care are in care because of a parent's incarceration (Allard & Lu, 2006). This chapter discusses child welfare legislation and policies that impact these CIP and describes the findings of a recent study of foster care caseworkers who manage such cases. These caseworkers, whose practice is framed by child welfare legislation, play pivotal roles in the lives of these CIP and their families. Despite this, researchers have argued that child welfare policies are relativity silent about the challenges caseworkers face in implementing child welfare legislation in such cases (Allard & Lu, 2006; Halperin & Harris, 2004). This chapter will examine the policies that guide foster care case management in CIP cases and a recent study that examined the challenges case managers face in completing their legislatively mandated responsibilities and their perspective regarding working with CIP.

LEGISLATION AND POLICIES

The Adoption Assistance and Child Welfare Act of 1980 (AACWA) (P.L. 96–272) laid much of the groundwork for current child welfare practice. AACWA was passed, in part, as a response to reports of "foster care drift," wherein children lived "in limbo," in unplanned long-term foster care and were often moved from one foster home to another (Gelles, 1998). This law mandated that "reasonable efforts" be made to prevent foster care placements when possible, as well as to reduce the length of placements when they do occur. The intended short-term nature of foster care was emphasized. Caseworkers were to develop case plans for children at risk of being removed from their home, and for children who had been removed from their parental homes within six months of the child's removal. These case plans indicate the complex needs of the children involved, and recommend appropriate intervention services. The plans also delineate tasks that parents must accomplish to rectify identified problems such as a mental health evaluation, completion of substance abuse treatment, a parenting class, and/or an anger management class and obtaining secure employment and safe housing. Permanency planning was expected as a means of arranging permanent living situations for children that offer security, continuity, and longevity. Court or administrative reviews of the progress made in each case toward establishing permanence through parent-child reunification or alternative accommodations, such as adoption, were mandated when a child had been in care for six months. A permanency hearing was mandated after 18 months.

Parent-child reunification is encouraged when there is evidence of a parent's capacity to provide a suitable living situation for their child and when the parent makes timely progress toward rectifying the problems that prompted their child's placement. Parent contact with their child and participation in the case planning and court review processes are noteworthy as deterrents to accusations of disinterest or abandonment and dilute efforts to initiate termination of parental rights (TPR) proceedings. In cases involving an incarcerated parent, permanency planning calls for an assessment of the nature and quality of the parent-child relationship and caretaking prior to the parent's incarceration, and the potential for appropriate parental caretaking after the period of incarceration (Beckerman, 1998; O'Donnell, 1999). Although a parent's incarceration may not reflect a weak relationship with their child, disinterest, or an inability to function as a capable parent, there is concern that parent-child bonds might be weakened by family and community disapproval of the parent's criminal activities, barriers to parent-child contact, and the length of the parent's incarceration (Hairston, 1998; Nurse, 2002; Western & McLanahan, 2007).

The 1997 passage of The Adoption and Safe Families Act (ASFA) (P.L. 105–89) provides guidelines for current child welfare practice. As in AACWA, ASFA authorizes funding for family preservation programs and promotes reasonable efforts to prevent a child's removal from their parental home. Reasonable efforts are also expected to reunify foster children with their parents, but contrary to past policies, specific findings that such efforts are made are not required. ASFA indicates a primary concern that the children receive "safe and proper care." Criteria that define when efforts for family preservation or family reunification are expected, and when courts are to make permanency decisions based on safety consideration are provided.

ASFA mandates a shorter timeline than AACWA to expedite the movement of foster children into permanent living situations. Court reviews are mandated after six months of out-of-home care. Permanency hearings are mandated after 12 months of a child's placement. TPR proceedings must be initiated when a child has been in care for 15 out of 22 months or when a court has determined that a child is an "abandoned infant." TPR proceedings are also expected when a parent will be absent from a child's life through much of their childhood, except when the child is being cared for by a relative, when a determination has been made that the child welfare agency involved did not provide services necessary for the child's safe return to their family, or when there is a "compelling reason" that termination is not in the child's best interests.

Reflecting the legislation's emphasis on expediting permanency, ASFA encourages the use of concurrent planning in which planning for parent-child reunification and alternate permanent living situations, such as adoption or guardianship with relatives, occur simultaneously. Adults who qualify as permanent guardians or adoptive parents are identified and approved in the event reunification is determined inadvisable or unlikely. ASFA offers financial incentives to states, local communities, and courts for increasing the number of adoptions. States are required to use cross-jurisdictional resources for adoptive and permanency placements. Federal assistance is denied when the placement of a child for adoption outside a state's jurisdiction is impeded (Westat, 2001).

Placement in a foster home with foster parents interested in adoption or in a home with relatives or a close family interested in permanent guardianship or adoption is encouraged. These are viewed as a means of providing both short-term temporary caretaking and a venue for long-term permanency. Although ASFA expects that relative foster parents meet licensing standards established for non-relative caretakers, states can, on a case-by-case basis, waive such standards. The assumption of legal custody of foster children by relatives is also viewed as a means of reducing foster care and administrative costs (Westat, 2001).

Such arrangements are also seen as a means of circumventing the trauma that accompanies placement with a stranger and of reinforcing a child's sense of identity as they remain connected with their family history and culture. It is also noteworthy that when children are in the care of relatives their parents may be exempted from mandates to terminate their parental rights (Westat, 2001).

Other recent legislation also encourages relative care. The 1996 Personal Responsibility and Work Opportunity Reconciliation Act (P.L. 104–93) indicates that when children are being placed in foster care, preference should be given to relatives who meet state standards for such care. The Fostering Connections to Success and Increasing Adoptions Act of 2008 (P.L. 11–351) further encourages relative care by mandating that relatives be informed within 30 days of a child's removal from their parental home and by offering financial assistance to relatives who pursue guardianship (Allen, DeVooght, & Geen, 2008). Studies have indicated, however, that relatives may resist the assumption of caretaking and becoming permanent guardians or adoptive parents because of the costs involved and distaste for having child welfare agencies involved in their lives. In response to these concerns, many states have simplified the procedures for securing kinship assistance, and have implemented guardianship programs for relatives.

ASFA and its expectation for concurrent planning has been described as an initiative that promises to minimize the negative impact of separation and loss on foster children by reducing the length of time children are in placement, the number of times children move from home to home, and the number of relationship disruptions they experience (Ott,1998). Tartara (1993) found that although most children in out-of-home care were reunified with their families within two years of their placement, as many as 25% of the children lingered in care without realistic plans for family reunification or adoption. George, Wulczyn, and Harden (1994) reported that children placed in care at a young age tend to remain in care longer and live in multiple homes during their years in care. Concurrent planning is seen as giving priority to children's developmental need for permanency and reducing the likelihood of children lingering in foster care. The relatively prompt securing of a permanent living situation acknowledges "theories about the nature of a child's sense of time," children's need for "secure attachment and bonding," and "the impact of separation, loss, and grief on child development."

Historically, caseworkers have been taught to plan in a relatively sequential fashion, initially working with parents toward reunification with their child and initiating efforts to pursue TPR and adoption or other permanency options when reunification as an option has been ruled out (Ott, 1998; Schene, 2001). This approach has been criticized because with this passage of time, parents "become alienated from their child and the case-planning process" and children's "length of stay in foster care has been prolonged unnecessarily" (Ott, 1998, p. 1). In contrast, concurrent planning calls for educating the network of children's relatives and family friends early in the case-planning process about the role they can play as a source of continuity and permanency in these children's lives. Interested and capable parties can be identified earlier in order to facilitate timely movement toward permanency (Katz, Spoonemore, & Robinson, 1994; Westat, 2001).

At the same time, ASFA has been criticized as moving "away from the promotion of aggressive family reunification efforts and attempts to alter permanency planning priorities in a way that is consistent with an emphasis on child safety" (Herring, 2000, p. 330). ASFA has been described as punitive to parents who must address complex problems in an unrealistically short amount of time (Lee, Genty, & Laver, 2005). ASFA's mandated timeframe for moving to TPR has also been criticized as falsely assuming that there are adoptive homes available for the children involved and thus creating "a new version of being in limbo" for children who might prefer being in long-term foster care (Westat, 2001).

Foster care cases involving CIP present unique challenges. Case planning includes an assessment of the extent and quality of parents' caretaking, the role of support systems prior to and during their incarceration, as well as the feasibility of parents' caretaking after their release from prison. Case plans specify goals such as post-incarceration family reunification, and alternatives such as permanent guardianship with a relative and initiation of TPR proceedings.

There is an inherent tension between the legislatively mandated time line for permanency decisions and the ability of an incarcerated parent to achieve family reunification. Prison sentences often exceed the timeline imposed by ASFA for initiating TPR proceedings if a child is in non-kinship care, and for achieving parent-child reunification (Allard & Lu, 2006; Halperin & Harris, 2004). The time served in a federal prison for drug offenses has, for example, increased in the past two decades, from an average of 30 months to 66 months (Scalia, 2001). In part, this trend reflects the passage of the 1986 Anti-Drug Abuse Act (P.L. 99–570), which imposed lengthy mandatory minimum sentences for drug-related offenses that disproportionately impact women (Johnson & Waldfogel, 2002).

Lee, Genty, and Laver (2005) conducted a study that examined the likelihood of increased instances of TPR of incarcerated parents as a result of ASFA's mandated timelines and the lengthening of prison sentences. Interest in the study was in part prompted by concern that federal courts do not "ordinarily permit 'family ties' as an appropriate reason to lower a sentence" and because increasing numbers of nonviolent drug offenders who in the past would have been on probation or in a community correctional facility were sentenced to lengthy periods of incarceration and faced the possibility of TPR. The study involved interviews with judges, attorneys, and child welfare agency representatives. These respondents expressed concern that "ASFA affects children of incarcerated parents differently than other children" (p. 8). They noted the likelihood that in CIP cases, permanency planning might become synonymous with adoption and reunification might become "the exception" because the problems present are often too challenging to address within the legislatively mandated timeframes.

Lee, Genty, and Laver (2005) also examined state laws and court record files and found that 36 states had TPR statutes that specified parental incarceration as a factor; 25 of these states identified the length of incarceration as a major factor. The study also found that although in the five years prior to the passage of ASFA, the number of cases filed for TPR that involved an incarcerated parent increased from 169 to 218. During the five years following passage of ASFA, the number of such proceedings increased from 260 to 909.

CASEWORKERS' DECISION MAKING

A recent study was conducted by this writer to gain insight into the factors case managers take into consideration during case planning with

CIP, the extent to which case managers receive training for working with CIP cases, and the amount of contact that imprisoned parents have with their children and case managers. The study examined how case managers approach the tensions posed by child welfare policies and a parent's incarceration. The interviews questioned case managers about their preparation for working with CIP cases, the characteristics of the CIP and their parents in their caseload, and the factors taken into consideration during case planning.

The study employed a sample of convenience. Email and phone contact was made with child welfare agencies across Florida inviting case manager participation. The foster care system in Florida has been privatized and the 31 persons who agreed to participate were housed in six private nonprofit agencies in different parts of the state. These case managers had been working in their current agency setting for between three and 66 months, and were managing caseloads that included between 7 and 36 children. At the time of the interview, the respondents were responsible for a total of 90 CIP, with each case manager responsible for between one and eight CIP cases.

The case managers' primary responsibilities included making recommendations of where children should be placed, monitoring the safety of children in care, and monitoring case plans. Case managers also assisted with referrals and transportation for children for services such as dental and medical care and therapy, and for family members for substance abuse treatment and therapy, as well as monitoring the use of such services. They attended court hearings, prepared court documents, and served as advocates in the courtroom. Home visits were reportedly conducted at least once a month but could be weekly if needed, depending on the presence of risk factors. Examples of other responsibilities were participating in staff meetings about cases, maintaining communication with other agencies, visiting with parents, performing home studies, supervising sibling visits and parent-child visits, attending school meetings as needed, as well as preparing children for adoption and working with pre-adoptive families.

Most of the study participants interviewed were women (84%). About half (55%) of the participants were White, 39% were Black, and 7% were biracial or multiracial. Of the respondents, 20% indicated their ethnic background – 10% were Hispanic and 10% were Caribbean. All of the respondents had a bachelor's degree, which had been completed since 2000 (74%) or during the 1980s (6%) or 1990s (20%). Most respondents had majored in psychology or human services (32%), criminal justice or criminology (18%), or social work (13%). Some respondents indicated that they had completed an internship or fieldwork in child welfare (22%) or corrections (19%).

All case managers reported that they engage in concurrent permanency planning, were mindful of the timeline to be followed regarding TPR, and recognized the emphasis placed on arranging relative care and facilitating permanency goals. They were aware of agency manuals regarding child welfare policies and of attorneys who worked with their agencies when there was ambiguity. When asked whether they had received training in how to manage CIP foster care cases, two respondents (7%) said there had been formal training in their current agency setting and three (10%) indicated receiving training in an agency in which they had previously been employed. They reported that this training had been beneficial with one respondent noting that, "You're able to learn what needs to be done, and learn about topics like 'giving parents services.'" Most respondents described receiving informal training that was described as "really OJT [on-the-job-training]," noting that, "when a case comes up like this" they consult with a coworker or supervisor, or "discuss it when we have our unit meeting." The remaining case managers indicated that when they have a question about a CIP case they asked supervisors and colleagues about their experiences managing such cases.

CIP and Their Parents

The average age of the 90 CIP described by the case managers was 7, with an age range from less than 1 year to 17. Most of the children were girls (56%). They were racially diverse, with 38% of the children being White, 40% Black, and 22% biracial/multiracial. Of the multiracial children, 18% were Hispanic, 3% were Caribbean, and one was Native American. All but one of the children was born in the U.S. This child, born in Cuba, was a citizen.

Most of the CIP had a father (69%) or mother (18%) in prison. The remaining 13% had both parents in prison. These children had been in a median of two out-of-home care settings, with 43% in one home and 30% in two homes. More than half (59%) of the children were in kinship care at the time of the interview. About half (55%) of the children had one or more siblings in foster care. All but one set of siblings were in the same care setting.

The median age of the mothers of the CIPs was 26, ranging in age from 18 to 44. The father's median age was 31, ranging from 21 to 52. Most of the mothers (78%) and fathers (62%) were White. Of the mothers, 17%

were Black, and 38% of the fathers were Black. An additional 6% of the mothers were biracial/multiracial. Six (7%) of the mothers and eight (9%) of the fathers were Hispanic. One mother and three fathers were Caribbean.

The mothers were in prison for a wide range of crimes such as violation of parole or probation; eluding law enforcement; purchasing, possession, or trafficking of cocaine or other drugs; prostitution; grand theft; credit card fraud federal; violating terms of drug court; battery on a pregnant minor, elderly woman, or law enforcement officer; assault of mental health group home staff; armed robbery; murder of a daughter; and child abuse. The fathers were in prison for first degree murder; violation of parole or probation; battery; aggravated assault; burglary; grand theft; criminal mischief; trafficking in stolen property; forgery; manufacture, sale, possession, delivery, and/or trafficking of cocaine or other drugs; driving with suspended or cancelled license; gun charges; escape; armed robbery; forgery; obstructing justice; attempted kidnapping; passing worthless checks; domestic violence; and sexual relations with a minor.

Case managers reported having some contact with these mothers (61%) and fathers (74%). In most cases, there had been correspondence with the mothers (83%) and fathers (80%). In the remaining cases, contact was maintained through attorneys or time was allocated for a case manager-parent meeting following court hearings when a parent was present. The primary purpose of these contacts was to discuss and share copies of case plans and inform parents of their children's health status, school performance, and adjustment to foster care.

Parent-Child Visits

Most case managers felt that incarcerated parents should be in contact with their children unless they committed an egregious offense or were disinterested. One study participant stated:

> I do believe they have a right to see their children. They should try to have a bond with their parent. They have a right to know that person. The court didn't put restriction on contact in this case, and I think that's good.

Most (61%) of the mothers and 41% of the fathers had some type of contact with their children. Visitation was the exception, however, for both mothers (7%) and fathers (7%). Contact typically took the form of correspondence or phone calls. In cases where visits did not occur, a host of reasons were provided by case managers. In three cases the parents' rights had been terminated. In another three cases, the court had ordered "no contact" because of the nature of the parent's relationship with the child or the nature of the crime committed. In some instances, the parent had just been sentenced, or their requests for visits had just been approved and visits were expected to begin shortly. In 12 cases, visitation was not seen as viable because it would be taxing on the children involved and staff to travel great distances.

In numerous cases there was no expectation of visits. Numerous reasons were provided for this. In some instances there were strong feelings among case managers to not encourage such visits because children should not be exposed to a prison setting. In other instances, visits were not considered because the children involved had not expressed an interest in visiting or because there was no court order mandating visits. It was also not uncommon for judges to rule against visits as a punitive action. In one case, for example

> The father is married to a school principal who got in touch with his attorney, begging for visits. The judge determined no visits because of the length of the sentence. He said that he needed to pay for what he did, which includes losing contact with his child. The new wife fought harder than I've seen anyone fight but to no avail.

Case Plan Goals and Factors Impacting Goal Selection

The case managers all reported that they utilized a concurrency planning approach. In all cases, the "default" or initial case plan goal was parent-child reunification, unless the parent has been involved in egregious activities such as the murder of a spouse or child, or sexual abuse of a child. In almost half of the cases the primary case plan goal at the time of the interview was reunification with the incarcerated parent (22%) or with a non-incarcerated parent (25%). All of the case managers were aware of TPR regulations but reported that when a child has two parents, it is not common practice to move forward to TPR a parent's rights, even if that parent is incarcerated. As explained by one case manager,

> The policy is to wait for all parents involved to resolve their issues before moving for TPR. We move to TPR all of them at same time. If one parent is completing tasks and the other is not, we do not move to TPR because it is cumbersome. Usually we move to TPR after five months if neither parent

is completing tasks. But we don't wait for the six month deadline because it always takes longer and then we are not in compliance.

Other children had a case plan goal of permanent guardianship with a relative or close family friend (28%), adoption by a relative (7%), and adoption by a non-relative (9%). The major factors identified as prompting these goals were the length of a parent's sentence, the nature of their crime, or a determination that the incarcerated parent would be unable to provide a stable home upon their release from prison, had neglected their children prior to their incarceration, and/or had a serious drug or alcohol abuse problem.

The case goal had not been established in 6% of the cases because the incarcerated parent had not yet been sentenced. In 2% of the cases, because of the child's age, the goal was independent living.

Policy and Practice Changes

Of the 31 case managers interviewed, 19 identified incarcerated parents' inability to complete case plan expectations as one area of case management that is problematic and in need of attention. Case managers felt that incarcerated parents should have the opportunity to complete the tasks specified in their case plan. They did not assume that incarcerated parents were disinterested in completing their assigned case plan tasks but acknowledged that parents may become disillusioned and noncompliant. One case manager stated,

> I take pictures of his son and give them to the father to get him "on board." I'm working with the father to drum up his interest. His compliance level says otherwise and I don't blame him.

Reflecting on their experiences with parents who had been completing their tasks prior to their incarceration, two case managers noted,

> I wish they could get services inside a prison. He was doing them when he was outside. It's not fair. He can't do services. Everyone else [who is not in prison] gets a shot unless it's egregious.

Several case managers reported that correctional institutions do not routinely offer the range of services specified in case plans and that when services are available, there is often a waiting list.

> We can't give parents services because prisons don't have them.
>
> There needs to be more services available to parents while incarcerated so they can work the case plan while jailed. I would like them to have more opportunities in prison, like parenting [and substance abuse] classes. They have some of these in some places, but there is a long waiting list.
>
> The opportunity for the parent to really work a case plan is really not there. The things they really need to do are not offered at every facility. They are kind of behind the eight ball. They "kind of" put the parents in the negative.

Case managers also reported that they submit referrals to correctional institutions, requesting that parents participate in the types of programs specified in their case plans. The absence of a relationship with staff in the corrections system had made it difficult, however, to learn about the services available within the prison housing that parent, and to monitor the parent's participation and completion of programs. Study participants described frustration, noting:

> I would like to ask the father to do tasks like parenting, home skill classes, and mental health evaluation. This all depends on what the facility has. I don't know who I should call at the facility to find out.
>
> I called and asked to see what services exist in the prison and no one calls back. It's frustrating. The prison doesn't answer the phone or call back, and I have to drive to the prison.
>
> How do you find out what prison offers? Some believe case managers are supposed to find out what's available. They expect us to do referrals. Some believe lawyers should find out. It's a mess.
>
> This is my first out-of-state case. It is very hard to get information about the services they are in and if they completed them satisfactorily. I have to work through the telephone and attorney.
>
> I believe there should be a court order where we can have access to any kind of record when a parent is in prison. They should make sure to update [the] system so we know where a parent is. We should have the same access to DOC [Department of Corrections] as we have to the school system. Each foster child is coded in the school system and information is updated often. When he was in a treatment center in the community, I could reach him and staff easily. We were able to arrange visits with the child. Contact with prison needs to better so we can communicate. Incarcerated parents are "out of reach."

Case managers also described challenges to arranging for parents to be present during court hearings. Case managers are not informed when parents are transferred from one correctional facility, and case managers are thus unable to monitor their location. This information is needed to notify parents of upcoming court hearings and arrange visits. In addition, inmates are sanctioned for each day, or portion thereof, that they are not within the correctional facility serving their sentence. The latent function of this regulation is that parents are discouraged from attending court hearings.

> Parents are moved around a lot. We cannot find them. We cannot find them to get them to come to court.
> It is hard to get parents MRT'd (Motion to Release Transportation). They lose a day of time or privileges for going to court. They have to add time if they go to court.
> I wish the parents would be more cooperative but they don't want to be transported because they don't want to lose time.

Five of the 31 case managers interviewed expressed frustration that their efforts to develop case plans and indicate tasks parents should complete were futile. In many cases they felt that reunification was not realistic. They felt that the timeline established by legislation allowed too much time to pass before a permanent living situation could be arranged for CIP. They felt that too often current policies favor "incarcerated parents' rights" rather than "children's rights."

CHAPTER SUMMARY

Current child welfare legislation mandates reductions in the length of time children are in foster care and emphasizes the importance of concurrent permanency planning. Foster children are expected to move quickly into more permanent living arrangements such as adoption and permanent guardianship. The study findings indicate that reunification is the default case plan when a parent is incarcerated, until the details of each case are clarified and concurrent planning can be initiated. The timeframe imposed by legislation, however, typically precludes serious consideration of parent-child reunification for large numbers of incarcerated parents and presses for termination of parental rights (Johnson & Flowers, 1998). Exceptions to this are cases in which children are in kinship care, whereby relatives are encouraged to become permanent guardians or adopt the child in their care. Parental rights may not have to be terminated, and family members may work to sustain ties between the child and parent during their incarceration or following their release. Kinship care allows for maintaining some level of parent-child relationships.

Foster care caseworkers and the incarcerated parents with whom they work experience unique challenges. Regulatory and administrative constraints within the correctional system impede professional autonomy and decision making. The study findings indicate that most case managers tend to accept the parameters of child welfare presented by legislation and are dispassionate about the contextual limitations these pose for their ability to work with CIP cases. They accept the premise that parents might not be able to complete the tasks prescribed in their case plans. Features of the correctional system serve as obstacles to parents' ability to complete tasks and as obstacles to the sharing of information by correctional institutions with child welfare staff. The sharing of information about what services are available, how parents can access these services, and when tasks are completed by imprisoned parents is erratic and often absent.

Staff also have minimal experience and training in how to handle these situations. The study findings suggest a pattern of practice referred to by Munro (2008) as "tunnel vision," in which case managers consider a "narrow range of options when facing a decision" (p. 195). The findings also reflect a complacent acceptance of the limitations imposed by legislation and an acceptance of the premise that parents might not be able to complete the tasks prescribed in their case plans. This suggests a need, previously articulated by Gambrill (2008), to address what appear to be dysfunctional policies and practices.

Previous studies have found an absence of adequate rehabilitation opportunities in many correctional settings, which interferes with incarcerated parents' ability to respond to court or case plan expectations. Case manager-parent contact and parent-child contact are also compromised by the time, cost, and inconvenience involved, despite the importance of such contact for maintaining family relationships, providing case managers with opportunities to assess family relationships and the strong correlation between contact and successful family reunification (Hess & Mintun, 1992; Simms & Bolden, 1991). Correctional facilities are often located far from the children's home communities and do not offer hospitable settings for visits or meetings, and case managers acknowledge that they sometimes feel that they might not be following what they perceive to be "best practices" by not extending themselves to engage incarcerated parents and facilitate parent-child relationships (Currence & Johnson, 2003; Simmons, 2003). Kowoitz-Margolies and Kraft-Stolar (2006) found that case managers may be reluctant to handle CIP foster care cases because they are seen as requiring more work than other cases and as unlikely to result in family reunification. Some case managers also may have negative attitudes about visits between CIP and their parents, noting that children should not be exposed to prison settings. Case managers also may be reluctant to visit incarcerated parents, finding the screening process that precedes entrance into a correctional facility humiliating.

Many of the case managers interviewed in the current study recommended changes in correctional and child welfare policies. An examination of corrections policies regarding transporting of inmates was called for, as well as a review of the history and rationale for "docking" inmates if they spend some of their sentence time to attend court hearings or meetings. The study findings also suggest the need for prison programs that educate parents about child welfare legislation and about the benefits of contact with one's child.

The study found that despite the importance of parent-child contact for maintaining parental rights and promoting child and family wellbeing, there remains considerable variability in how child welfare agencies and correctional facilities deal with incarcerated parents and their families. Few child welfare agencies have formal policies for working with CIP, and correctional institutions lack initiatives that address the needs of incarcerated parents. As noted by Johnson and Waldfogel (2008), there is a clear need for the development of agency or state-level guidelines for working with CIP to reduce the tensions between the goals of child welfare and criminal justice agencies.

REFERENCES

Allard, P. E., & Lu, L. D. (2006). *Rebuilding families, reclaiming lives. State obligations to children in foster and their incarcerated parents.* New York: New York University School of Law Brennan Center for Justice.

Allen, T., DeVooght, K., & Geen, R. (2008 December). *State kinship care policies for children that come to the attention of child welfare agencies. Findings from the 2007 Casey kinship foster care policy survey.* Washington DC: Child Trends.

Beckerman, A. (1998). Charting a course: Meeting the challenges of permanency planning for children with incarcerated mothers. *Child Welfare, 77*(5), 513–530.

Currence, P. L. J., Johnson, W. E., Jr. (2003). *The negative impact of incarceration on black fathers.* Retrieved June 13, 2009, from www.rcgd.isr.umich.edu/prba/perspectives/winter2003/currence.pdf.

Dallaire, D. H. (2007). Children with incarcerated mothers: Developmental outcomes, special challenges and recommendations. *Journal of Developmental Psychology, 28*(1), 15–24.

Gambrill, E. (2008). Decision making in child welfare: Constraints and potentials. In Lindsey, D., & Al Shlonsky, A. (Ed.). *Child welfare research.* 175–193. New York: Oxford University Press.

Gelles, R. J., (1998). The Adoption and Safe Families Act of 1997 rightly places child safety first. *Brown University Child and Adolescent Behavior Letter, 14*(4), 1–3.

George, R. M., Wulczyn, F. H., & Harden, A. W. (1994). *A report from the multi-state foster care data archive: Foster care dynamics 1983–1993.* Chicago: Chapin Hall Center for Children at the University of Chicago.

Glaze, L. E. & Maruschak, L. M. (2009, January updated). *Parents in prison and their minor children.* Washington DC: U.S. Department of Justice, Office of Justice Programs, Bureau of Justice Statistics. Retrieved June 13, 2009, from http://www.ojp.usdoj.gov/bjs/pub/pdf/pptmc.pdf.

Hairston, C. F. (1998). The forgotten parent: Understanding the forces that influence incarcerated fathers' relationships with their children. *Child Welfare, 77*(5), 617–640.

Halperin, R., & Harris, J. L. (2004). Parental rights of incarcerated mothers with children in foster care: A policy vacuum. *Feminist Studies, 30*(2), 339–352.

Herring, D. J. (2000). Adoption and Safe Families Act - Hope and its subversion. *Family Law Quarterly, 34,* 329–358.

Hess, P., Mintun, G., Moehlman, A., & Pitts, G. (1992, January/February). The Family Connection Center: An innovative visiting program. *Child Welfare, 71,* 77–88.

Johnston, D. (2006). The wrong road: Efforts to understand the effects of parental crime and incarceration. *Criminology & Public Policy, 5*(4), 703–719.

Johnston, D. (1995). *Effects of parental incarceration.* In K. Gabel, & D. Johnston (Eds.). Children of incarcerated parents (pp. 59–88). New York: Lexington Books.

Johnson, J. M., & Flowers, C. N. (1998). You can never go home again: The Florida legislature adds incarceration to the list of statutory grounds for termination of parental rights. *Florida State University Law Review, 25*(2), 335–350.

Johnson, E. I., & Waldfogel, J. (2002). Parental incarceration: Recent trends and implications for child welfare. *Social Service Review, 76*(3), 460–522.

Johnson, E. I., & Waldfogel, J. (2008, Spring). Trends in parental incarceration and implications for child welfare. *CW360⁰: A comprehensive look at a prevalent child welfare issue. Children of incarcerated parents.* Saint Paul, MN: University of Minnesota, Center for Advanced Studies in Child Welfare, 6–7.

Katz, L., Spoonemore, N. & Robinson, C. (1994). *Concurrent planning: From permanency planning to permanency action.* Mountlake Terrace, WA: Lutheran Social Services of Washington and Idaho.

Kowoitz-Margolies, J., & Kraft-Stolar, T. (2006). *When "free" means losing your mother: The collision of child welfare and the incarceration of women in New York State.* New York: Correctional Association of New York.

Lee, A. F., Genty, P. M., & Laver, M. (2005). *The impact of the Adoption and Safe Families Act on children of incarcerated parents.* Washington DC: Child Welfare League.

Munro, E. (2008). Lessons from research on decision making. In Lindsey, D., & Shlonsky, A. (Eds.) *Child welfare research.* 175–193. NY: Oxford University Press.

Nurse, A. M. (2002). *Fatherhood arrested.* Nashville, TN: Vanderbilt University Press.

O'Donnell, J. M. (1999). Involvement of African-American fathers in kinship foster care services. *Social Work, 44*(5), 428–441.

Ott, A. B. (1998, September 30). Tools for permanency. Tool #1: Concurrent permanency planning.. Hunter College School of Social Work of the City University of New York. National Resource Center for Foster Care & Permanency Planning. Retrieved June 13, 2009, from http://www.hunter.cuny.edu/socwork/nrcfcpp/downloads/tools/cpp-tool.pdf.

Poehlmann, J. (2005). Representation of attachment relationships in children of incarcerated mothers. *Child Development, 76*(3), 679–696.

Scalia, J. (2001, August). *Bureau of Justice Statistics. Special report. Federal drug offenders. 1999 with trends 1984–99.* Washington DC: U.S. Department of Justice. Office of Justice Programs. Retrieved June 13, 2009, from http://www.cs.indiana.edu/sudoc/image_30000096190149/30000096190149/pdf/fdo99.pdf.

Schene, P. (2001 May). *Implementing concurrent planning: A handbook for child welfare administrators.*

Portland, MN: National Child Welfare Resource Center for Organizational Improvement. Institute for Child and Family Policy. Edmund S. Muskie School of Public Service, University of Southern Maine.

Simmons, C. W. (2003). *California law and the children of prisoners.* Sacramento, CA: California Research Bureau, California State Library.

Simms, M. D., & Bolden, B. J. (1991). The family reunification project: Facilitating regular contact among foster children, biological families, and foster families. *Child Welfare, 70*(6), 679–691.

Swann, C. A., & Sylvester, M. S. (2006). The foster care crisis: What caused caseloads to grow? *Demography, 43*(2), 309–335.

Westat Chapin Hall Center for Children, University of Chicago. (2001, December). *Assessing the context of permanency and reunification in the foster care system.* Retrieved June 13, 2009, from http://aspe.hss.gov/hsp/fostercare-reunif01.

Western, B., & McLanahan, S. (2007). *Fathers behind bars: The impact of incarceration on family formation.* Princeton, NJ: Princeton University Center for Research on Child Wellbeing.

Wright, L. E., & Seymour, C. B. (2000). *Working with children and families separated by incarceration. A handbook for child welfare agencies.* Washington DC: Child Welfare League Association Press.

ADDITIONAL RESOURCES

Books, Manuals, Newsletters, and Reports

Adalist-Estrin, A. (2003). *Visiting mom or dad: The child's perspective.* Jenkintown, PA: Families and Corrections Network. Retrieved June 13, 2009, from http://www.fcnetwork.org/cpl/CPL105-VisitingMomorDad.pdf.

Adalist-Estrin, A. (2003). *What do children of prisoners and their caregivers need?* Jenkintown, PA: Families and Corrections Network. Retrieved June 13, 2009, from http://www.f2f.ca.gov/res/pdf/WhatDoChildren.pdf.

Bernstein, N. (2005). *All alone in the world. Children of the incarcerated parents.* NY: New Press.

Bloom, B., Owen, B., & Covington, S. (2003, June). *Gender-responsive strategies. Research, practice and guiding principles for women offenders.* Washington, DC: National Institute of Corrections. U.S. Department of Justice. Retrieved June 13, 2009, from http://www.nicic.org/pubs/2003/018017.pdf.

Brooks, S. (2008, Summer). *Out of the shadows: What child welfare workers can do to help children and their incarcerated parents.* Reaching Out. Current Issues in Child Welfare Practice in Rural Communities (newsletter). Davis, CA: UC Davis Extension, University of California, The Center for Human Services, Northern California Training Academy. Retrieved June 13, 2009, from http://humanservices.ucdavis.edu/News/pdf/074_140.pdf.

Coalition for Women Prisoners. (2008). *My sister's keeper. A book for women returning home from jail or prison.* NY: Correctional Association of New York. Retrieved June 13, 2009, from http://www.correctionalassociation.org/publications/download/wipp/MySistersKeeper_Re-EntryGuide.pdf.

Family to Family tools for rebuilding foster care. Family to Family Toolkit – Partnerships between corrections and child welfare: Collaboration for change, part two. Baltimore, MD: Annie E. Casey Foundation. Retrieved June 13, 2009, from http://www.f2f.ca.gov/res/pdf/PartnershipsBetween.pdf.

Hammer, V., & Bucci, M. (2008). *Florida manual for incarcerated parents.* Newberry, FL: Florida.

Institutional Legal Services. Retrieved June 13, 2009, from http://www.f2f.ca.gov/res/pdf/FloridaManual.pdf.

Hess, P. (2003). *Visiting between children in care and their families: A look at current policy.* From http://www.hunter.cuny.edu/socwork/nrcfcpp/info_services/family-child-visiting.html.

Hunter College School of Social Work. National Resource Center for Foster Care and Permanency Planning. Retrieved June 13, 2009, from http://www.hunter.cuny.edu/socwork/nrcfcpp/downloads/visiting_report-10-29-03.pdf.

Johnson, E. I., & Waldfogel, J. (2002, July 17). *Children of incarcerated parents: Cumulative risk and children's living arrangements.* NY: Columbia University School of Social Work.

La Vigne, N. G., Davies, E., Brazzell, D. (2008, February). *Broken bonds: Understanding and addressing the needs of children with incarcerated parents.* Washington DC: Urban Institute Justice Policy Center. Retrieved June 13, 2009, from http://www.f2f.ca.gov/res/pdf/BrokenBonds.pdf.

Mumola, C. (2000, August). Special report: Incarcerated parents and their children. Washington, DC: U.S. Department of Justice, Office of Justice Programs, Bureau of Justice Statistics. Retrieved June 13, 2009, from http://www.ojp.usdoj.gov/bjs/pub/pdf/iptc.pdf.

Osborne Association. (1993) *How Can I Help? A Three-Volume Series on Serving Special Children,* New York, NY: Author.

Osborne Association. (2007). Visiting tips for families: Supporting children visiting their parents. NY: NYC Initiative for Children of Incarcerated Parents, Osborne Association. Retrieved June 13, 2009, from http://www.f2f.ca.gov/res/pdf/VisitingTipsFor-Families.pdf.

Rise – A Magazine By and For Parents in the Child Welfare System. Available http://www.risemagazine.org/pages/about.html.

Ross, T., Khashu, A., & Wamsley, M. (2004, August). *Hard data on hard times. An empirical analysis of maternal incarceration, foster care, and visitation.* NY: Vera Institute of Justice. New York City Administration of Children's Services. Retrieved June 13, 2009, from http://www.vera.org/publication_pdf/245_461.pdf.

San Francisco Partnership for Incarcerated Parents. (2003). *San Francisco children of incarcerated parents: A bill of rights.* Stockton, CA: Author. Retrieved June 13, 2009, from http://www.sfcipp.org.

Seymour, C., & Hairston, C. F. (2001). *Children with parents in prison. Child welfare policy, program, and practice issues.* Edison, NJ: Transaction Publishers.

Travis, J., McBride, E. C., & Solomon, A. L. (2003). *Families left behind: The hidden costs of incarceration and reentry.* Washington, DC: Urban Institute. Retrieved June 13, 2009, from www.urban.org/UploadedPDF/310882_families_left_behind.pdf.

Videos

Champagne and The Talking Eggs. (2003). Sma Distribution.

Girl Scouts Beyond Bars. (2005). Mobilus Media.

White Oleander. (2003). Warner Brothers.

Children's Books

Blomquist, G. M., & Blomquist, P. B. (1990). *Zachary's new home:* A story for foster and adopted children. NY: Magination Press.

Woodson, J. (2002). *Our gracie aunt.* NY: Hyperion.

Woodson, J. (2002). *Visiting day.* NY: Scholastic Press.

Service Planning and Intervention Development for Children of Incarcerated Parents

SUSAN D. PHILLIPS

This chapter describes two different frameworks that are often implicit in service planning and intervention development efforts for children of incarcerated parents. The strengths and limitations of each framework are discussed and examples are provided of programs and services that fit within these frameworks.

Two factors helped set the stage for the current push to develop services and interventions for children of incarcerated parents. One was the unprecedented increase in the number of children with parents in prison that resulted from the "mass incarceration" policies of the 1980s and 1990s. The other, and perhaps more potent factor, was concern that children of incarcerated parents would become "the next generation of inmates" (e.g., Hagan, 1996).

There has been interest in intergenerational incarceration for decades. Early researchers hypothesized that inmates' sons became involved in delinquency because they mimicked their fathers' criminal attitudes and behaviors (Glueck & Glueck, 1950; McCord & McCord, 1958). This led to a body of research on the relationship between parent criminality and delinquency. Obviously, researchers cannot follow parents around to directly observe them committing criminal acts, so they instead used reports of arrests as proxies for parents' criminal behaviors. Some researchers differentiated between arrests for misdemeanors and arrests for felonies (the latter typically carry prison sentences) to distinguish parents' involvement in more serious crimes.

Research on parent criminality suggests that children whose parents become involved with criminal authorities (but not exclusively those whose parents go to prison) are more likely than are other children to become involved in delinquency (Farrington, Jolliffe, Loeber, Stouthamer-Loeber, & Kalb, 2001; Leve & Chamberlain, 2004; Murray & Farrington, 2005; Robins, 1978; Sirpa, 2002; U. S. Department of Justice, 1988). Throughout the 1990s, distorted findings from this research were used to raise concerns about the unintended consequences "mass incarceration" policies were having on inmates' children and became the impetus for specialized services for children of incarcerated parents.

Unfortunately, selling services for children of incarcerated parents by promoting the idea that these children will become the next generation of inmates reinforced the stereotypical belief that "the apple doesn't fall far from the tree" and fostered a mistaken perception that delinquency is commonplace, if not inevitable, among children whose parents go to prison. Anyone interested in developing services or designing interventions for children of incarcerated parents must understand that there is no evidence that children of incarcerated parents are all doomed to have serious problems. When researchers say that children whose parents are involved with criminal authorities are more likely than other children to become involved in delinquency, it does not mean that all or even most of them will get in trouble with the law. It simply means that if you divide all children into two groups—those whose parents have been arrested and those whose parents have not—you will find a higher percentage of children who become involved in delinquency within the group whose parents were arrested. Similarly, if we divide all adults into two groups—those who buy lottery tickets and those who do not—you will find a higher percentage of people who win the lottery among those who buy tickets. We all know, however, that most people who buy lottery tickets do not win.

Theories of delinquency have evolved over time. We now know that many different child, parent, family, and community factors play a role in young people becoming involved in delinquency and that the effect of those risk factors can be diminished by protective factors. One of the legacies of research on parent criminality, however, is that researchers came to think of parent criminality as simply a marker for various other risk factors that tend to co-occur with parental arrest (e.g., poverty, single-parent households, parent-child separation, unemployment, substance abuse, mental illness, and so forth). It was not until prison populations began skyrocketing in the 1980s and advocates for inmates began doggedly asking questions about what was happening to the millions of children whose parents were in prison that researchers began seriously considering the possibility that parental incarceration might actually be the cause of some of the risk factors associated with parent criminality (e.g., disruptions in care, poverty, and so forth) and directly or indirectly influence the risk for delinquency (Murray & Farrington, 2005; Phillips, Erkanli, Keeler, Costello & Angold, 2006).

The push for services and interventions for children of incarcerated parents has gained momentum over the years as advocates, researchers, policy makers, and service providers began paying attention to what happens to children at various points in their parents' progression through the criminal justice system. Two different (but not necessarily antagonistic) conceptual frameworks are implicit in discussions about services and interventions for children of incarcerated parents. One is a social justice framework, or more specifically a procedural justice framework. From this perspective, the goal of interventions and services is to eliminate, or at least minimize, the adverse consequences criminal processes may have for offenders' children for the sake of equity. The other is a developmental epidemiologic framework. From the developmental epidemiologic perspective, the purpose of intervention is to prevent serious childhood emotional and behavioral problems. This chapter describes the nature of service planning and intervention development from these two perspectives and introduces readers to some of the different types of services that currently exist for children of incarcerated parents.

Procedural Justice

What It Is

Procedural justice is concerned with the fairness of processes for settling conflicts (Lind & Tyler, 1988). In the case of children with parents in prison, the issue is the lack of justice inherent in the procedures for settling conflicts between the state and parents who violate the law. The root of this injustice lies in unintended and potentially adverse consequences parental arrest and incarceration can have for children

(Clear, 1996; Hagan & Dinovitzer, 1999; Lange, 2000; Lee, 2005). The procedural justice orientation is clearly seen in the title of one of the seminal reports on incarcerated parents' children, *Why Punish the Children?* (McGowan & Blumenthal, 1978).

Services and Interventions

From a procedural justice perspective, the aim of services and interventions is to eliminate, or at least minimize, the adversity children experience because of their parents' involvement in criminal justice procedures (e.g., arrest, sentencing, incarceration, and release). Initially, advocacy and service planning efforts focused on sentencing reforms and on support for children and families during a given episode of parental incarceration; interest in interventions associated with parental arrest and parents' release from prison came later.

Sentencing drew attention because of the role sentencing reforms played in the exponential growth in prison populations that took place in the 1980s and 1990s. These reforms made more crimes punishable by imprisonment, increased the time people spend in prison, and took away discretion judges previously had to consider an individual's family circumstances when passing sentence (Tonry & Petersilia, 1999). They had a particularly acute effect on the number of people sent to prison for nonviolent drug crimes and on the number of women in prison (Caplow & Simon, 1999). In response, advocacy groups began a national campaign in 1995 to make drug treatment an alternative to incarceration for mothers convicted of nonviolent drug offenses (JusticeWorks Community, nd). That campaign continues until today.

More recent efforts to influence sentencing focus on modifying the pre-sentencing investigations that are already conducted by courts. Advocates are urging that these include a family impact component describing the effects different sentences are likely to have on defendants' children and recommendations about the least detrimental sentencing alternative for children (e.g., San Francisco Children of Incarcerated Parents Partnership, 2003). Individuals in various organizations around the country also regularly testify to similar information or provide similar reports in local jurisdictions, although not necessarily as part of institutionalized court reforms (e.g., Center for Children of Incarcerated Parent).

Direct services for children (as opposed to policy reforms) are typically connected to periods during which parents are in jail or prison. The objectives of these services are to help (1) children sustain relationships with their incarcerated parents, (2) cope with their parents' incarceration, or (3) support family members who are caring for incarcerated parents' children. Some organizations provide services that address multiple of these objectives (e.g., Forever Families, Project SKIP, Peanut Butter and Jelly, Arkansas Voices for Children), whereas others have a more limited range of services. Names of several organizations that provide services or offer training and consultation on service development are found in Table 10.1.

Efforts to help children sustain relationships with their incarcerated parents take many forms. Some community groups provide transportation so children can visit their parents in prison (e.g., Families in Crisis; Friends Outside; Lutheran Social Services of Illinois; Pulaski Heights United Methodist Church; also see Virginia Commission on Youth, 2002). Others operate playrooms or other child-friendly areas within prisons and jails (e.g., Centerforce, Cook County Sheriff's Women's Justice Services, Pittsburgh Child Guidance Foundation; also see Kazura & Toth, 2004) or programs that give children an opportunity to take part in normal parent-child activities while visiting with their parent in jail or prison. Some of these activities include Scouting (e.g., Girl Scout of America; also see Block, 1999; Moses, 1995) and various reading and literacy programs (e.g., Pennsylvania Prison Society, also see Bassett, nd; Martin, 1995; McCorkle & Mulroy, 2007; Urrutia, 2004). Still others help children stay in touch with their parents through mail, or more recently videoconferencing (e.g., Nefsis, nd; also Pennsylvania Prison Society).

There are also organizations that help children cope with their parents' imprisonment. Some try to reduce children's sense of stigmatization or help them deal with their feelings about their parents' incarceration. One strategy is to bring children together to engage in recreational or leisure activities with the expectation that during the course of those activities children will learn that they share a mutual experience—the incarceration of a parent—and feel less alone (e.g., KARE, Lutheran Social Services of Illinois). Intervention also sometimes takes the form of support groups or mutual aid groups that bring children together specifically to discuss their experiences stemming from their parents' incarceration (e.g., Families in Crisis, also see Springer, Lynch, & Rubin, 2000). These groups are sometimes led by individuals within the organization who have clinical skills or who are experts in child development, but these types of services are also sometimes provided through partnerships with other organizations (e.g., Center for Children of Incarcerated Parents, KARE Family Center, Project SKIP). A growing trend is

Table 10.1

ORGANIZATIONS THAT PROVIDE SERVICES FOR CHILDREN OF INCARCERATED PARENTS AND/OR CONSULTATION AND TRAINING ON PROGRAM DEVELOPMENT

Program/Organization*	Web Address
Amachi (mentoring)	www.amachimentoring.org
Arkansas Voices for Children	www.arkvoicesforchildren.org
Big Brothers, Big Sisters	www.bbbs.org/site/c.esJQK5PFJnH/ b.1717047/k.F9D4/Mentoring _Children _of_Incarcerated_Parents.htm
Center for Children of Incarcerated Parents	www.e-ccip.org/
Centerforce	www.centerforce.org/programs/
Community Works	www.community-works-ca.org/index.html
Cook County Sheriff, Women's Justice Services	www.cookcountysheriff.org/womens _justice_services/wjs_main.html
Family and Corrections Network	www.fcnetwork.org/read.html
Families in Crisis	www.familiesincrisis.org/
Forever Family	www.foreverfam.org/kids.php
Friends Outside	www.friendsoutside.org/
Girl Scouts of America	www.girlscouts.org/program/program_ opportunities/community/gsbb.asp
KARE Family Center	www.arizonaschildren.org/programs/ specialprograms.html
Lutheran Social Services of Illinois	www.lssi.org/Service/ConnectionsVisits ToMomsDadsInPrisonandSupport Programs.aspx
Montana Alliance for Families Touched by Incarceration	www.mafti.org/partners.htm
National Partnership for Children of Incarcerated Parents	www.nationalborpartnership.net/
New Hampshire Department of Corrections	www.nh.gov/nhdoc/fcc/books.html
Osborne Association	www.osborneny.org/youth_family _services.htm
Peanut Butter & Jelly Family Services	www.pbjfamilyservices.org/
Pennsylvania Prison Society (Project SKIP)	www.prisonsociety.org/index.shtml
Pima Prevention Partnership	www.thepartnership.us
Pittsburg Child Guidance Foundation	foundationcenter.org/grantmaker/ childguidance/initiative.htm
Pulaski Heights United Methodist Church (MIWATCH)	www.fumclr.org/index.php? fuseaction=p0007.&mod=22
San Francisco Children of Incarcerated Parents Partnership	www.sfcipp.org/whoweare.html

*Information in this table is provided as a starting point for readers who want to learn more about service and intervention models. It is not an exhaustive list of services, nor is it an endorsement of any particular service model or intervention.

to situate support groups in school settings (e.g., Peanut Butter and Jelly, Project SKIP, Community Works). For teens, there are also opportunities to take part in youth-lead activities to educate people about their experiences and to promote policy reforms (e.g., Osborne Association, Community Works).

As the result of a multimillion dollar investment by the federal government during the Bush administration, a growing number of organizations began operating mentoring programs for children with incarcerated parents (e.g., Amachi, Big Brothers-Big Sisters). These programs are intended to provide children with a consistent relationship with a supportive adult outside of their family.

Other service programs indirectly help children of incarcerated parents by providing support and resources to relatives who care for children while their parents are serving time. Some organizations distribute information for adults explaining how to talk to children about parental incarceration in developmentally appropriate terms and helping them anticipate children's emotional and behavioral reactions to parental incarceration (e.g., Center for Children of Incarcerated Parents, Family and Corrections Network, Montana Alliance for Families Touched by Incarceration, Osborne Association, Virginia Commission on Youth, 2002). A number of children's books are also available to help children understand parental incarceration. These are listed on a several Web sites (e.g., Family and Corrections Network; New Hampshire Department of Corrections).

Many children live with grandparents or other relatives while their parents are incarcerated (although not necessarily because their parents were sent to prison). Relatives have traditionally faced many barriers to obtaining resources and support for the children in their care. In response, a number of organizations have emerged that offer case management services, support groups, or advocacy for relative caregivers (e.g., KARE Family Center, Forever Family). There have also been successful advocacy efforts to reform policies so that family members can access resources through the child welfare system without states having to take custody of children.

In addition to sentencing reforms and programs to support children while their parents are in prison, organizations in several locales have recently begun working with law enforcement agencies to institute training on how officers should interact with children who are present when their parents are taken into custody. These may be coupled with procedural reforms to assure that children are adequately cared for in the aftermath of their parents' arrest (e.g., Pittsburgh Child Guidance Foundation; Pima Prevention Partnership; also see Nieto, 2002; Nolan, 2003). These procedural changes can be as simple as allowing parents to make extra phone calls if needed to make arrangements for their children or as involved as hiring "civilian" transportation services to take children to child-friendly settings to wait for someone to pick them up.

The period following release from prison is also increasingly garnering attention. Family reentry has become a hot topic in recent years, partly because of anticipation that federal funding would become available to support services at this point in the criminal justice continuum. Because of barriers people with felony convictions face in obtaining employment and housing, services often concentrate on helping parents meet basic survival needs. It is rare for programs to specifically address children's adjustment to their parents' return from prison, although there are some programs that include inmates' families in the preparations for inmates being released from prison.

The Bill of Rights for Children of Incarcerated Parents

A timely example of the application of the procedural justice perspective in service planning efforts is found in *The Bill of Rights for Children of Incarcerated Parents* (San Francisco Children of Incarcerated Parents Partnership, 2008; see also National Partnership for Children of Incarcerated Parents). The rights set out in this document are not rights in the legal sense—they are not established by law. Instead, they are a set of guiding principles for how children should ideally be treated by individuals and systems when their parents are arrested and incarcerated. These rights map to the major junctures in the criminal justice process. For example, *The Bill of Rights* includes the right for children to be kept safe when their parents are arrested, to be considered when decisions are made about their parent (e.g., sentencing), and to be well cared for while their parents are serving time (Table 10.2).

Groups throughout the country are finding *The Bill of Rights* a useful tool around which to organize advocacy and service development efforts, but before *The Bill of Rights* can be "adopted," its principles must first be translated into specific goals for policy and practice change (e.g., training for law enforcement officers so children are kept safe when their parents are arrested). The particular rights that groups focus upon are often determined by the particular mix of organizations that are working together. Unfortunately, their success in bringing about

Table 10.2

THE BILL OF RIGHTS FOR CHILDREN OF INCARCERATED PARENTS

1. I have the right to be kept safe and informed at the time of my parent's arrest.
2. I have the right to be heard when decisions are made about me.
3. I have the right to be considered when decisions are made about my parent.
4. I have the right to be well cared for in my parent's absence.
5. I have the right to speak with, see, and touch my parent.
6. I have the right to support as I struggle with my parent's incarceration.
7. I have the right not to be judged, blamed, or labeled because of my parent's incarceration.

reform is often limited by a lack of resources. Nonetheless, these groups have gained considerable practical knowledge when it comes to strategies for gaining support for services and are succeeding in instituting changes (Phillips, 2008).

Limitation

A major limitation of the procedural justice approach as it is typically applied in developing services and interventions for children of incarcerated parents is that it does not account for the fact that some children experience multiple episodes of parental arrest and incarceration. It also typically does not address the risk to children posed by parent problems (e.g., drug addiction, lack of job skills) that may be associated with repeat arrests.

Rather than progressing through the criminal justice system in a linear fashion (e.g., arrest, sentencing, incarceration, release), many parents actually loop through the system. Consistent with this, the majority of parents in prison at any given time have served prior sentences. Moreover, about 50% of people released from prison are rearrested within just three years of their release. Any particular episode of parental arrest and incarceration, therefore, exists in the context of a parent's overall criminal career and the problems that contribute to his or her repeated arrest.

Despite its limitations, the procedural justice framework provides a valuable lens for looking at parents' involvement in criminal justice system processes. It highlights the fact that the decisions we make as a society about criminal justice policies for adults have consequences for children. It also provides a starting point for examining those consequences and taking steps to either eliminate them or make them less noxious. It complements the developmental epidemiologic perspective by adding knowledge of children's experiences stemming specifically from their parent's involvement with criminal authorities.

The Developmental Epidemiology Perspective

What It Is

Developmental epidemiology is concerned with the origins, course, and prevention of serious childhood emotional and behavioral problems. The procedural justice and developmental epidemiologic perspectives are not necessarily antagonistic, but they can lead to a different appraisal of the services and interventions children need and why they need them.

From the developmental epidemiologic perspective, a given episode of parental incarceration is only one of many risk factors that might be operating in children's lives to increase their chances of developing serious emotional and behavioral problems. Other possible risk factors include poverty, parental substance abuse, parental mental illness, witnessing violence, being the victim of child neglect or abuse, family instability, and other parent, family, and community risk factors. Many of these risk factors are found more commonly among parents who become involved in the criminal justice system than among other parents. Several programs include elements that are informed by developmental epidemiology (e.g., Center for Children of Incarcerated Parents, Project SKIP, Peanut Butter and Jelly).

To illustrate the difference in the procedural justice and developmental epidemiologic perspectives, consider the incarceration of parents who were involved in their children's lives before being sent to prison. The procedural justice perspective focuses on the unfairness of depriving children of a relationship with their parents. From the developmental epidemiologic perspective, incarceration-induced parent-child separation is a potential cause of grief reactions, attachment disorders, or other emotional and behavioral problems. In either case, intervention might include helping children sustain a relationship with their parents. Within the developmental epidemiology framework, other treatments may also be indicated if children have already developed problems (e.g., unresolved grief). On the other hand, the procedural justice perspective is not concerned necessarily with whether children will develop problems because of separation from their parents or the clinical treatment of serious emotional and behavioral problems. From the procedural justice point of view, services are warranted simply because children should not be punished along with their parents.

The Nature of Services and Interventions

Looked at from the developmental epidemiologic perspective, any particular instance of parental arrest or incarceration is an isolated incident in the course of a child's development. The developmental epidemiologic perspective calls into focus the complete constellation of risks to which children may be exposed during their childhoods. From this perspective, children who experience parental arrest and incarceration are potentially in need of services beyond those that are developed to mitigate the adverse consequences of criminal justice system processes. For instance, the developmental epidemiologic perspective would suggest that in addition to visitation programs and other forms of services for children whose parents are in prison, it is also important for correctional facilities to provide incarcerated parents with substance abuse treatment, mental health services, domestic violence interventions, parent skill training, and other indicated interventions while incarcerated. In contrast, only a fraction of parents who might benefit from these services receive them while they are serving time. Moreover, incarceration-specific services for children are often developed and operated in isolation from prison-based programs that might address parent problems that place children at risk for adverse outcomes.

The developmental epidemiologic perspective also calls attention to the fact that not all children with incarcerated parents are exposed to the same risk factors. Denise Johnston, a pioneer in interventions for children of incarcerated parents, noted a decade ago that there is no risk factor or problem that is universal among children with parents in prison. Recent research confirms that, in fact, there are identifiable subgroups of children who are exposed to very different categories of risk factors for which different types of interventions are indicated (Phillips & Erkanli, 2008; Phillips, Erkanli, Costello, & Angold, 2007). For instance, the major risk factor for some children is child abuse and neglect; for others it is familial substance abuse and mental illness, and for others it is extreme poverty. Accordingly, children of incarcerated parents can be susceptible to developing problems for various different reasons. The developmental epidemiologic perspective suggests the need for a careful assessment of the risk factors operating in any given child's life and for services and interventions that target those specific risk factors.

The group of children who are perhaps most vulnerable to developing serious problems are those who live in families in which many different risk factors are present. Past research shows that as the number of risk factors in a child's life increase, the chances of children developing serious problems grows exponentially (Biederman et al., 1995; Johnson & Waldfogel, 2002). If the goal of services and interventions for children of incarcerated parents is to prevent children from developing serious problems, services that make parental arrest and incarceration less noxious for children may not be sufficient alone to alter the outcomes of the youth who are at greatest risk. These children and their families will need coordinated or integrated services from multiple systems.

Limitation

One of the drawbacks of the developmental epidemiologic framework is that the consequences of parental arrest and incarceration for children may not register as a problem if they do not contribute significantly to the risk of children developing problems. Systems that routinely work with children and families such as the child mental health system, schools, medicine, child welfare, and juvenile justice already have substantial knowledge about the efficacy and effectiveness of services and interventions to prevent serious childhood problems, but may not understand how parental arrest and incarceration affect children and families. In fact, the imprisonment of a parent may be seen as reducing children's risk exposure (e.g., parental substance abuse or mental illness) when in fact there can be a trade-off between children's exposure to certain risk factors because their parents are in the home (e.g., substance abuse) and their exposure to other risk factors (e.g., reduced household income or disrupted parent-child bonds) because the criminal justice system takes their parent out of the home. Nonetheless, the developmental epidemiologic framework is valuable for what it can tell us about the totality of children's experiences and the subgroup of children with incarcerated parents that are at highest risk for adverse outcomes.

WHAT WORKS?

In this era of evidence-based practice, a common question about services and interventions is "what works." Unfortunately, there is no clear answer to this question when it comes to services for children of incarcerated parents. First, it is rare for programs to collect data on children's outcomes. Prison-based programs, for example, may evaluate how parents respond to an intervention, but not their children. This is partly because of how difficult it is to directly study children whose parents are in prison (Miller, 2006). As a result, evaluations of programs that purportedly benefit children of incarcerated parents are largely limited to process evaluations describing barriers to program implementation.

Second, before we can learn what works, we have to first define what "works" means. As this chapter illustrates, there are competing perspectives on the ultimate aim of services and interventions for children of incarcerated parents. These give rise to varied criteria for evaluating the impact of programs. Moreover, the question we should be asking is "what works for which children?" Different subgroups of children have different needs. The intervention needs of children who are victims of physical or sexual abuse, for instance, may be different than the needs of children whose families are primarily struggling with poverty. That fact withstanding, a lesson to be drawn from the discussions that have taken place about children of incarcerated parents is that although the needs of individual children may vary, they all have the same "rights."

Programs for children of incarcerated parents need the tools and knowledge to assess the specific needs of individual children and referral mechanisms to help children gain access to resources that will meet their needs. This is not to suggest that these programs must be all things to all children, but they can be a conduit through which children obtain needed services. At the same time, those in service systems that traditionally serve children also need to be aware of the unique issues related to parental incarceration, such as the stigma associated with incarceration, the economic barriers faced by parents with convictions, and the stress incarceration places on family relationships.

Finally, the field lacks any type of central clearinghouse that people can turn to for a comprehensive synthesis of information about the nature or effectiveness of services for children of incarcerated parents. In fact, information about the existence of services and interventions typically spreads through a loosely linked informal network of advocates, researchers, and service providers. Outsiders who are interested in implementing a service or developing an intervention will find a considerable amount of information on the internet, but this information may not provide the level of detail necessary to replicate a service or even to assess its appropriateness for a particular setting or group of children. The list of organizations in Table 10.1 above, although not exhaustive, will help individuals connect with organizations that can at least share their experiences and knowledge and help individuals locate more specific information.

FUTURE DIRECTIONS

Both a procedural justice and a developmental epidemiology perspective can be identified in discussions of services and interventions for children of incarcerated parents. A major contribution of the procedural justice perspective is that it highlights the consequences adult criminal justice processes have for children. Services born from this perspective might be considered universal prevention efforts (if we look at them through the developmental epidemiologic lens). They target the entire subgroup of children whose parents are involved with criminal justice authorities regardless of any particular child's individual level of risk. Services that primarily aim to make a parent's involvement in the criminal justice system less noxious for children may be beneficial to children, but they may not be sufficient alone to improve the outcomes for the subgroup of children who are at greatest risk for developing serious problems, or to help children who have already developed serious problems. Ultimately, service planning can benefit from both perspectives. Universal prevention should be commonplace, but linked with mechanisms that channel children and families to more targeted or multifaceted interventions when needed. At the same time, systems that provide targeted interventions (e.g., children's mental health, the child welfare system) can improve their response to children by learning about the specific consequences of parental arrest and incarceration for children.

CHAPTER SUMMARY

Interest in providing services and interventions for children whose parents are involved with the criminal justice system has been growing. Two different perspectives have permeated discussions about services for these children, and each has something to contribute to understanding the nature of the services these children need. One of the limitations of service development efforts has been the tendency to conceive of children of incarcerated parents as a homogeneous group, when in reality the needs of children and their families vary. Individual service providers and organizations may be limited as to which of these needs they can address by virtue of the nature of their organizations; nonetheless "big picture" thinking is critical. Mechanisms need to be in place to determine the specific needs of individual children and to link them and their family members to the full array of services they need. It is also important to establish mechanisms for programs and providers to share information with one another; particularly information about the effects their efforts have on children. At the same time, it is important to revise criminal justice policies and practices so that they do the least harm possible to children.

REFERENCES

Bassett, L. (nd) Motheread/Fatheread: A family literacy program of Humanities Washington. Retrieved April, 2009, from http://www.newhorizons.org/strategies/literacy/bassett.htm

Biederman, J., Milberger, S., Faraone, S. V., Kiely, K., Gutie, J., Mick, E., et al. (1995). Family-environment risk factors for attention-deficit hyperactivity disorder: A test of Rutter's indicators of adversity. *Archive of General Psychiatry, 2*, 464–470.

Block, K. J. (1999). Bringing Scouting to prison: Programs and challenges. *Prison Journal, 79*, 269(215).

Caplow, T., & Simon, J. (1999). Understanding prison policy and population trends. In M. Tonry & J. Petersilia (Eds.), *Prisons* (pp. 63–120). Chicago: University of Chicago Press.

Clear, T. R. (Ed.). (1996). *Backfire: When incarceration increases crime.* New York: Vera Institute of Justice.

Farrington, D. P., Jolliffe, D., Loeber, R., Stouthamer-Loeber, M., & Kalb, L. M. (2001). The concentration of offenders in families, and family criminality in the prediction of boys' delinquency. *Journal of Adolescence, 24*, 579–596.

Glueck, S., & Glueck, E. (1950). *Unraveling juvenile delinquency.* Cambridge, MA: Harvard University Press.

Hagan, J. (1996). *The next generation: Children of prisoners.* New York: Vera Institute of Justice.

Hagan, J., & Dinovitzer, R. (1999). Collateral consequences of imprisonment for children, communities, and prisoners. In M. Tonry & J. Petersilia (Eds.), *Crime and Justice: A Review of Research.* Chicago: University of Chicago Press.

Johnson, E. I., & Waldfogel, J. (2002). *Children of incarcerated parents: Cumulative risk and children's living arrangement.* New York: Columbia University.

JusticeWorks Community. Mothers in prison, children in crisis (MIPCIC) Retrieved April, 2009, from http://www.justiceworks.org/natcamp.htm

Kazura, K., & Toth, K. (2004). Playrooms in prison: Helping offenders connect with their children. *Corrections Today, 66*, 128–132.

Lange, S. (2000). The challenges confronting children of incarcerated parents. *Journal of Family Psychotherapy, 11*(4), 61–68.

Lee, A. (2005). Children of inmates: What happens to these unintended victims? *Corrections Today, June,* 63–95.

Leve, L. D., & Chamberlain, P. (2004). Female juvenile offenders: Defining an early-onset pathway for delinquency. *Journal of Child & Family Studies, 13,* 439–452.

Lind, E., & Taylor, T. (1988). *The social psychology of procedural justice.* New York: Plenum.

Martin, S. L. (1995). The Motheread Program: Literacy invention for incarcerated women. *Corrections Today, 57,* 120.

McCord, J., & McCord, W. (1958). The effects of parental role model of criminality. *Journal of Social Issues, 14,* 66–75.

McCorkle, K., & Mulroy, M. (2007). Field notes for ABLE staff: A family literacy program behind bars. Retrieved April, 2009, from http://www.pde.state.pa.us/able/lib/able/ fieldnotes07/fn07flbehindbars.pdf

McGowan, B., & Blumenthal, K. (1978). *Why punish the children?* New York: Children's Defense Fund.

Miller, K. M. (2006). The impact of parental incarceration on children. An emerging need for effective interventions. *Child and Adolescents Social Work Journal, 23,*472–486.

Moses, M. C. (1995). A synergistic solution for children of incarcerated parents. *Corrections Today, 57,* 124–128.

Murray, J., & Farrington, D. P. (2005). Parental imprisonment: Effects on boys' antisocial behaviour and delinquency through the life course. *Journal of Child Psychology and Psychiatry, 46,* 1269–1278.

Nefsis. (nd). Video conferencing expedites court arraignments and helps increase visitation. Retrieved April, 2009, from http://www.nefsis.com/Best-Video-Conferencing-Software/applications-arraignment.html

New Hampshire Department of Corrections. The Family Connections Center: List of books for children of incarcerated parents. Retrieved April, 2009, from http://www.nh.gov/nhdoc/ fcc/books.html

Nieto, M. (2002). *In danger of falling through the cracks: Children of arrested parents.* Sacramento: California Research Bureau, California State Library.

Nolan, C. M. (2003). *Children of arrested parents: Strategies to improve their safety and well-being.* Sacramento: California Research Bureau, California State Library.

Phillips, S. D. (2008). *The Bill of Rights for Children of Incarcerated Parents Technical Assistance Project: Contextual Factors.* Chicago, IL: Jane Addams College of Social Work.

Phillips, S. D., & Erkanli, A. (2008). Differences in patterns of maternal arrest and the parent, family, and child problems encountered in working with families *Children & and Youth Services Review, 30,* 157–172.

Phillips, S. D., Erkanli, A., Costello, E. J., & Angold, A. (2007). Differences among children whose mothers have a history of arrest. *Women & Criminal Justice, 17*(2/3), 45–63.

Phillips, S. D., Erkanli, A., Keeler, G. P., Costello, E. J., & Angold, A. (2006). Disentangling the risks: Parent criminal justice involvement and children's exposure to family risks. *Criminology and Public Policy, 5*(4), 677–702.

Pima Prevention Partnership. (2007). *Arizona children of incarcerated parents Bill of Rights project: Report and recommendations.* Tucson, AZ: Pima Prevention Partnership.

Robins, L. N. (1978). Sturdy childhood predictors of adult antisocial behaviour: Replications from longitudinal studies. *Psychological Medicine, 8,* 611–622.

San Francisco Children of Incarcerated Parents Partnership. (2008). San Francisco Children of Incarcerated Parents Partnership: Who We Are. Retrieved June 5, 2008 from http://www.sfcipp.org/whoweare.html

Sirpa, S. K. (2002). Familial criminality, familial drug use, and gang membership: Youth criminality, drug use, and gang membership – What are the connections? *Journal of Gang Research, 9,* 11–22.

Springer, D. W., Lynch, C., & Rubin, A. (2000). Effects of a solution-focused mutual aid group for Hispanic children of incarcerated parents. *Child and Adolescent Social Work Journal, 17,* 431–442.

Tonry, M., & Petersilia, J. (1999). Prisons research at the beginning of the 21st century. In M. Tonry & J. Petersilia (Eds.), *Prisons.* Chicago: University of Chicago Press.

U. S. Department of Justice. (1988). *Survey of youth in custody (NIJ113365).* Washington DC: Bureau of Justice Statistics.

Urrutia, S. (2004). Words Travel: A model family-strengthening and literacy program. *Corrections Today, April,* 80–83.

Virginia Commission on Youth. (2002). *Children of incarcerated parents. Available from* http://coy.state.va.us/docs/Incarcerated%20Parents.pdf. Richmond, VA: Author.

11

The Challenges of Family Reunification

YVETTE R. HARRIS
VANESSA HARRIS
JAMES A. GRAHAM
GLORIA J. OLIVER CARPENTER

In previous chapters of this book, we have discussed a variety of programs designed to provide support to incarcerated parents and their children. Many of these individuals, especially mothers, will return to their roles as parents, and face numerous challenges. Thus the challenge of maternal child family reunification is the focus of this chapter.

The chapter begins with an overview of the statistics on parent child reunification outcomes and continues with a discussion of the challenges and barriers to successful family reunification and a discussion of the proposed components of family reunification programs. The chapter concludes with suggestions for framing research questions and directions on family reunification programs in the twenty-first century.

Why focus on mothers? As stated in chapter one, incarcerated mothers in comparison to incarcerated fathers prior to their incarceration are more likely to be the primary caretaker for their children, and assume the major responsibility for the financial and social welfare of their children (Bloom & Steinhart, 1993). Furthermore, children experience more emotional trauma when their mothers are arrested, incarcerated, and reenter their lives than when the fate is similar for their fathers (Macintosh, Myers, & Kennon, 2006). Lastly, as the statistics in the next paragraph indicate, the number of mothers in prison and jails is on the rise. Thus, focusing on the challenges mothers face as they reunify with their children and families is of top concern to policymakers, practitioners, and social science researchers.

In 2007, approximately 65,600 female inmates were mothers to minor children, and this number represents an increase of 131% since 1991 (Bureau of Justice Statistics, 2008). Of these mothers, 60% report living with their children prior to arrest, and many expect to resume some form of their parenting role after incarceration (Arditti & Few 2008). However, the resumption of their parenting role is in part determined by the placement of their children during their incarceration, the length of their incarceration, and a host of other proximal and distal factors.

Previously incarcerated mothers encounter challenges in maintaining parental rights and reuniting with their children once they are released from prison. These mothers placed their children with relatives or foster parents during their absence. Under the federal Adoption and Safe Families Act of 1997, states reserve the right to terminate the parental rights of parents with children placed in foster care after fifteen months of their initial enrollment (Humphrey, Turnbull, & Turnbull, 2006). Only six states have statutes in place to reunite incarcerated mothers and their children (Hayward & DePantfilis, 2007).

According to Testa and Slack (2002), the percentage of mothers reunifying with their children is higher when their children are placed with grandparents than when their children are placed in foster care. Figure 11.1 presents information on reunification outcomes.

As Figure 11.1 illustrates, about 20% of children reunify with their mothers, and the majority are adopted or remain in foster care. A minority of these children will exit the system, remain under some form of relative guardianship (SG), or live independently (IL).

It may be the case that some mothers will seek full custody of their children, and others will seek to have partial contact or periodic visiting

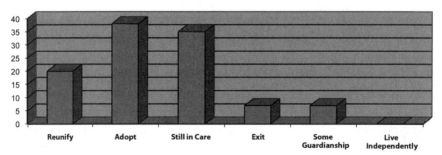

Figure 11.1 Reunification outcomes source: *Corrections Today* (2006)

with their children (Maluccio, Abramczyk, & Thomlinson, 1996). Regardless of the reunification goals and outcomes, it is clear that most mothers and their children will attempt some form of reconnection after the mother has been released from prison. Therefore, identifying the barriers to successful reunification and providing solutions and programs are paramount to ensuring better outcomes for children of incarcerated parents, their mothers, and their temporary caregivers.

Family reunification presents a host of challenges not only for the reentering mother, but also for her children and the current caregivers of her children. In the next section of the chapter we discuss those

Figure 11.2 Challenges for the reentering mother

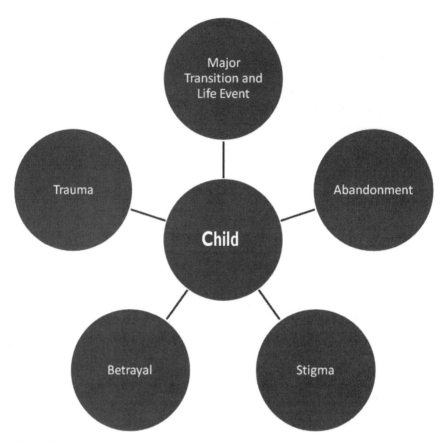

Figure 11.3 Challenges for the children of the reentering mother

challenges. Figures 11.2–11.4 provide a conceptual model of those challenges experienced by the mothers, their children, and the caretakers.

We begin the discussion with maternal challenges.

CHALLENGES FOR THE REENTERING MOTHER

Adjustment to Non-Prison Life

Overcoming the structure, regimentation, loss of independence, and culture of the prison environment takes time. According to Haney (2003), ex-offenders must "take off the prison psychology" and develop a new identity as they adjust to non-prison life and undo the psychological harm caused by prison.

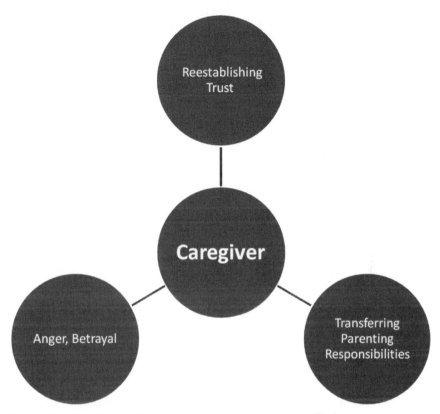

Figure 11.4 Caregiver challenges

In the particular case of mothers, this may involve a transition from external "other" control to one of internal self-control and independent decision making. Because they are unaccustomed to independent decision making and independent problem solving, these mothers often find it difficult to organize the daily lives of their children and to negotiate the multiple demands that are placed on them as the primary caregivers of their children (Brown & Bloom, 2009). This process is doubly challenging for mothers because they "go through two transitions" at once: they are working to be successful at their own reentry process and adapting to their families' and friends' adaptive responses to their return.

Education, Income, and Employment

Unfortunately, some of these mothers failed to finish high school or receive their GED prior to their arrest. Although an estimated 62% of mothers had their diploma or GED at their time of prison admission (Bureau of Justice Statistics, 2008), few mothers participate in the GED programs that are provided in prison during their incarceration (Harlow, 2003).

Of these mothers, 76% report that they were not employed full time prior to their arrest, and 35% had incomes less than $600.00 per month before their incarceration (Brown & Bloom, 2009). Most employers are reluctant to hire ex-offenders and often link a criminal background with an increased probability for engagement in subsequent criminal activity (i.e., theft, physical endangerment, substance abuse, and other negative behaviors). Several states prohibit ex-offenders with drug offenses from occupations that involve child care, elder care, and health care. This places many mothers at a disadvantage, because the majority of women are incarcerated for drug-related crimes (Brown & Bloom, 2009; Richie, 2001).

As a result of their education level, their lack of work experience, and their criminal record, they are unable to secure employment with benefits to support and sustain a family. Thus, as you can see, they face numerous challenges to economic self-sufficiency, which is vital in establishing and maintaining a nurturing and safe environment for their children.

Access to Public Benefits and Housing

In some instances, mothers with criminal records also are denied access to public benefits, such as welfare cash assistance (Temporary Aid for Needy Families), food stamps, and federal housing assistance, which may be key to their transition to self-sufficiency (Laughlin, Arrigo, Blevins, & Coston, 2008). These restrictions apply mostly to individuals who have committed drug-related crimes. The Personal Responsibility and Work Opportunity Reconciliation Act permanently denies assistance to individuals who are convicted of a drug-related felony (Montoya & Atkinson, 2002). As stated earlier, drug-related offenses comprise the majority of crimes committed by women with criminal records, and therefore a significant number of them will likely face challenges in accessing such benefits (Brown & Bloom, 2009).

Physical Health and Mental Health Issues

Many mothers enter prison with a host of serious health problems, ranging from HIV/AIDS to hypertension, diabetes, asthma, and reproductive health problems (Richie, 2001). Although several ex-offenders report receiving health care while in prison, many of them are released with their healthcare needs unmet (Richie, 2001), and they state that they are unable to secure ongoing health care services upon their release from prison. The lack of access to health care impacts the quality of their health and directly influences their ability to sustain employment. Without access to health care they face a greater probability of reincarceration.

In the general population it is estimated that 12% of females have some type of mental disorder, compared to 9% of males. The trend continues with female inmates (73% in state prisons) having higher rates of mental health problems compared to their male counterparts (55% in state prisons) (Bureau of Justice Statistics, 2006).

A significant percentage of mothers who lived with their minor children before their incarceration experienced either physical/sexual abuse (59.7%), had mental health problems (72.8%), or substance abuse problems (63.6%). These rates were higher for mothers who did not live with their minor children at their time of arrest (72.4%, 57.6%, 75.3%, and 81.5% respectively) (Bureau of Justice Statistics, 2008).

In state prisons an estimated 27% of females received some type of therapy/counseling, and 22% were on psychotropic medications (Bureau of Justice Statistics, 2001). Few reported receiving adequate treatment (i.e., counseling, or medication) for their mental health problems (Ardetti, & Few 2008), and others reported that the quality of mental health services was poor, inconsistent, or ineffective. Some refused any type of treatment because of "distrust of the system" or refused medical management of their mental health problems because of their concern of being "altered" while on medication, preferring to stay in their current mental state.

Women who are incarcerated due to a drug offense or have had a drug addiction may be even more reluctant to consume a prescribed medication for fear of developing another addiction. In addition to those problems, these mothers must cope with such feelings as worthlessness and low self-esteem, all of which impact their availability to parent and the quality of their parenting. They may also feel guilty about being emotionally and physically absent from their children's lives (Grella & Greenwell, 2006). Physically unhealthy mothers and mothers with persistent mental health problems are unable to resume an effective parenting role.

Ongoing Substance Abuse Issues

According to the Bureau of Justice (2006), 60% of incarcerated women have substance abuse issues and 59% were using drugs at the time of their arrest. Although drug treatment programs are offered in prison, they are frequently criticized because they employ a "male prisoner" model and fail to take into account the unique drug use and health issues of female offenders. Women in comparison to men use harder drugs (e.g. cocaine), and use drugs to cope with sexual abuse, physical abuse, or some life trauma. Many reenter without having received adequate treatment for their substance abuse, and as a consequence are more likely to reuse (Shivy, Wu, Moon, Mann, Holland, Eacho, 2007).

PARENTING CHALLENGES

Although several of the parenting programs discussed in previous chapters of this book are designed to provide mothers with knowledge of child development and skills and tools to effectively parent, these programs are conducted under supervision, with their parenting process monitored, and they are provided with feedback. However, that structure and support are virtually nonexistent in the real world of parenting once they are released from prison. The lack of support, feedback, and monitoring makes "real world parenting" on the home front a daunting task for most mothers being released from prison (Kennon, Macintosh, & Myers, 2009).

There are other challenges that these mothers face with their roles as parents. Those include a history of "disrupted parenting" due to repeated cycles of incarceration. Hence they are unaware of the critical milestones in their children's lives (i.e., birthday's, school transitions, academic milestones, and developmental issues).

In addition, the incarcerated parent returns home to children who have aged, and the incarcerated parent is unaware of the developmental changes or not prepared to parent them. Here is an excerpt from a conversation with a mother that aptly captures this experience: "Before I went to prison, I was able to parent a 6-year-old and now that he's 12, I'm not sure what to do" (Coen & Harris, 2009, Personal Communication).

These mothers are also returning to a "revised family system" without clear roles and responsibilities for them. Consequently, they must confront a process of reestablishing bonds (Brown & Bloom, 2009) and parental authority with children despite having limited contact with them while in prison. They must redevelop the attachment relationship because in many cases, the children have formed an attachment relationship with their current caregivers and may be unwilling to transfer "filial affection" to their mothers (Taylor, 1996). The reestablishment of the attachment relationship is further complicated when the children have experienced multiple placements (Mackintosh, Myers, & Kennon 2006).

Lastly, they are returning to children who exhibit mild to severe emotional problems, including anger management issues, attention deficit disorder, oppositional defiant disorder, bi-polar disorder, and depression, to name a few. These children present unique parenting challenges and many mothers are not prepared to parent children with such extreme mental health problems.

COMMUNITY AND NEIGHBORHOOD CHALLENGES

The neighborhoods that these mothers return to, as Chung and McFadden indicate in Chapter 5, are poor, with little to no employment opportunities or support services, and are high-risk, where criminal activity continues. Women of color returning from jail or prison do not feel embraced by their communities (Marbley & Ferguson, 2005), and this lack of community support may impact the quality of their reentry and their ability to create a safe parenting environment for their children. Thus, the neighborhoods are not conducive to their growth and development as parents, and may present additional challenges as they resist "entering back into a former lifestyle."

CHALLENGES FOR CHILDREN OF REENTERING MOTHERS

Children of incarcerated parents are a hidden segment of our society. They are the casualties and collateral damage of parental incarceration, and as stated in previous chapters, experience a range of mental health, behavioral, and cognitive problems. Unfortunately there are few comprehensive services available to them, and many are not emotionally prepared to cope with a parent's reentry into their lives. For some, maternal reentry represents another disruption in their lives, and they confront the problems discussed below. However the degree to which they experience those challenges is determined by their age, cognitive level, and the quality of emotional support available to them.

Major Life Event and Transition

As illustrated in the Figure 11.3, from a child's perspective the return of a parent from prison represents a significant life event and transition in their lives. As a result of the mother reentering the parenting role, the child must adjust to changes in household arrangements, parental authority, as well as family income and family resources. These children experience a wide range of emotions in anticipation or in reaction to these changes, including happiness, anger, sadness, shame, excitement, and fear. Acting out behavior may increase as a response to the anticipation in the change of the family structure. Depending on the length of incarceration, many of these children have grown up without their mothers in their lives, and might rebel against any parenting attempts. According to the Bureau of Justice (2008), "more than a third of minor children will reach age 18 while their parent is incarcerated."

Other children may not have their mothers return to their homes, but these mothers will still assume an active role in their lives. This may be stressful for them as well, and they will also exhibit a range of emotional and behavioral problems.

Trauma

In addition to the aforementioned issues, children may also have unresolved trauma as a consequence of witnessing the arrest of their mothers. One in five was present at the time of their mother's arrest (Seymour, 1998), and more than half of the children were under the age of seven and in the sole care of the mother at the time.

Abandonment

They may also deal with unresolved abandonment issues. Children who were in school at the time of the arrest may return home to an empty house, unaware of the reason for the mother's absence. Depending on the crime, mothers may not have time to arrange for alternative guardianship while they are incarcerated. Children left in undesired custody situations (abuse, neglect) may blame the mother, causing challenges in the later reunification process.

Stigma

Many children have to cope with the stigma of having a mother in prison. As Holmes et al. state in Chapter 2, they experience disdain and negative comments from peers, teachers, and other adults, and isolation within their neighborhoods. This results in feelings of shame and loss, and influences their willingness to reunite with their mothers.

Feelings of Betrayal

A small percentage of children, specifically adolescents, were arrested with their mothers, although they were not participants in the crime (Brown & Bloom, 2009). Consequently, depending on the type of crime, the adolescent may be unable to pursue certain types of employment or receive assistance. When children are arrested for their unwitting or forced involvement in their parents' criminal activities, the reunification process can become more difficult due to the greater likelihood of the children feeling betrayed, used, or angry.

CHALLENGES FOR CARETAKERS

The feelings of caregivers in reaction to the reentry of mothers into the lives of their children are often unexplored in the social science research. Caregivers serve a pivotal role in assisting children of incarcerated parents to adjust to their mothers' arrest, incarceration, and reentry. Like these children, some of the caregivers struggle with feelings of abandonment, betrayal trauma, and anger. They must cope with their own unresolved relationship issues with the reentering mother and work on rebuilding a functional relationship with the reentering mother in the context of a family. The degree to which caregivers experience those feelings depends on the custodial arrangements (if they are grandparents, foster care parents, fathers, or other relatives assuming parenting responsibilities for the children), and their relationship with the returning mother.

Given that most caretakers of children of incarcerated parents are grandparents, usually grandmothers, we focus the discussion on their experiences (Baydar & Brooks-Gunn, 1998). In addition to the issues discussed below, grandparents face a host of financial and emotional challenges and are rarely provided with support or emotional validation (Holmes, et al. 2010). Some grandmothers report experiencing feelings of alienation, and few receive social or government assistance (Hayslip, 2002).

Reestablishing Trust

Many times caretakers, especially grandparents, have been the target of the mother's criminal activity (i.e., stealing, forging checks), and issues of trust must be reestablished. This takes time and effort.

Transferring Parenting Responsibilities

Many caregivers struggle with the challenge of transferring the parenting responsibilities to the returning mother. They have misgivings about the ability of the mothers to demonstrate that they are responsible parents who can at some point in time assume an effective parenting role in their children's lives. Some express concerns about the potential damaging influence of reunification on the children's emotional well-being, and a few state that reunification "is more trouble than it is worth." (Harris, 2009)

Given the challenges discussed in the previous section for reentering mothers, their children, and families, it is necessary to develop reunification programs that assist these mothers, their children, and current caretakers to successfully make the transition from prison. These programs should be comprehensive, and community-based programs designed with flexibility to take into account the mother's cultural background and developmental level.

The welfare-to-work demonstration programs of the 1980s and 1990s serve as prime models for designing mother-child reunification programs. These programs were intended to offer comprehensive assistance to mothers to "move them from welfare dependency to work." For example, programs such as JOBS and New Chance provided services that aided young and poor mothers in completing their education and securing employment. In addition, parenting classes and life skills classes with an emphasis on relationships were offered as well.

Proposed Components of Maternal-Child Family Reunification Programs

Figure 11.5 describes the proposed components for family reunification programs. The degree to which features are included in a program is determined in part by the type of reunification the parent and child will have, and in part determined by the parental cultural background.

As the figure illustrates, such core features should include the following elements.

Pre-Release Preparation

Pre-release preparation involves providing the mothers prior to their release from prison with what Karfgin (2002) refers to as a "discharge plan." The discharge plan is a document that outlines the activities that they are to accomplish within the first 30 days after their release

Figure 11.5 Suggested components of a maternal-child family reunification program

from prison and identifies challenges they will encounter upon release, offering solutions to those challenges. Many reentering mothers express anxiety about returning to their communities and their parenting role. The goal of the discharge plan would be to offset that anxiety with concrete suggestions on coping consistent with the day and week after release from prison, especially focusing on the parenting challenges that they will encounter. This discharge plan would provide information on local services that offer public assistance, housing, education, employment opportunities, community mentors, and community resources. The overall goal of the prerelease plan is to help these mothers begin their adjustment and transition to the non-prison world.

Post-Prison Support

This is essentially a form of "reentry managed care." Post-prison support should come in the form of providing assistance in completing forms, scheduling appointments, and connecting the mothers with support services discussed below (i.e., mental health counseling, access to health care, substance abuse treatment, parenting classes, education, employment, community support, and legal assistance). Post-prison support should last for one year after the mothers are released from prison. Mothers who transition off of probation and parole and those who are released from prison without the constraints of probation and parole represent special cases; however, this support should be offered to assist them with their continuing and changing reentry needs.

Mental Health Counseling

A critical component of the program should be to provide mental health services to these mothers in the form of evaluation and counseling. These mothers should be evaluated upon release, and evaluated for a year following their release from prison. Counseling should focus on such issues as depression, self-esteem, relationships, and violence prevention.

Access to Health Care

One of the most prevalent concerns expressed by reentering mothers is access to health care (Richie 2009). Although some women have access to medical care while they are incarcerated, they typically do not have ongoing attention to their health care needs upon release from prison.

Substance Abuse Treatment

As we stated earlier in the chapter, a significant percentage of women leave prison with continuing substance abuse issues. We suggest that substance abuse treatment be provided along with counseling and programs tailored to address the unique needs of these parenting women. Petersilia (1990) suggests designing substance abuse treatment programs from a social learning perspective that emphasize social skill building, role playing, and interpersonal cognitive skill training. The most effective treatment programs using this orientation should provide follow-up for several months after mothers have completed the program.

Access to TANF

Other public assistance efforts that should be extended to provide mothers with access to public assistance include TANF, food stamps, and public housing. For some, depending on the offense, this would entail changes in the laws that restrict their receipt of public assistance.

Parenting Classes

Reentering mothers need assistance in rebuilding the parent-child relationship. The parenting classes should be offered on an ongoing basis for these mothers and their children, and structured so that the classes address the following issues: household management, cooking, comparative shopping, budgeting, and housekeeping. In addition, mini modules could provide information on specific parenting issues such as discipline, with a focus on discipline at the different ages, monitoring homework, and other academic environmental support issues for the children. For the mothers who have not resumed custodial care of their children, there should be modules to assist them in developing their co-parenting role. According to Richie (2009), when women are offered adequate support for being a parent, having even a noncustodial relationship with one's children can be an important stabilizing force in women's lives as they make difficult transitions. Parenting classes taught by women from the same cultural and economic background as the mothers seem to be the most effective (Schaffner, 1997).

Lastly, the mothers should be provided with a parenting mentor who is available to monitor their parenting, offer suggestions, and model parenting behavior.

In addition to the issues presented above, we propose that reunification programs should have an advocacy component to them. That component would support legislation that removes legal barriers, and prescribe strategies to reintegrate mothers into their communities. These components are briefly discussed below.

Remove Legal Barriers and Provide Legal Assistance

This would require changes in laws that prohibit ex-offenders who have committed certain crimes from receiving TANF funds, food stamps, as well as the restrictions on housing. Following the directions and suggestions spelled out in the "Second Chance Act" is a first step. In addition, the mothers should be provided with legal assistance to help them renegotiate custody arrangements and secure child support payments

Community Involvement and Support

The quality and the type of community support is instrumental to successful family reunification. The community can serve as a surrogate family for the reentering mothers, their children, and families, as well as provide avenues for social and economic support. However, as previously mentioned, incarcerated individuals frequently return to neighborhoods that have the fewest resources to sustain their successful reentry and reunification. For those at-risk mothers and low-resource communities, there should be a recommitment to community development (see Chung & McFadden, Chapter 5) with an emphasis on the following ideals: Communities should be equipped and remodeled to provide educational opportunities and employment services, and safe, secure, and affordable housing. A one-stop-shopping model approach should be adopted to offer healthcare services and substance abuse treatment within a central location in the community. La Bodega de la Familia is an example of a community-based model that provides one-stop-shopping comprehensive services with a specific focus on substance abuse treatment for reentering individuals and their families. Providing these mothers with these services in a familiar environment might reduce the alienation and isolation that some report feeling when they are released from jail or prison.

Assistance for Children of Reentering Mothers

Assistance for children would involve providing them with reentry counseling. This counseling could focus on what to expect when their mother returns home from prison and on assisting them in "working through" some of their unresolved issues pertaining to their mother's arrests and incarceration. To ensure their optimal functioning, ongoing support services should be provided for them, either in a school setting, a summer camp setting, or in the form of individual counseling.

Assistance for Current Caregivers

We propose that support for caregivers come in the form of parenting classes and address such issues as co-parenting, transferring responsibility, and developing healthy family relationships.

FRAMING QUESTIONS AND DIRECTIONS FOR MATERNAL-CHILD REUNIFICATION FAMILY PROGRAMS IN THE TWENTY-FIRST CENTURY

First, research must be grounded in theoretical perspectives that emphasize a family systems perspective or an ecological perspective (Bowen, 1966; Bronfenbrenner, 1986). Both perspectives take into account the individual, family, neighborhood, and community influences that impact adjustment for the returning mothers, their children, and their current caretakers.

Second, multi-method (qualitative and quantitative) and interdisciplinary approaches must be employed to address a problem as complex as family reunification. The former provides a vehicle to explore the voices of those affected by incarceration, and the latter expands the lens through which we view the success or lack thereof of family reunification.

Third, reunification programs must be rigorously evaluated in order to determine which components are the most effective and least effective in facilitating successful maternal-child family reunification. Any program developed must take into consideration the cultural background and age of these mothers and their children, and be anchored in such a context. Programs should be tailored to meet the unique needs of adolescent mothers who are reentering the lives of their children. Programs should also be designed to meet the unique needs of those in poverty, women in general, and African American mothers and other mothers of color.

Fourth, programs must be adapted to meet the reunification goals of the mothers, children, and their current caretakers. For some of the reentering mothers who have never had custody of their children, their goal of successful reunification may be to establish a pattern of consistent visitation and to assume a peripheral parenting role. On the other hand, for individuals who have had custody of their children prior to their incarceration, their goal may be to resume a full-time parenting role.

CHAPTER SUMMARY

The focus of this chapter was to discuss the challenges inherent in the family reunification process. The chapter began with an overview of the reunification outcomes statistics, and continued with a discussion of the challenges facing returning mothers. This section highlighted their education, income, and employment challenges. Many of these mothers have little "real world" work experience, few have completed their education, and many do not qualify for government assistance.

The chapter continued with a discussion of the challenges that children of incarcerated parents face. Children of incarcerated parents experience a range of emotions as they adjust to their mother's arrest, incarceration, and reentry into their lives. Yet there are few comprehensive programs available for them. For many of them, the mother's return to their lives represents a major transition and life event, and they must cope with the trauma of the parental incarceration, the stigma, and the resulting abandonment issues. Caregivers play an integral role in the adjustment of children to maternal reunification. How they cope with trust issues and transferring parental responsibility were discussed as well.

The next section of the chapter focused on the components of a successful reunification program. Those included providing services for the returning mother, her children, and their caregivers. The chapter concluded with a discussion of framing research questions and direction on family reunification programs in the twenty-first century.

The reentry process of formerly incarcerated individuals, especially mothers, has become a growing area of research and should become one of the focal points of research for the next decade.

REFERENCES

Arditti, J. A., & Few, A. L. (2008). Maternal distress and women's reentry into family and community life. *Family Process, 47*(3), 303–321.

Arditti, J. A., & Few, A. L. (2006). Mothers' reentry into family life following incarceration. *Criminal Justice Policy Review, 17*(1), 103–123.

Baydar, N., & Brooks-Gunn, J. (1998). Profiles of grandmothers who help care for their grandchildren in the united states. *Family Relations, 47*(4, The Family as a Context for Health and Well-Being), 385–393.

Bloom, B. & Steinhart, D. (1993). *Why punish the children: A reappraisal of the children of incarcerated mothers in America.* San Francisco: National Council on Crime & Delinquency.

Bowen, M (1966). The use of family theory in clinical practice. Comprehensive Psychiatry, 7, 345–374.

Bronfenbrenner, U. (1986). Ecology of the family as a context for human development: Research Perspectives. Developmental Psychology, 22, 723–742.

Bureau of Justice Statistics. (2006). *Drug use and dependence, state and federal prisoners, 2004: Special report.* Washington DC: U.S. Department of Justice.

Bureau of Justice Statistics. (2006). *Mental health problems of prison and jail inmates: Special report.* Washington DC: U.S. Department of Justice.

Bureau of Justice Statistics. (2008). *Parents in prison and their minor children: Special report.* Washington DC: U.S. Department of Justice.

Brown, M., & Bloom, B. (2009). Reentry and renegotiating motherhood: Maternal identity and success on parole. *Crime & Delinquency, 55*(2), 313–336.

Cohen, L., & Harris, Y. R. (2009). Mother's Perception of Parenting: A Personal Interview.

Grella, C. E., & Greenwell, L. (2006). Correlates of parental status and attitudes toward parenting among substance-abusing women offenders. *The Prison Journal, 86*(1), 89–113.

Hanlon, T. E., Carswell, S. B., & Rose, M. (2007). Research on the caretaking of children of incarcerated parents: Findings and their service delivery implications. *Children and Youth Services Review, 29*(3), 348–362.

Haney, C. (2003). The psychological impact of incarceration: implications for post prison adjustment. In J Travis and M. Waul, (eds.), *Prisoners Once Removed: The Impact of Incarceration and Reentry on Children, Families and Communities.* Washington DC: Urban Institute.

Harlow, C. (2003). Education and correctional populations. Washington DC, bureau of Justice Statistics, NCJ 195670.

Harris, Y. R. (2009). Interview with grandparent of a child with both parents incarcerated.

Hayslip, B., Emick, M., Henderson, C., & Elias, K. (2002). Temporal variations in the experience of custodial grand parenting: A short term longitudinal study. *The Journal of Applied Gerontology, 21*, pp. 139–156.

Hayward, A., & DePanfilis, D. (2007). Foster children with an incarcerated parent: Predictors of reunification. *Children and Youth Services review, 29*, 1320–1334.

Henriques, Z. W., & Manatu-Rupert, N. (2001). Living on the outside: African American women before, during, and after imprisonment. *The Prison Journal, 81*(1), 6–19.

Humphrey, K. R., Turnbull, A. P., & Turnbull III, H. R. (2006). Impact of the adoption and safe families act on youth and their families: Perspectives of foster care providers, youth with emotional disorders, service providers, and judges. *Children and Youth Services Review, 28*(2), 113–132.

Kargin, A. (2002). Attachment and Reunification: Building Parental Skills. GANNS Newsletter, retrieved on September 22, 2009 from www.gainsctr.com.

Kennon, S., Mackintosh, V., & Myers, B. (2009). Parenting Education for Incarcerated Mothers. *The Journal of Correction 60.* 10–30.

La Vigne, N. G., Naser, R. L., Brooks, L. E., & Castro, J. L. (2005). Examining the effect of incarceration and in-prison family contact on prisoners' family relationships. *Journal of Contemporary Criminal Justice, 21*(4), 314–335.

Laughlin, J. S., Arrigo, B. A., Blevins, K. R., & Coston, C. T. M. (2008). Incarcerated mothers and child visitation: A law, social science, and policy perspective. *Criminal Justice Policy Review, 19*(2), 215–238.

Mackintosh, V. H., Myers, B. J., & Kennon, S. S. (2006). Children of incarcerated mothers and their caregivers: Factors affecting the quality of their relationship. *Journal of Child & Family Studies, 15*(5), 579–594.

Maluccio, A. N., Abramczyk, L. W., & Thomlison, B. (1996). Family reunification of children in out-of-home care: Research perspectives. *Children and Youth Services Review, 18*(4–5), 287–305.

Marbley, A. F., & Ferguson, R. (2005). Responding to prisoner reentry, recidivism, and incarceration of inmates of color: A call to the communities. *Journal of Black Studies, 35*(5), 633–649.

Montoya, I. D., & Atkinson, J. S. (2002). A synthesis of welfare reform policy and its impact on substance users. *American Justice, Drug Alcohol Abuse, 28*(1), 133–146.

Petersilia, J .(1999). Parole and Prisoner Reentry in the United States. In Prisons, Crime and Justice: A Review of Research, vol 26, (ed) M Tonry, J Petersilla, pp. 479–529. Chicago: University of Chicago Press.

Richie, B. E. (2001). Challenges incarcerated women face as they return to their communities: Findings from life history interviews. *Crime & Delinquency, 47*(3), 368–389.

Schram, P. J., Koons-Witt, B. A., Williams, F. P. III, & McShane, M. D. (2006). Supervision strategies and approaches for female parolees: Examining the link between unmet needs and parolee outcome. *Crime & Delinquency, 52*(3), 450–471.

Seymore, C. (1998). Children with parents in prison: Child welfare policy, programs, and practice issues. *Child Welfare, 77,* 1–14.

Schaffner, L. (1997). Families on probation: Court ordered parenting classes for parents of juvenile offenders. *Crime and Delinquency, 43,* 412–437.

Shivy, V. A., Wu, J. J., Moon, A. E., Mann, S. C., Holland, J. G., & Eacho, C. (2007). Ex-offenders reentering the workforce. *Journal of Counseling Psychology, 54*(4), 466–473.

Taylor, S. D. (1996). Women offenders and reentry issues. *Journal of Psychoactive Drugs, 28* (1), 85–93.

Testa, M., & Slack, K. (2002). The gift of kinship foster care. *Children and Youth Services Review, 24,* 79–108.

ADDITIONAL RESOURCES

Videos

Makeba's Story. YouTube. This short video appears on YouTube and is written and directed by a young woman who had to cope with the challenges of parental incarceration and reunification. She provides suggestions to her peers and offers guidance on ways to manage the challenges that the reentering parent, the family, and the child will encounter.

Documentaries on Children of Incarcerated Parents

A Sentence of Their Own. Filmmaker, Edgar Barens. This film chronicles the damaging impact incarceration has on families and makes visible the gradual descent of a family doing time on the outside.

Inside/Out and *What Does He Do in There?* Barry Zack, Center Force. This video is designed for children and tracks a day in the life of a prisoner in San Quentin State Prison to answer questions posed by visiting children.

When the Bough Breaks. Filmmaker, Jill Evans Petzel. This film explores the emotional impact on children whose mothers are incarcerated for nonviolent crimes. Filmed over the course of a year, children in three Missouri families tell their stories.

Web Sites for Reentry Support Programs

Center Point Inc. is a private, not-for-profit corporation that provides a multidisciplinary continuum of social rehabilitation services for men, women, and women with dependent children. Services include outpatient, inpatient, vocational, and consultation treatment to develop individual, personal, social, and moral responsibilities in every person served. To learn more about the Center Point Inc. program, go to www.cpinc.org.

La Bodega de la Familia is a community based comprehensive program that provides services to formerly incarcerated inmates who are going through the recovery process. To learn more about La Bodega go to www.vera,org/bdf

Additional Readings

Arditti, J. A., & Few, A. L. (2008). Maternal distress and women's reentry into family and community life. *Family Process, 47*(3), 303–321.

Arditti, J. A., & Few, A. L. (2006). Mothers' reentry into family life following incarceration. *Criminal Justice Policy Review, 17*(1), 103–123.

Cohen, L. P. (2006). A law's fallout: Women in prison fight for custody. *The Wall Street Journal, 247*(47)

Hanlon, T. E., Carswell, S. B., & Rose, M. (2007). Research on the caretaking of children of incarcerated parents: Findings and their service delivery implications. *Children and Youth Services Review, 29*(3), 348–362.

Hayslip, B., Emick, M., Henderson, C., & Elias, K. (2002). Temporal variations in the experience of custodial grand parenting: A short term longitudinal study. *The Journal of Applied Gerontology, 21*, pp. 139–156.

Mackintosh, V. H., Myers, B. J., & Kennon, S. S. (2006). Children of incarcerated mothers and their caregivers: Factors affecting the quality of their relationship. *Journal of Child & Family Studies, 15*(5), 579–594.

Research and Intervention Issues for Moving Forward with Development in Children of Incarcerated Parents

12

GLORIA J. OLIVER CARPENTER
JAMES A. GRAHAM
YVETTE R. HARRIS

As the growth rate of the prison population has increased over the past few decades, so too has the growth rate of the population of children of incarcerated parents (CIP) (Bureau of Justice Statistics, 2003; Mumola, 2000). In addition to individual normative developmental tasks, CIP often face challenging circumstances and are considered to be at varying levels of risk for negative outcomes (Phillips & Erkanli, 2008).

Despite the growing attention over the past decade, no one agency is responsible for CIP, and research data are sparse and inconsistent. Because of the legal, psychological, and social implications of the parent-child separation (e.g., guardianship, child trauma related to separation or parents' arrest, financial burden, stigma, peer pressure, etc.), a number of different systems are often involved in the care and well-being of CIP. There is a unique inclusion of family, community, and state systems that influence the development of children of incarcerated parents. These systems are discussed in chapters 2, 5, and 6 of this text.

As we attempt to understand these children using a developmental perspective, we must include an understanding of the systemic context. This context exerts direct and indirect influences on CIP. Furthermore, a developmental perspective necessitates an evaluation of factors and an understanding of processes that contribute to resiliency and success in this vulnerable population. As discussed in the early chapters of this text

277

(e.g., chapters 2, 5, & 6), Bronfenbrenner's Ecological Systems Model (2001) provides a comprehensive framework for understanding CIP. This model allows us to focus on the different systems affecting the child directly and indirectly at any given point in development. Thus, we are able to understand change that occurs over time as a process rather than as distinct events. We can also understand environmental and psychological issues that contribute to risk and resiliency for the child. Furthermore, this ecological model allows us to implement appropriate interventions and legislative policies that will support optimal development. Understanding multiple variables that define the child's context beyond parental incarceration—variables that may have been present before the parent's arrest—is critical to understanding this population and providing effective interventions.

This chapter summarizes research presented throughout the text, while highlighting important issues fundamental to our understanding of this population. The chapter calls for an examination of context and resiliency mechanisms for normative development. In addition, indirect influences on CIP are considered as important pathways for facilitating success. Attention is placed upon our conceptual framework and approach to exploring the lives of CIP. Finally, the chapter presents recommendations for future research and intervention development with this heterogeneous group.

As stated elsewhere in this volume, multiple issues are salient throughout child development for CIP. Likewise, it is important to understand the child's reactions and adjustments to the different periods of the parent's incarceration (i.e., before, during, or after incarceration). Different dynamics may occur at all stages of the incarceration process. Research indicates that incarcerated parents (mothers in particular) lived in poverty, were single, ill-prepared to raise their children, and were chronic abusers of drugs and/or alcohol to the extent that their parenting was compromised before the incarceration (Hanlon, Blatchley, Bennet-Sears, et.al., 2005). These factors contribute to a vulnerability in CIP that puts them at risk for a deviant lifestyle and an intergenerational cycle of abuse before parental incarceration becomes an issue (Hanlon, et.al., 2005; Greene, Haney, & Hurtago, 2002; Covington, 2002). Once the incarceration has occurred, the child is likely to experience a heightened sense of stress due to the separation as well as other factors that may have been at issue before the incarceration (e.g., poverty, instability, discrimination, limited access to emotional and social support, etc.). Incarcerated persons are often viewed as unfit for society and undeserving of positive attention and resources; thus, their children are also affected and often denied support and attention. Reports have indicated that even when CIP have the support of social workers, they are often not receiving emotional support or outlets to discuss their parent's imprisonment (Philbrick, 2002). Without this needed support, CIP and particularly those who are adolescents can develop higher levels of aggression, perennial delinquent activity, and increased risks for intergenerational incarceration (Bernstein, 2005; Eddy & Reid, 2003). During parental incarceration, children are faced with the need to adjust to their loss and sometimes adapt to their new lifestyle. They must find a renewed sense of balance and identity while adjusting to change. This process continues during the reentry period when the parent rejoins the family (Travis & Waul, 2003; Parke & Clarke-Stewart, 2003).

To fully understand the effects of these stressors for children, we must explore the individual's internal context, which contributes to his or her ability to cope (Boss, 1986; Bronfenbrenner, 2001). Although this point is underemphasized in the prevention and intervention literature, it is an essential component of any effort to reach children and facilitate effective coping skills. Age, gender, and developmental trajectories are primary factors that contribute to the child's coping skills. Individuals are active agents who contribute to their own development (Bronfenbrenner, 2001). For example, facilitating realistic and adaptive meaning-making skills prompted by the negative life experiences of CIP has life-long implications for strength building and character development (Erikson, 1959; Kegan, 1982). These researchers acknowledge that an individual's own interpretation of the negative events or contradictions he or she experiences in life and the meaning he or she derives from those experiences play a key role in future character development and resiliency processes (Colby & Damon, 1992; Kegan, 1982).

INTERVENTION

Current intervention efforts focus on facilitating resiliency for CIP through proximal processes. Research on attachment and parent-child relationships, as well as on parenting styles and parent education is plentiful and tends to provide the framework for evidence-based intervention. For example, most intervention is child-focused, parent-child focused, or parent-education focused. Child-focused interventions typically take the form of support groups, mentoring programs, and therapeutic counseling services. These interventions commonly focus on the child's socio-emotional functioning, and are often driven by a proven theoretical foundation, including client-centered theory (Rogers, 1957), attachment theory (Bowlby, 1988), resiliency (Masten & Coatsworth, 1998), or other theories focused on optimal development. Chapters 7, 8, and 10 present a more comprehensive focus on the frameworks and theories that guide intervention with this population.

Recent initiatives over the last two decades have focused on reaching children within the school system, because this is considered a typical environment where they spend the majority of their day. Thus, academic and social emotional problems related to the parent's incarceration are often revealed at school. This system (i.e., school) offers a definite gateway of access to CIP, and services are likely to be delivered by competent professionals (teachers, guidance counselors, psychologists, etc.). Despite the potential benefits of school-based interventions, the work with CIP within the school system is under-documented and likely to be neglected. A review of the current literature revealed very few school-based intervention programs targeting CIP (Lopez & Bhat, 2007; Springer, Lynch, & Rubin, 2000; Springer, Pomeroy, & Johnson, 1999; Johnston, 1992; 1993). Without a doubt, more work is needed in this area. School-based interventions represent an opportunity to reach children in a safe and familiar place. Several types of initiatives can be implemented within the school, including mentoring programs, solution-focused or coping therapies, peer support, and prevention programs.

There are other programs providing general support through socioemotional interventions. Community programs that offer mentoring, tutoring, and extracurricular activities are essentially providing the support and stability needed for CIP. Examples of these programs include Big Brothers, Big Sisters, Girl Scouts, Volunteers of America, the Salvation Army, and other community-based programs (Mid-Atlantic Network, 2003). The current inter-agency initiative to motivate adults to connect with children at the family, school, and community levels (Bush, 2008) demonstrates the importance of supporting youth in their development, meeting them where they are (developmentally, geographically, and contextually), and identifying needs for specific prevention and intervention efforts. Much of the criticism regarding intervention questions the efficacy of work that may or may not be developmentally and culturally appropriate (Miller, 2006). Practitioners call for interventions with a more specific focus that incorporate differences in children's reactions that may be due to child gender, ethnicity, age, and cognition, as well as ecological factors that may influence child coping (Miller, 2006; Hanlon, et al., 2005; Hanlon, Carswell, & Rose, 2007).

Consistent with its assertion that there are gender-specific reactions to incarceration, the literature suggests that children (regardless of gender) exhibit "acting out" behaviors when a man enters prison, and "acting in" behaviors when a woman enters prison (Breen, 1995; Fritsch & Burkhead, 1981). Unfortunately, more research is needed to understand the correlates of a child's reaction to incarceration and the intervention strategies that would address these issues.

Major attention should be given to the child's status and problems prior to the parent's imprisonment and to their use as a baseline to support stability and successful development (Dalley, 2002). For example, many children are faced with adjusting to multiple homes, parenting styles, and school placements, and others may be experiencing a different type of adjustment if the incarcerated parent was not the primary caregiver before imprisonment.

Likewise, interventions focused on parenting and education strategies should acknowledge the parent's skills prior to his or her incarceration as well as changes in the quality and consistency of parenting responsibilities brought on by the incarceration (Hanlon, et.al., 2007). Parent education programs should focus not only on parenting skills, but should also include a focus on self-improvement mechanisms, such as increasing self-esteem and confidence, as well as impulse control and insight awareness (Gonzalez, Romero, & Cerbana, 2007). Interventions focused on repairing and building parent-child relationships are often initiated with the intent of reducing problematic behaviors in CIP. This area of intervention, however, could be enhanced by preventive efforts at the judicial level. Specifically, a consideration of children's needs, as indicated in chapters 2 and 3, in the sentencing and pre-sentencing process could alleviate much of the burden placed upon parent-child relationship interventions. This would include a consideration of the distance between the child's home and the prison when a facility is being selected, a consideration of alternate sentencing placements to support family-friendly environments, and the availability of resources to support the child in adjusting to a new living situation as well as eventual family reunification (Nesmith & Ruhland, 2008). Research has found that when children have access and direct contact with their incarcerated parent, they are more likely to feel connected with that parent and to have less stress and worry related to the separation (Nesmith & Ruhland, 2008). In addition, there is often a smaller burden on the caregiver who is left to help the child understand and cope with the separation from the parent.

As indicated earlier, programs and interventions targeting families of CIP have developed from a variety of agencies. Bouchet (2008) asserts that, although this primarily stems from resources and funding, quality and effectiveness of services are also of concern. Many agencies may not have practitioners who are competent to work across cultures and across other specific dynamics (i.e., social stigma & child policies) that may be affecting this heterogeneous population. In addition, many programs struggle to exist beyond a few years, which limits evaluation of the program's effectiveness and potential for documenting successful outcomes. Thus, these challenges with practice and intervention also hinder the research conducted in this area.

RESEARCH

Unfortunately, research on CIP faces some of the same constraints as research on other understudied populations. That is, conceptual and methodological limitations impact our ability to understand our participants from a normative developmental perspective and to explore within-group characteristics that would help us to identify the myriad of risk and protective factors that promote resiliency (Brooks-Gunn, 1998; McLoyd, 1998). As indicated in earlier chapters, these conceptual and methodological limitations are illustrated via recruitment methods, researcher bias and incompetency, lack of culturally-sensitive measures, and inaccurate descriptions and definitions of the sample of interest (Sue, 1999; Brooks-Gunn, 1998; McLoyd, 1998).

Perhaps a starting point for correcting these conceptual and methodological limitations in interventions and research would be our conceptual framework for CIP. In addition to Bronfenbrenner's ecological approach, frameworks utilizing a positive, strengths-based perspective that recognizes developmental change as a process within an environment would help to sort out the complexities of this population. A framework such as the youth development theory would emphasize the need to understand the environment and context that are needed for optimal development to occur (Perkins, Borden, Keith, Hoppe-Rooney, & Villaruel, 2003). Similarly, the developmental epidemiology perspective (as discussed in chapter 10) recognizes the child as an active agent, coping with parental incarceration as one of several risk factors. This perspective encourages in-depth research to investigate the categories of risk factors that may be contributing to prevailing problems (Phillips &

Erkanli, 2008; Johnson & Waldfogel, 2002). Furthermore, the developmental epidemiology approach supports targeted interventions based on the child's cumulative and distinct risk factors.

As we embark upon this challenge of targeted intervention, it is important to consider the child as an active agent with strengths and resources to be utilized. This notion advances intervention through research drawn from the literature on child development and resiliency. Because of the many systems that have an impact on this population, the study of CIP necessitates an inclusion of theories from different disciplines. This inclusion represents the heterogeneity within the population, and the needs of these children on multiple levels.

As noted in chapter 9, practitioners who provide services to this population have a unique responsibility vis-à-vis the population and the agencies. This responsibility entails extensive effort to meet the children where they are (e.g., understanding cultural differences, discerning distinct risk factors, and facilitating developmental growth). These professionals are most likely to be conversant in the legislative policies, which adds to the need for advocacy and intervention.

In addition to the need for an inclusion of disciplines, the work in this field needs collaboration among practitioners and researchers. This combined effort would help to build effective programs and document outcomes that would be useful in research and practice, as we move forward with this underserved and understudied population. Furthermore, this type of collaboration would help us to understand the unique dynamic among the cumulative and distinct risk factors experienced by children of incarcerated parents.

CHAPTER SUMMARY

In this volume we have come to understand the developmental challenges and supports available for children of incarcerated parents. A focus on the contextual systems is integral to understanding children of incarcerated parents. In addition, research has called our attention to the importance of understanding the child's lifestyle before the parent's incarceration (Hanlon, 2005) and using the child as an active agent in the process of coping and meaning-making (Kegan, 1982). This textbook singles out these direct and indirect influences on the child for continued research that extends beyond narrow definitions and methods of inquiry.

The distinct and cumulative risk factors that can infuse the lives of CIP contribute to atypical pathways that present opportunities for intervention and the fostering of resiliency. As we unravel these developmental pathways, implications for clinical intervention are prevalent and discussed throughout the text. Most importantly, this text calls attention to opportunities for intervention at individual and systems levels. At the individual level, clinical issues with CIP evolve around the child's developmental status as he or she copes with environmental influences. Likewise, as indicated in chapters 5 and 9, there are intervention opportunities in relation to systems within the communities and the legislative process. Similar to the magnitude of the need for research, the clinical implications for CIP are considerable and extend beyond any one traditional view of intervening. The information presented in this textbook helps us to understand this as we formulate plans for developmental success with CIP.

REFERENCES

Bernstein, N. (2005). *All alone in the world: Children of the incarcerated.* New York: New Press.

Bouchet, S. M. (2008). *Children and families with incarcerated parents.* Baltimore, MD: The Annie E. Casey Foundation.

Bowlby, J. (1988). *A secure base: Parent-child attachment and healthy human development.* New York: Basic Books.

Boss, P. (1986). Family stress: Perception and context. In M. Sussman & S. Steinmetz, (Eds.), *Handbook on marriage and the family (pp. 695–723).* New York: Plenum Press.

Breen, P. (1995). Bridging the barriers. *Corrections Today, 57, 7,* 98–99.

Bronfenbrenner, U. (2001). Human development, bioecological theory of. In N. J. Smelser & P. B. Baltes (Eds.), *International encyclopedia of the social and behavioral sciences* (pp. 6963–6970). Oxford: Elsevier.

Brooks-Gunn, J., Rauh, V., & Leventhal, T. (1999). Equivalence and conceptually anchored research with children of color. In H. E. Fitzgerald, B. M. Lester, & B. Zuckerman (Eds.), *Children of color: Research, health and policy issues* (pp. 25–51). New York, NY: Garland.

Bureau of Justice Statistics, (2003). *Sourcebook of criminal justice statistics online: Section 6, Persons under correctional supervision (31st ed).* New York: Author. Retrieved on September 16, 2009 from http://www.albany.edu/sourcebook/index.html

Bush, G. (2008). Executive order: Improving the coordination and effectiveness of youth programs. http://www.whithouse.gov/news/releases/2008/02/20080207-15.html

Colby A. & Damon, W. (1992). *Some do care: Contemporary lives of moral commitment.* New York: The Free Press.

Covington, S. S. (2002). A woman's journey home: Challenges for female offenders and their children. Paper presented at the From Prison to Home Conference hosted by the U.S. Department of Health and Human Services and The Urban

Institute, Bethesda, MD. Retrieved September 16, 2009, from http://aspe.hhs.gov/hsp/prison2home02/Covington.htm

Dalley, L. P. (2002). Policy implications relating to inmate mothers and their children: Will the past be prologue? *The Prison Journal, 82, 2,* 234–268.

Eddy, J. M. & Reid, J. B. (2003). The adolescent children of incarcerated parents: A developmental perspective. In J. Travis, & M. Waul, (Eds.) *Prisoners once removed: The impact of incarceration and reentry on children, families, and communities.* Washington DC: The Urban Institute Press.

Erikson, E. (1959). Identity and the life-cycle. *Psychological Issues, 1,* 18–164.

Fritsch, T. A., & Burkhead, J. D. (1981). Behavioral reactions of children to parental absence due to imprisonment. *Family Relations, 30, 1,* 83–88.

Gonzalez, P., Romero, T., & Cerbana, C. B. (2007). Parent education program for incarcerated mothers in Colorado. *Journal of Correctional Education, 58, 4,* 357–373.

Greene, S. Haney, C., & Hurtago, A. (2002). Cycles of pain: Risk factors in the lives of incarcerated mothers and their children. *The Prison Journal, 80,* 3–19.

Hanlon, T. E., Blatchley, R. J., Bennett-Sears, T., O'Grady, K. E., Rose, M., & Callaman, J. M. (2005). Vulnerability of children of incarcerated addict mothers: Implications for preventive intervention. *Children and Youth Services Review, 27,* 67–84.

Hanlon, T. E., Carswell, S. B., & Rose, M. (2007). Research on the caretaking of children of incarcerated parents: Findings and their service delivery implications. *Children and Youth Services Review, 29,* 348–362.

Johnson, E. I. & Waldfogel, J. (2002). *Children of incarcerated parents: Cumulative risk and children's living arrangements.* NY: Columbia University School of Social Work.

Johnston, D. (1992). Children of offenders. Pasadena, CA: Pacific Oaks Center for Children of Incarcerated Parents.

Johnston, D. (1993). The Therapeutic Intervention Project: A report to funders. Pasadena, CA: Pacific Oaks Center for Children of Incarcerated Parents.

Lopez, C. & Bhat, C. S. (2007). Supporting students with incarcerated parents in school: A group intervention. *The Journal for Specialists in Group Work, 32, 2,* 139–153.

Kegan, R. (1982). *The evolving self: Problem and process in human development.* Cambridge, MA: Harvard University Press.

Masten, A. S. & Coatsworth, J. D. (1998). The development of competence in favorable and unfavorable environment: Lessons from research on successful children. *American Psychologist, 53,* 205–220.

McLoyd, V. C. (1998). Changing demographics in the American population: Implications for research on minority children and adolescents. In V. C. McLoyd & L. Steinberg (Eds.), *Studying minority adolescents: Conceptual, methodological, and theoretical issues* (pp. 3–28). Mahwah, NJ: Erlbaum.

Mid-Atlantic Network of Youth and Family Services. (2003). *Mentoring children of prisoners program: 2003 Grantee Profiles.* Pittsburgh, PA.

Miller, K. (2006). The impact of parental incarceration on children: An emerging need for effective interventions. *Child and Adolescent Social Work Journal, 23, 4,* 472–486.

Mumola, C. J. (2000) Incarcerated parents and their children: U.S. Department of Justice.

Nesmith, A. & Ruhland, E. (2008). Children of incarcerated parents: Challenges and resiliency, in their own words. *Children and Youth Services Review, 30,* 1119–1130.

Parke R. D. & Clarke-Stewart, K. A. (2003). The effects of parental incarceration on children: Perspectives, promises, and policies. In J. Travis, & M. Waul, (Eds.) *Prisoners once removed: The impact of incarceration and reentry on children, families, and communities.* Washington DC: The Urban Institute Press.

Perkins, D. F., Borden, L. M., Keith, J. G., Hoppe-Rooney, T. L., & Villaruel, F. A. (2003). Community youth development: Partnership creating a positive world. In F. A. Villaruel, D. F. Perkins, L. M. Borden, & J. G. Keith (Eds.), *Community youth development: Programs, policies, and practices.* Thousand Oaks, CA: Sage.

Phillips, S. D. & Erkanli, A. (2008). Differences in patterns of maternal arrest and the parent, family, and child problems encountered in working with families, *Children and Youth Services Review, 30,* 157–172.

Rogers, C. R. (1957). The necessary and sufficient conditions of therapeutic personality change. *Journal of Consulting Psychology, 21,* 95–103.

Springer, D. W., Lynch, C., & Rubin, A. (2000). Effects of a solution-focused mutual aid group for Hispanic children of incarcerated parents. *Child and Adolescent Social Work Journal, 17,* 431–442.

Springer, D. W., Pomeroy, E. C., & Johnson, T. (1999). A group intervention for children of incarcerated parents: Initial blunders and subsequent solutions. *Groupwork, 11,* 54–70.

Sue, S. (1999). Science, ethnicity, and bias: Where have we gone wrong? *American Psychologist, 54,* 1070–1077.

Travis, J. & Waul, M. (2003). Prisoners once removed: The children and families of prisoners. *Prisoners once removed: The impact of incarceration and reentry on children, families, and communities.* Washington DC: The Urban Institute Press.

Recommendations from Children of Incarcerated Parents

**RESEARCHED AND COMPILED BY
TRISHA FERRER, JULIO RAY, ANTHONY PEIRCE,
DAVIAN, AND ANTHONY**

VISITING

Youth Perspectives:

"I never got to visit my parents"

"From the time I was seven years old to nine years old I didn't see my mother . . ."

"I went with my brother's mother to go visit my father. Yo, he denied our visit and we had to sit outside in the hot ass sun for three hours for the visit to be over. That's not funny. She was pregnant and they said she had to sit on the curb. I was so upset."

Youth Recommendations:

1 Revise security procedures for youth under 18 who are entering the prisons.
   a No unwanted touches.
   b No dehumanizing security measures.
   c Should be age and gender appropriate.
2 Visiting room/environment should be comfortable, interactive, and youth friendly.
3 More visiting. Support programs that facilitate visiting.

4 No more arbitrary rules that prevent children from seeing their family members in prison.

5 Guards cannot change rules and visitors should be fully informed of the procedures.

COPS

Youth Perspectives:

"One time we were asleep, the whole house was asleep. They came into the house with a gun out and they . . . they're just allowed to come to your house whenever. So they came, came to the house with this gun out in the middle of the night. The team just came in and stormed in the room. My brother, he looks like he's really old, like, not really old, but he looks older for his age so they thought he was the man of the house. So they arrested him and he was trying to explain to them "I'm not the man of the house, I'm the son" but they kept hitting him with the bat so he could stay still. Like that's why his whole right side is fucked up, but so my mother like, they was OD-ing 'cause they messed up the whole house. They tore down everything, they put everything inside out . . . My mom was trying to act as calm as possible so that she wont traumatize me. Like she was trying to get me dressed so that they could take me to my grandmother's house . . ."

Youth Recommendations:

1 Cops should have clear procedures to follow when conducting a raid in which children under the age of 18 are in the house:
  a Come into the home in a respectful manner.
  b Avoid drawing guns if kids are around.
  c Ask parents/kids the number of an immediate family member or close friend.
  d Wait with the child until a guardian arrives to care for them.

ACS (ADMINISTRATION FOR CHILDREN'S SERVICES)

Youth Perspectives:

"When my mom got locked up they took me away from my family and I was in foster care for like six years. I was with my two sisters and they split up my other sisters. And that wasn't a good thing."

Youth Recommendations:

1 Try harder to keep families together:
   a Consult the family about who should be placed together or where they should be placed if separation is unavoidable.
   b Facilitate visiting between siblings, incarcerated family members, and other family members.
   c Try to keep siblings informed when one is moved to a new placement.
   d Keep family members in as close a distance as possible.

EMOTIONS

Youth Perspectives:

"I sort of you know, me I feel like angry and confused 'cause when my mother got arrested I didn't know what was going on."
"It was depressing."
"I had mixed feelings."
"It was annoying."
"When my mother went to jail, I was rebellious to people I was with. I was angry at her for not coming back to get me and I was disappointed with her. There was a little bit of hate also and I felt resentful because I had to seek responsibility for my little brothers and sisters."

Youth Recommendations:

1 Offer people support to deal with the variety of emotions that come with parental incarceration.
2 Keep youth informed to avoid the confusion and depression that often comes with feeling like prison has made you lose control of your life.
3 Support/fund programs where youth can be with other youth experiencing familial incarceration.

KEEPING COMMUNICATION OPEN

Youth Perspectives:

"Maybe if you had, like, more sessions like this with people like with our problem or whatever, it would be easier for people to be more open-minded and speak. And maybe it would be like, I don't know, different than it was for me. I went on my own."

"My sister helped, because it was my sister who was the one who gave me the envelopes, the papers, and the stamps and everything. I didn't know how to do that, I was young. I mean, I was seven years old."

Youth Recommendations:

1   Need more ways to communicate with parents that are affordable and convenient (no high-priced phone calls, need access to envelops and stamps, etc.)
2   Children should be informed by facilities if parents are moved so that they can remain in contact.
3   More supportive groups that help children understand their experience with parental incarceration. This understanding may help them communicate better with their families.
4   An interactive Web site should be developed so that youth could communicate with other youth who are going through the same thing.

POST-RELEASE SUPPORTS

Youth Perspectives:

"We always argue, so for me it's like a big change 'cause I'm so used to my grandmother . . ."

"Right, 'cause you've—you're restricted to do certain things. You can't get a job anywhere. Like you be able, you might have the smarts for it, but you don't have the qualifications just because you went to jail."

"My mom just came out in December from like, she's been there since I was 12. So I ain't never know her that much. So now that she's out I get to chill or do whatever, and its like I'm still a little kid to her, and I still feel like I'm a little kid because she babies me."

Youth Recommendations:

1   Family therapy for children and parents upon release.
2   A pre-release program for parents that is co-created by children of incarcerated parents that helps them think through potential

difficulties that they may have when transitioning back into their children's lives.

3 More comprehensive pre-release and post-release supports (housing, jobs, etc.) for parents and kids so that they can have a smoother transition back into their children's lives.

4 Fun and interactive programs for parents and kids to do together when they are released.

SCHOOLS

Youth Perspectives:

"Teachers don't have to know, but well, they don't ask you."

"I didn't tell anyone in school because everybody had their mother, and my mother was in prison."

"I told my second grade teacher 'cause she asked me where was my mother and I had to tell her."

Youth Recommendations:

1 Schools should be a place of potential support:
   a Counselors should be trained to be sensitive to the needs of youth dealing with familial incarceration.
   b If a child begins to have a sudden drop in grades, counselors or teachers should consider asking about familial incarceration as one possible cause.
   c Help and support should be offered, not punishment.
   d In-school supportive programs should be created for youth that are dealing with incarceration.

INCARCERATION OF MULTIPLE FAMILY MEMBERS

Youth Perspective:

"I'll go. In 1996, my father got sentenced for five years. I was seven years old. In 1997 my uncle went in for four years. I was turning eight. In 1999, my cousin got sentenced for a year. I was nine. In 2006, my brother got arrested for possession of a weapon. The case is still pending. And in 2006, I got arrested for a week. I got arrested for a week . . ."

Youth Recommendations:

1 Youth who live in communities targeted by cops/prisons need support to deal with the multiple family members getting locked up (mothers, fathers, cousins, uncles, brothers).
2 Interventions are needed to help youth who have had multiple family members incarcerated to avoid incarceration themselves.

Appendix B
Equations Pertaining to Multilevel Models

The equations pertaining to Hypotheses 1 and 2 (Chapter 6) predicting the living arrangements of children of incarcerated mothers and fathers are the same, and are represented by level 1 and level 2 equations, listed below. The level 1 structural models predicting the log odds of living in one of the three living arrangements compared to category 4 (living with the other parent) are as follows (grand mean centered variables are noted in equations in italics):

$$\eta_{mij} = \beta_{0j\,(m)} + \beta_{1j\,(m)} * (\text{Female})_{ij} + \beta_{2j\,(m)} * (Age)_{ij}$$

In the level 2 structural model, a random effect or between-incarcerated-parent variation is specified in Equation 1 below for living in category 1 (e.g., incarcerated mother) compared to living with the other parent (category 4). The random component in the other level 2 equations below is constrained to zero (Raudenbush & Bryk, 2002, p. 328). All other level 1 regression coefficients are fixed in these analyses.

1. $\beta_{0j(1)} = \gamma_{00(1)} + \gamma_{01(1)} * (\text{Hispanic}) + \gamma_{02(1)} * (\text{African American}) + \gamma_{03(1)} * (\text{Married}) + \gamma_{04(1)} * (\text{Separated/Divorced/Widowed}) + \gamma_{05(1)} (Number\ of\ Children) + u_{oj(1)}$

2. $\beta_{0j(2)} = \gamma_{00(2)} + \gamma_{01(2)} * (\text{Hispanic}) + \gamma_{02(2)} * (\text{African American}) + \gamma_{03(2)} * (\text{Married}) + \gamma_{04(2)} * (\text{Separated/Divorced/Widowed}) + \gamma_{05(2)} (Number\ of\ Children)$

3. $\beta_{0j(3)} = \gamma_{00(3)} + \gamma_{01(3)} * (\text{Hispanic}) + \gamma_{02(3)} * (\text{African American}) + \gamma_{03(3)} * (\text{Married}) + \gamma_{04(3)} * (\text{Separated/Divorced/Widowed})) + \gamma_{05(3)} (\textit{Number of Children})$

4. $\beta_{qj(m)} = \gamma_{q0(m)}, q = 1, \ldots, 2$

The equations representing the multilevel models pertaining to Hypotheses 3 to 6 testing parental expectations to live with children upon release are represented by the following equations. The level 1 structural model predicting the log odds of parental expectations to live with children upon release from prison is

$$\eta_{ij} = \beta_{0j} + \beta_{1j}(\text{Female})_{ij} + \beta_{2j}(Age)_{ij}$$

The full level 2 or between-parent model is as follows:

$$\beta_{0j} = \gamma_{00} + \gamma_{01}(\text{Hispanic}) + \gamma_{02}(\text{African American}) + \gamma_{03}(\text{Lived with Parent}) + \gamma_{04}(\text{Lived with Relative}) + \gamma_{04}(\text{Lived in Other Arrangement}) + \gamma_{05}(\text{Married}) + \gamma_{06}(\text{Separated/Divorced/Widowed}) + \gamma_{07}(\textit{Number of Children}) + \gamma_{08}(\text{Sentence Length}) + u_{oj}$$

This population average random-intercept model tests the structural embeddedness of parental expectations. All other level 1 coefficients are fixed in these analyses.

Index

Note: Page references ending in "*f*" (e.g., 8*f*) indicate a figure; those ending in "*t*" indicate a table.